The Fruits of Exile

The Carolina Lowcountry and the Atlantic World
*Sponsored by the Program in the Carolina Lowcountry
and the Atlantic World of the College of Charleston*

Money, Trade, and Power
Edited by Jack P. Greene, Rosemary Brana-Shute,
and Randy J. Sparks

The Impact of the Haitian Revolution in the Atlantic World
Edited by David P. Geggus

London Booksellers and American Customers
James Raven

Memory and Identity
Edited by Bertrand Van Ruymbeke and Randy J. Sparks

This Remote Part of the World
Bradford J. Wood

The Final Victims
James A. McMillin

*The Atlantic Economy during the Seventeenth
and Eighteenth Centuries*
Edited by Peter A. Coclanis

From New Babylon to Eden
Bertrand Van Ruymbeke

Saints and Their Cults in the Atlantic World
Edited by Margaret Cormack

Who Shall Rule at Home?
Jonathan Mercantini

To Make This Land Our Own
Arlin C. Migliazzo

Votaries of Apollo
Nicholas Michael Butler

Fighting for Honor
T. J. Desch Obi

Paths to Freedom
Edited by Rosemary Brana-Shute and Randy J. Sparks

*Material Culture in Anglo-America:
Regional Identity and Urbanity in the Tidewater, Lowcountry, and Caribbean*
Edited by David S. Shields

The Fruits of Exile
Edited by Richard Bodek and Simon Lewis

The Fruits of Exile

Central European Intellectual
Immigration to America in
the Age of Fascism

Edited by
Richard Bodek and Simon Lewis

The University of South Carolina Press

© 2010 University of South Carolina

Published by the University of South Carolina Press
Columbia, South Carolina 29208

www.sc.edu/uscpress

Manufactured in the United States of America

19 18 17 16 15 14 13 12 11 10   10 9 8 7 6 5 4 3 2 1

Library of Congress Cataloging-in-Publication Data

The fruits of exile : Central European intellectual immigration to America in the age of fascism / edited by Richard Bodek and Simon Lewis.
   p. cm. — (The Carolina lowcountry and the Atlantic world)
   Includes bibliographical references and index.
   ISBN 978-1-57003-853-2 (cloth : alk. paper)
   1. United States—Civilization—Foreign influences. 2. National socialism and intellectuals—Europe, Central. 3. Intellectuals—United States—History—20th century. 4. Intellectuals—Europe, Central—History—20th century. 5. Political refugees—United States—History—20th century. 6. Europe, Central—Emigration and immigration—United States—History—20th century. 7. United States—Emigration and immigration—Europe, Central—History—20th century. I. Bodek, Richard, 1961– II. Lewis, Simon, 1960–
   E169.1.F865 2010
   973—dc22

2009029425

This book was printed on Glatfelter Natures, a recycled paper with 30 percent postconsumer waste content.

Contents

Acknowledgments   vii
Preface   ix

The *Eclipse of Reason* and the End of the
   Frankfurt School in the United States   1
   James Schmidt

Max Horkheimer and "The Jews and
   Europe": A Reevaluation   29
   Richard Bodek

Selective Affinities: On U.S. Reception of
   Hans Kelsen's Legal Theory   40
   Jeremy Telman

From *Bildung* to Planning: Karl Mannheim
   as a Refugee   59
   Colin Loader

The Obscure Sea Change: Hermann Broch,
   Fascism, and the United States   71
   Donald Wallace

Fighting Windmills on Broadway: Max Reinhardt's
   Exile in the United States   91
   Gudrun Brokoph-Mauch

Schoenberg in the United States Reconsidered:
   A Historiographic Investigation   102
   Sabine Feisst

When the Nobel Prize Was Not Enough: Jewish Chemists
   from the Nazi Regime as Refugees in the United States   127
   Yael Epstein

At Home with Nietzsche, at War with Germany:
   Walter Kaufmann and the Struggles of Nietzsche
   Interpretation   156
   David Pickus

Negotiations: Learning from Three Frankfurt Schools   177
   David Kettler

Budapest—Berlin—New York: Stepmigration from
   Hungary to the United States, 1919–1945   197
   Tibor Frank

Contributors   223
Index   227

Acknowledgments

The editors of this book would like to thank David Cohen, dean of the Addlestone Library, for giving us access to the library's collection of émigré prints, Martin Perlmutter, director of Jewish Studies at the College of Charleston, for graciously providing facilities, and Todd McNerney, chair of the Department of Theatre, for organizing and directing the performance of *Copenhagen*.

We would also like to thank our students for providing us with an interesting atmosphere in which to teach and write, the Departments of German, History, Music, and Political Science, and the Humanities Council[SC] for generous financial support.

Finally, we would like to our two sets of children for keeping everything in perspective: Richard Bodek's Benjamin and Zachary and Simon Lewis's Megan, Zoë, and Oliver.

Preface

This collection examines how the study of the European intellectual exile has changed in the years since the publication of Bernard Bailyn and Donald Fleming's edited collection, *The Intellectual Migration: Europe and America, 1930–1960* (1969) and H. Stuart Hughes' classic work, *The Sea Change* (1975). Whereas these first two volumes have as their concern documenting the fundamental impact these émigrés had on U.S. culture, *Fruits of Exile* is intended to provide a forum for interdisciplinary discussion and exploration. The work here also explores the contributions to U.S. thought by disciplines and intellectuals that the two previous studies were not able to document. The essays for this volume were chosen for their intellectual coherence and indication of where new work on the intellectual immigration is going and where it can go. One of the interesting findings of more recent work is just how rocky the soil was that eventually nurtured these "fruits of exile."

The volume's first section explores the experience of some social scientists—and their works—in the United States and Great Britain. Although James Schmidt, Richard Bodek, Jeremy Telman, and Colin Loader all indicate the enormous influence that German refugees had on English speakers/ social thought, they also show the enormously difficult time that this work had gaining initial acceptance.

Schmidt's essay tells the tale of Max Horkheimer's book, *Eclipse of Reason*. This volume, which was intended to have pride of place among the Frankfurt School's work in English, was totally misunderstood by U.S. critics and faded into almost total obscurity, overshadowed by *Dialectic of Enlightenment*.

Continuing the focus on the work of Horkheimer, Bodek asserts that the essay "The Jews and Europe," which has been criticized as representing little more than an embarrassingly wrong prequel to *Dialectic of Enlightenment,* his fundamental collaboration with Theodor Adorno, ultimately represented a strong analytical statement about the nature of anti-Semitism in the modern world, one that informed both his own later work and the work of others who followed him.

Telman analyzes the legal positivism of Hans Kelsen, a legal theorist whose work barely made a ripple in U.S. legal thought. It seems that Kelsen's pure theory of law had few, if any, points of contact with legal pragmatism in the United States. Nevertheless Telman argues that it is now high time for the "sea change" represented by Kelsen's ideas of indeterminacy to influence this country's legal theory.

Loader explains the story of Karl Mannheim, exiled in Britain. While in exile, Mannheim devoted much of his thought and writing to trying to adapt the German concept of *Bildung* to a more open, democratic society by attaching it to sociological concepts when he found himself in exile. Mannheim believed that U.S. and British societies were experiencing the same kinds of disintegration as had Germany. In a situation similar to that of Kelsen and Horkheimer, Mannheim found himself to be peripheralized for being too German and too theoretical for his host country.

The second group of essays looks at a writer, a theatrical director, and a composer who found refuge in the United States. It too shows the different kinds of responses that émigrés could encounter. In his essay on the political theory of the novelist Hermann Broch, Donald Wallace examines Broch's critical appreciation of the U.S. democratic system. In Broch's view, although the country was founded on the principle of individual rights—rather than on citizens' duties to the state—it lacked a safeguard that would protect individuals from one another. Ultimately, according to his reading of Broch, Wallace contends that these safeguards would have to be located in a nonmaterialistic ethos.

Gudrun Brokoph-Mauch tells of Max Reinhardt's experience of the U.S. theatrical scene. When visiting the United States before the ascendancy of fascism in Germany, Reinhardt was hailed as a genius. Later, however, when forced to try to rebuild a career in the United States, he quickly saw the tumbling of his reputation and the failure of his projects to re-create the U.S. theater.

Sabine Feisst tells an altogether happier story of Arnold Schoenberg's exile. Although earlier literature has stressed Schoenberg's hardships, Feisst convincingly demonstrates Schoenberg's continued creativity and his vast influence on U.S. music. In this piece Feisst shows one of the relatively few positive creative relationships between émigré and the United States in this era.

The third and final quartet of papers looks at relatively understudied individuals and groups. Much of the importance of Yael Epstein's essay on the history of science lies in her pathbreaking shift of attention from physicists to chemists. She shows the importance of émigré chemists, especially the younger ones, to polymer science in the United States.

David Pickus's work on Walter Kaufmann goes a long way toward illuminating how this enigmatic scholar contributed to our understanding of the work of Friedrich Nietzsche. Especially fascinating is his study of Kaufmann's critical analysis of Stefan George and Nietzsche's reception.

David Kettler provides a firsthand account of his own experience of Americanization as a German-Jewish youth, and his indebtedness to the older generation of émigré scholars under whom he studied. He uses himself as an example in his study of the whole cohort of "second wave" refugees. By opening the question of intellectual legacies and continuities, he provides problems to solve, and ideas to consider, to generations of scholars to come.

Finally Tibor Frank shows how the process of Magyarization in the World War I era, and then intermediate exile to the Weimar Republic, prepared Hungarian Jews for the trials of immigration to the United States in the 1930s. Yet, even with this experience, the émigrés still found the transition to the United States, with its depressed economy and anti-Semitism, daunting. Frank's piece provides a fitting finale, as it shows both the possibilities inherent in immigration and the hurdles that these European exiles had to jump before they could fully enjoy the fruits of exile.

James Schmidt

The *Eclipse of Reason* and the End of the Frankfurt School in the United States

On May 22, 1947, Leo Lowenthal stepped out of an elevator on the sixth floor of the New York office of Oxford University Press and—as he wrote to Max Horkheimer that night—discovered that "a surprise expected [sic] me": "You remember that there is a showcase next to the entrance door where the Press exhibits their newest publications. There was nothing else in the case but your book. Fourteen copies of it, and an extremely funny astronomical symbolism, showing a sun in its various ecliptical stages."[1] The book that surprised Lowenthal was *Eclipse of Reason*, a work that—as Horkheimer explained in its preface—was intended "to present in epitome some aspects of a comprehensive philosophical theory developed by the writer during the last few years in association with Theodore [sic] W. Adorno."[2]

Lowenthal reported to Horkheimer that Oxford was "proud and happy with the book because they think it is one of the few serious publications that have come out in this country for a number of years."[3] Indeed expectations for the book ran high in Horkheimer's circle during the spring of 1947. Shortly after its publication, Lowenthal wrote Horkheimer that his Columbia University colleagues Robert Merton and Paul Lazarsfeld "are highly excited and studying the book with great passion."[4] A few months later, Lazarsfeld himself wrote Horkheimer and hailed the book as "a real step forward. . . . The book is written in such a way as to make it understandable to many people and will undoubtedly also influence many readers. As a matter of fact, I, myself, have never so clearly understood before some of your basic ideas."[5] Such praise would seem to confirm Lowenthal's initial assessment of the manuscript from a year and a half earlier: "You have achieved a document which, for the first time in the English language, can give an adequate idea about the impression of one philosopher's voice in the desert of streamlined society of today. Since I believe in the presence of unknown spiritual friends even on this continent, I look forward to the time when people will contradict the smooth critics who see in Ernst Cassirer the non plus ultra of philosophical thinking in this epoch."[6] On that May morning when Lowenthal stepped from the elevator, it was not unreasonable to hope that Horkheimer's book might achieve the sort of success with educated readers that Cassirer had recently attained with his posthumously published *Essay on Man* and *Myth of the State*. The ultimate fate of Horkheimer's book, however, must have been a disappointment. A few reviews appeared—some positive, some negative—and the book soon lapsed into obscurity.

Today *Eclipse of Reason* is viewed as a postscript to the work now seen as the magnum opus of the Frankfurt School's U.S. exile: *Dialectic of Enlightenment*. Rolf Wiggershaus's treatment in his history of the Frankfurt School is typical: the section dealing with *Eclipse of Reason* carries the title "Horkheimer's 'Dialectic of Enlightenment.'"[7] Commentators who have dismissed Horkheimer's book are in good company: the author himself had misgivings. While drafting the series of public lectures that were the basis for the book, Horkheimer wrote to his lifelong friend and colleague Friedrich Pollock, wondering whether the results were worth the effort: "Reading a page of these lectures as I now start to dictate them, and comparing it with a page of my own texts, I must say it is almost a crime."[8] Two years later, as he worked to turn the lectures into a finished manuscript, he was still plagued by doubts. He confessed to Pollock, "It is not the English exoteric version of thoughts already formulated which matters, but the development of a positive dialectical doctrine which has not yet been written."[9]

Nevertheless this peculiar fruit of the Frankfurt School repays closer scrutiny. The writing of the book reveals much about the years of this exile, and a peculiar circumstance enables us to know quite a bit about its genesis. Horkheimer wrote the book in California, but much of the copyediting and preparation of the manuscript took place under Lowenthal's supervision in New York. Lowenthal preserved much of his correspondence with Horkheimer, including extensive documentation of the writing, revision, publication, and reception of *Eclipse of Reason*. He made this material available to Martin Jay when he was writing *The Dialectical Imagination*, and, after the completion of that book, Jay arranged to have Lowenthal's papers deposited in the Houghton Library at Harvard University.[10]

In recounting the story of the Frankfurt School in the United States, commentators have rightly given pride of place to *Dialectic of Enlightenment*, the "message in a bottle" that Horkheimer and Adorno let slip into a world that was hardly aware of its existence.[11] Written in German and daunting in its complexity, this work has come to be seen as epitomizing the experience of this stalwart group of German-Jewish intellectuals who, driven from Germany, remained uncomfortable in the United States and—while awaiting the day when the madness that had descended upon Europe at last lifted—stubbornly persisted in "speaking a language that is not easily understood."[12] Yet if we look at the closing years of their exile from the perspective opened by Lowenthal's papers, things appear in a somewhat different light. They remind us of the hopes placed in this now-forgotten book, published by a prestigious New York firm, which attempted to articulate, for an anglophone audience, the philosophical position that animated *Dialectic of Enlightenment*. Thus if *Dialectic of Enlightenment* shows us Horkheimer and Adorno at their most uncompromising, *Eclipse of Reason* reveals an attempt, if not to compromise, then at least to find a language that was not so difficult to understand. Here, in other words, was a book intended as something other than a message in a bottle.

Troubled Times on Morningside Heights

Horkheimer closed the preface to *Eclipse of Reason* with the following words: "Finally, it is to be set down here, as an abiding recognition, that all of my work would have been unthinkable without the material assurance and the intellectual solidarity that I have found in the Institute for Social Research through the last two decades" (vii). The acknowledgment would seem as unexceptional as the location and date Horkheimer attached to the preface: "Institute for Social Research (Columbia University), March 1946." But here, as elsewhere in the record Lowenthal has left us, things turn out to be somewhat more complicated.

Institute for Social Research was the name of the corporate entity that the philanthropist Hermann Weil had established in 1924 at the University of Frankfurt. The institute took an avowedly Marxist perspective on economic and social questions, as did Weil's son, Felix, who—as a result of his father's largesse—was able to begin an academic career with the institute. Horkheimer became director in 1931 and, after Hitler seized power, went into exile with his colleagues and reconstituted the institute in 1934 at Columbia. The material assurance to which Horkheimer alluded in the preface had been drawn from the institute's endowment, which had been moved to accounts outside Germany prior to the collapse of the Weimar Republic and hence remained a source of support for the institute's associates throughout their exile. Testimony to the "intellectual solidarity" that the institute provided could be found in the rich corpus of work that Horkheimer and his associates produced for the institute's journal, the *Zeitschrift für Sozialforschung*, and in the various seminars at its building on Morningside Heights. In Anson Rabinbach's apt image, the institute was the ark that rescued Horkheimer and his colleagues from the flood that had engulfed Europe.[13]

However, by the time Horkheimer wrote his preface, the institute's relationship with Columbia had become so tenuous and its continued existence so questionable that he chose not to list the affiliation in his initial draft. The omission sparked a protest from Felix Weil when he read the page proofs with Horkheimer during a meeting in San Francisco in late October 1946.[14] Weil noted that "even Neumann and Marcuse"—individuals viewed by Horkheimer as peripheral to the institute— had dated their books from the institute, and Horkheimer immediately rectified the omission in a telegram to Lowenthal: "Since Preface dated March could possibly add Columbia University in parenthesis to Institute dateline, but only if really permissible. Otherwise suggest adding New York N.Y."[15]

The dating of the preface was critical because, in the period between its writing and Horkheimer's revision of the proofs, the institute had severed its ties with Columbia.[16] By the time Horkheimer was making his corrections, he was in contact with officials at the University of California, Los Angeles, in hopes of arranging for an affiliation between that university and the institute.[17] The negotiations, however, were still in limbo, and when *Eclipse of Reason* appeared in the spring of 1947, the institute was unaffiliated. Hence the significance of the preface's dating: it recalled a relationship that no longer existed.

The break with Columbia in the summer of 1946 resolved what had become a rather troubled relationship between the institute and the university. Horkheimer left for California in April 1941, seeking to free himself from his administrative responsibilities so that he could commence work on his long-projected book on "dialectical logic."[18] With Horkheimer's departure, the institute's continued viability became more and more uncertain. The decline of the U.S. stock market had taken its toll on the institute's endowment, and for several years Horkheimer and Pollock had been struggling to cut costs, including reducing stipends for the institute's less central associates and not-so-subtle efforts to persuade them to find other sources of income.[19] Lowenthal reported to Horkheimer that their colleague Franz Neumann doubted not only whether the institute could continue to maintain a presence in New York with Horkheimer in Los Angeles but also whether Horkheimer would ever be able to complete his magnum opus.[20] By January 1942 Horkheimer was contemplating the possibility of putting "our most drastical [sic] reduction plans into effect" and by November had settled on what he termed the "two room solution": the institute would confine its operations to two rooms and lease its remaining New York offices to other tenants. Herbert Marcuse and Neumann would be encouraged to take government positions. If any difficulties were encountered in implementing these plans, "we close down."[21]

The arrangement freed Horkheimer to pursue his collaboration with Adorno (who had left New York in November 1941) in Los Angeles and pushed Neumann and Marcuse (the latter had initially gone to California to work with Horkheimer but had returned to New York prior to Adorno's departure for Los Angeles) to peripheral roles in the institute. Pollock divided his time between Washington and New York (along with periodic visits to Los Angeles), though he appeared to Lowenthal to be so pessimistic about the prospects for success of any of the institute's research initiatives and so incapable of dealing with other people that his contribution to running the institute was marginal.[22] Lowenthal was left to run what remained of the New York branch, where his responsibilities included editing the last volumes of the institute's journal, maintaining contacts between the institute and Columbia, and editing the work that Horkheimer and Adorno had begun to produce in California. He also met with the financial planners retained to provide advice about investing the institute's shrinking endowment and visited the housing development in which the institute had invested, where he assisted real estate brokers during sales campaigns (the thought that, even today, there may be families living in suburban homes constructed with financing from a Marxist institute is surely one of the more unexpected legacies of the Frankfurt School's U.S. exile).[23] His most important role, however, was to be Horkheimer's eyes and ears in New York, and in this capacity he wrote Horkheimer letters almost daily (and sometimes more than once a day) about what was taking place.[24] From those letters it is possible to reconstruct the tensions that plagued the institute after Horkheimer's resettlement in Los Angeles.

The institute's relationship with Columbia's sociology department was a prime concern in Lowenthal's correspondence with Horkheimer. As recent studies by Thomas Wheatland have shown, the department had been instrumental in bringing Horkheimer and his colleagues to Columbia.[25] A few months after going into exile, the institute had contacted several U.S. colleges and universities about its members' research projects, sending copies of its journal, a preliminary report of the institute's studies on authority and the family, and a letter written by Erich Fromm and Julian Gumperz that raised the possibility of affiliation with a U.S. university.[26] The presentation, Wheatland argues, was particularly attractive to the Columbia sociologist Robert Lynd, who had been brought to the department in hopes that he might raise its profile in empirical research. An affiliation with the institute seemed to offer the department a way to strengthen its empirical research without incurring additional expenses. The department's interest in the institute was thus based on expectations that would quickly prove impossible to fulfill. Fromm's bitter dispute with Horkheimer and withdrawal from the institute in 1940 was particularly troubling for Lynd, both because of his own interest in Fromm's efforts to bridge the fields of psychoanalysis and sociology and because Fromm had been responsible for most of the empirical research that had first attracted Lynd to the institute's work.[27]

As the institute's financial situation worsened, its relationship with the sociology department became ever more important. During the spring and summer of 1941, Horkheimer sought to negotiate appointments within the department for some of the institute's members.[28] Lowenthal continued these efforts in Horkheimer's absence and more generally kept Horkheimer informed about tensions festering between the department's empirical wing, led by Lynd, and the more theoretical wing, led by its chairman, Robert MacIver. The presence of two other figures further complicated matters: both Paul Lazarsfeld and Neumann had rather complex relationships with the institute, and both would go on to distinguished careers at Columbia. Contacts between Lazarsfeld and the institute date from the mid-1930s, when he was involved in some of the empirical research for the institute's *Studies on Authority and the Family,* and his importance for the institute only increased with the departure of Fromm. Lynd had known and respected

Lazarsfeld for some years and had been instrumental in bringing Lazarsfeld's Radio Research project to Columbia, where it would eventually become the foundation for the university's Bureau of Applied Social Research.[29] Neumann—who, prior to the collapse of the Weimar Republic, had been politically active as a lawyer for the Social Democratic Party—had come to Columbia in 1936 after completing his doctoral studies with Harold Laski and Karl Mannheim at the London School of Economics. He served as a legal adviser to the institute's London branch and became an active participant in New York in the institute's seminars and discussions. While he was never close to Horkheimer, he became, after Fromm's departure, the member of the institute who commanded the greatest respect among Columbia's sociologists. Yet as Neumann's reputation rose among them, his future within the institute became ever more doubtful. As early as September 1939, Horkheimer had informed him that his stipend from the institute would be terminated within a year's time as part of the strategy for reducing costs, though—in response to a plea from Neumann for more time to consolidate his academic reputation—the termination date was eventually extended until the end of 1942.[30]

In hopes of improving relations with the sociology department and more generally increasing the visibility of the institute at Columbia, Horkheimer proposed a series of lectures by institute members.[31] He assumed that as director he would have the honor of delivering the first lecture. But, as Lowenthal informed him in a letter dated January 23, 1942, the department's preference was to have Neumann launch the series, thus raising the prospect that a "former member" would give the first of the institute's lectures.[32] The news could not have been more troubling to Horkheimer, who already feared that Neumann was seen as "the most important person at the Institute" at the very moment when Horkheimer was attempting to get rid of him.[33] Seeking clarification on how things stood, Lowenthal spent the evening of January 23 attending a going-away party for some members of Lazarsfeld's project who—with the entry of the United States into World War II—were leaving for positions in Washington or in the army. Learning that Lazarsfeld had spoken with Lynd about the institute's lectures, Lowenthal attempted to extract information from Lazarsfeld about where matters stood, a task that—as he later explained to Horkheimer—"was not so easy, since we both were a little bit drunk, and I had to pilot him out of the place of joy and to lure him into his private office." In a letter recounting the conversation to Horkheimer—written after the party ended—an apparently tipsy Lowenthal apologized for the somewhat rambling account, explaining "it's late and, as I told you in the beginning, it was quite a wet party."[34]

While Lazarsfeld assured Lowenthal that it would be wrong to assume that "any intrigue is under way against the Institute or its director, that any resentment or ill-feeling or conspiracy plays any role" in selecting the lecturer, his account of how things stood in the department must have alarmed Horkheimer. The department's preference for Neumann, as Lazarsfeld saw it, was the consequence of a yearlong struggle "between the more theoretical and the more empirical approach." The empirical wing was winning, and MacIver was losing his grip on the department: hence his desire to avoid conflicts with Lynd, who recognized that it would be an embarrassment not to give the initial lecture to Horkheimer and had spoken to MacIver about "how to get around Horkheimer." Lazarsfeld also revealed that the department was less interested in having a rotating series of lectures than in appointing one member of the institute to a position that could be renewed each year. As Lowenthal explained, the department had ranked Horkheimer at the bottom of the list of those it preferred to fill such a position. Neumann and Otto Kirchheimer (who would, like Neumann, eventually join the Columbia faculty) topped the list. Lazarsfeld thought that it might be possible, with much effort, to have the lectureship assigned to Lowenthal or, "with much more difficulty and against much more antagonism," to Adorno.[35]

His worst fears confirmed, Horkheimer responded: "I think you realize the impossible situation of our Institute working under the Directorship of a man, whom you yourself designate as illoyal to the highest degree and whose scientific ideas which I personally respect are in no way typical of our work. And Neumann—there is not the slightest doubt—will become the most important person in the Institute. He will appear as the one who does the work. . . . Not only in Columbia 'the more empirical approach' has won over 'the more theoretical,' also in our institute."[36] The only recourse Horkheimer could see was to cut Neumann's ties with the institute while attempting to make it clear that this step expressed no disregard for Neumann and to proceed with the "two room plan" at Columbia while building up the institute's Los Angeles branch.[37] In the fall of 1942 Horkheimer directed Lowenthal to sublet all but two of the institute's offices and to "crowd the two roof-rooms so much with books that nobody can work there." He proposed that the institute's name be removed from the door, "since it suggests activities which at present we cannot maintain."[38]

Horkheimer had an additional motive for paring down the institute's activities. His collaboration with Adorno had begun to bear fruit. The first chapter of "Philosophische Fragmente" (the original title of the work that would eventually be published as *Dialectic of Enlightenment*) had begun to take shape over the summer of 1942, and, in an August letter to Lowenthal, Horkheimer described the last months as "some of the most enlightening ones I ever lived through."[39] He toyed with the idea of turning over the institute's directorship to Pollock, and, back in New York at the start of September to secure financing for the institute, he sent Adorno a bitter assessment of the talents needed to do the job properly: "If, in addition to the glamour which a director of an Institute connected with Columbia University possesses, I should have at least some of the qualities which are expected of such a functionary, for instance, a mastery of the English language, a natural behaviour free of aggression, a grown up attitude etc., I have little doubt that there would not be the slightest difficulties to get the necessary amounts of money. I am, however, completely deprived of such talents."[40] Faced with the prospect of a fruitless pursuit of funding to keep the institute afloat, Horkheimer was inclined to eliminate the New York branch and turn his full attention to his work with Adorno in Los Angeles. However, because of the efforts of Neumann and Lazarsfeld, a temporary solution for the institute's financial difficulties emerged.

Neumann, who had been pursuing government positions in Washington, alerted Horkheimer during the summer of 1942 that a change in the directorship of the research department at the American Jewish Committee had revived the prospects for funding a research project on anti-Semitism that the institute had submitted several years earlier.[41] Lazarsfeld provided advice on how to frame the proposal to make it more attractive to the committee, and in March 1943 funding was approved.[42] While the grant provided the support needed to maintain not only a presence at Columbia but also the research project in Berkeley that would eventually produce *The Authoritarian Personality*, the new initiative proved a mixed blessing. Horkheimer found himself forced—as he complained to Lowenthal—to turn his attention "from philosophy to the project." The decision left him "very sad": "The last weeks and even months have been taken [up] by the most exhausting thinking which I ever did in my life. Besides of some aphorisms I have not written anything, but I think that I [have] arrived now at a definite theory of dialectics, at an aim for which I have been striving during so many years. The formulation of that theory would have taken me the next half year and now I must start conversations with innumerable people in order to organize some worthwhile empirical study. I won't be able to show a documentation of my work, not even a fragmentary one."[43]

Horkheimer was able to resume work with Adorno on "Philosophische Fragmente" that autumn, at which point they appear to have been completing the chapter on the "culture industry."[44] By the next January, however, Horkheimer viewed his situation as "absolutely impossible": "If we could devote our whole time to the work to which we decided to devote our lives, and which nobody besides us can do, we could present—in a year's time—a volume which would justify our whole existence. Now, not you alone, but also I, are splitting up our time and living under an almost senseless pressure."[45] The first version of "Philosophische Fragmente"—which would be distributed shortly before the end of 1944 in a mimeographed edition of five hundred copies—was more or less finished by the end of the spring. In his usual role of proofreader and censor, Lowenthal continued to work with the manuscript throughout the summer, struggling to find ways to untangle Horkheimer and Adorno's sentences and voicing reservations about passages that "may bring about the impression that democratic society is everywhere conceived as a preceding stage to fascism, and with formulations which, if taken out of context, and used maliciously, may create the impression that the program of free love is proclaimed."[46]

Acknowledging the enthusiastic letter that Lowenthal sent him after receiving the final draft of "Philosophische Fragmente," Horkheimer responded, "It is a fine thing that you like the book and I hope that the second part will still be much better."[47] That part was a proposed sequel—tentatively titled "The Rescue of Enlightenment"—on the "positive theory of dialectics" that was to be the ultimate fruit of Horkheimer's labors. However, no such work appeared, and the few notes that exist for it suggest that little work was done on it. The reason is not difficult to see: the research project on anti-Semitism would claim almost all of Horkheimer's and Adorno's time over the next few years. While the project ultimately brought Horkheimer and his associates the U.S. audience that had long eluded them, it was not without its cost. The "Rescue of Enlightenment" remained unwritten, and though Horkheimer and Adorno's philosophical fragments eventually were published as *Dialectic of Enlightenment,* the book still remained in important ways as incomplete as it was at the time of its initial appearance in mimeograph.[48] The most finished of the products of Horkheimer's California sojourn turned out to be the work that has commanded the least respect.

The Lectures and the Book

As Horkheimer explained in its preface, *Eclipse of Reason* began as a series of lectures he delivered at Columbia in February and March 1944. The impetus for the lectures was an invitation—in which Horkheimer's friend Paul Tillich may have had a hand—from Columbia's philosophy department.[49] Discussions of possible lecture topics began in January 1943, a year after Horkheimer's initial overture to the sociology department and several months before he sent Lowenthal the first samples of what would eventually become *Dialectic of Enlightenment.*[50] At the end of January, Horkheimer mailed Lowenthal outlines for six possible topics: "Society and Reason," "Philosophy and the Division of Labor," "Theories of Philosophy and Society," "Philosophy and Politics," "American and German Philosophy," and "Basic Concepts of Social Philosophy."[51] The choice of which set of lectures Horkheimer would deliver was left to Lowenthal, who appears to have discussed the alternatives with Tillich and eventually settled on the first topic.

It is worth reflecting for a moment on the ones Lowenthal did not choose. "Philosophy and the Division of Labor" recalled some of the themes broached in Horkheimer's first articles in the *Zeitschrift für Sozialforschung* and proposed to explore the "scientification of philosophy under modern industry," using psychology and sociology as examples; the final lecture would discuss attempts to unite philosophy and the social sciences. The proposed lectures on theories of philosophy and society went back even further and, like some of the courses Horkheimer gave at Frankfurt at the end of the 1920s, compared the "role of the philosopher in ancient and modern philosophy"; examined the utopias of More, Campanella, and Bacon; analyzed the "political theories of enlightenment and romanticism"; discussed the "Marxian doctrine of ideology"; and concluded with a lecture on "modern sociology of knowledge." The lectures on philosophy and politics were also framed as a straightforward historical account of "the dissolution of feudal society and the rise of modern philosophy," "absolutism and reason," the "French Enlightenment as a political movement," "philosophies of counterrevolution," and finally the "philosophy of modern democracy." The lectures contrasting U.S. and German philosophy, which Lowenthal judged as demanding too much from Horkheimer, proposed to begin with the different conceptions of philosophy in both countries and then contrast their views of history, culture and civilization, and freedom and authority, followed by speculation on the "function of philosophy in world reconstruction." Finally, the series "Basic Concepts of Social Philosophy" recalled the topics that Horkheimer had initially proposed to examine in his work on dialectical logic: society and the individual, progress and retrogression, freedom and necessity, ideas and ideologies, and the idea of justice.

In advising Horkheimer to discuss society and reason, Lowenthal selected the one topic on Horkheimer's list that would draw on his current work. While some of the other topics would have reprised themes that Horkheimer had long ago addressed and others would have required him to venture into areas that he had not yet explored, Lowenthal's choice was tailor-made to allow Horkheimer to pull together the work that he had been doing with Adorno. Lowenthal's advice is all the more striking because, at the time he tendered it, he would have been familiar only with the first product of Horkheimer's collaboration with Adorno, the 1941 essay "The End of Reason."[52]

The lectures were delivered between 4:10 and 6:00 P.M. on five successive Thursdays beginning on February 3, 1944, in a seminar room in Philosophy Hall that by Lowenthal's reckoning could hold from twenty-five to sixty people.[53] Prior to his departure for New York, Horkheimer voiced his usual misgivings about the undertaking in a letter to Pollock: "It is a great pity, it is almost a catastrophe that I have to interrupt my work in order to deliver lectures in a language which I do not master. I am quite aware that it is I who insisted on getting this appointment. I did it because of the well-known motives. Now I must bear the consequences. However, I want to state that the four months, one third of a year, which I sacrifice for this purpose, are a terrible investment. I could have devoted time to our philosophical work, which is now in a decisive state. Never in my life did I feel so deeply the victory of external life over our real duties. . . . The world is winning, even in our own existence. This makes me almost desperate."[54]

He informed Lowenthal that he would be arriving in New York with three of the five lectures drafted but not "checked over linguistically," and he hoped that Lowenthal would help him "in a day and night effort to achieve something which will represent a popular version of some of our views." He also requested that Lowenthal obtain the services of an "experienced American stylist to do the editing."[55] Lowenthal arranged to have two people work with Horkheimer on a final version of the lectures: Norbert Guterman, a fellow exile born in Warsaw, who had frequented surrealist and Marxist circles in Paris during the 1920s and had worked as a translator for the institute, and Joseph Freeman, an American who had also done editing and translating for the institute.[56]

As Horkheimer explained in a subsequent letter to MacIver, the lectures "were composed almost entirely during my stay in New York, that is, in the intervals between the Thursdays on which they were delivered. I did this because I wanted to adapt them to the specific interests of the audience."[57] The typescript of the final version of the lectures confirms that a significant portion of the manuscript responded to questions raised by the audience at previous lectures. The second lecture, for instance, contains an extended discussion of John Dewey prompted by a comment that Dewey's "philosophy of experience" might provide a "way out of the impasse" discussed in Horkheimer's first lecture.[58]

The lectures that Horkheimer delivered at Columbia differed in significant ways from the book that grew out of them. The topics of the five lectures that made up *Society and Reason* (*SR*) were as follows:

I. Reason as the basic theoretical concept of Western civilization.
II. Civilization as an attempt to control human and extra-human nature.
III. The rebellion of oppressed nature and its philosophical manifestations.
IV. The rise and the decline of the individual.
V. The present crisis of reason.[59]

The last three lectures most closely correspond to the contents of *Eclipse of Reason* and include material subsequently reworked in the book's last three chapters. Much of the fourth lecture appeared in the identically titled fourth chapter, though there were extensive revisions. The same can be said for the relationship between the fifth lecture and the book's closing chapter, "On the Concept of Philosophy," and—to a lesser degree—for the relationship between the third lecture and the third chapter, "The Revolt of Nature."[60] However, the first two lectures were subjected to revisions so extensive that even the passages retained in *Eclipse of Reason* appear in a context that differs markedly.

So much of the second lecture was taken up with responses to objections raised in discussing the first lecture that Horkheimer arrived at its announced theme only shortly after its midpoint and—after outlining the points he hoped to discuss—noted that he would have to survey this material "more sketchily than I planned since I have already devoted a considerable part of this lecture to answering objections" (*SR*, lecture 2, 18).[61] Likewise, rather little of the first lecture survived the revisions that produced *Eclipse of Reason*. Horkheimer's alterations may have been motivated in part by the objections that the lecture met at Columbia. With so much of the second lecture devoted to answering objections to the first one, it is hardly surprising that Horkheimer decided to frame things differently in the book's opening. Other revisions, however, may have been the result of Horkheimer's long-standing desire to conceal his political allegiances in his published works.

Among the material cut was an introduction noting that the title of the lectures "may be misleading" in that it might suggest that "I am designating those elements in our society which are irrational, so that I may proceed to suggest how to overcome the irrational ones and to achieve the identity of society and rationality." Such a project, he noted, had been central to the program of "European socialism": "But the period in which these theories originated is ours no longer. It was the time of the free market, universal competition, the so-called anarchy of production, and these theories advanced the principle of rationality against the prevailing anarchy. I do not say that these categories have lost their validity under the conditions of present-day economy, but a new problem has arisen in the meantime; rationality has permeated human life to a degree which those older schools did not anticipate" (*SR*, lecture 1, 1).

In other words Horkheimer returned to New York bearing the bitter message that he and Adorno had been preparing in California: the socialist dream of subjecting the irrationality of capitalist production to scientific planning had in effect been realized under the conditions of monopoly capitalism, but in the process its full monstrosity had become evident. This was a message whose cruel irony presupposed an audience that had once shared that dream. *Eclipse of Reason* (*ER*) was intended for different readers.

It is not clear when Horkheimer decided to publish the lectures. In a letter to MacIver of August 9, 1944, he was "still uncertain whether or not the lectures should be printed."[62] A possible impetus may have been provided by Lowenthal's letter of September 25, which reported that Lynd had informed him that "the University authorities feel that we have not 'come through in a big way' in the same sense as in Germany."[63] The need to raise the institute's profile with a significant publication could only have become more pressing in the coming year as the university began evaluating its relationship with the institute. Whatever the motivation, by the autumn of 1945 the book had been accepted at Oxford, and Horkheimer was at work revising the manuscript, with a promised delivery date of January 1946.

"Ends and Means," the first chapter, drew on the distinction between formal and substantive conceptions of reason that had been elaborated in *Society and Reason* but incorporated much new material, including an extended discussion of pragmatism (*ER*, 42–57). "Conflicting Panaceas," the second chapter, juxtaposed the neo-Thomist understanding of reason to naturalist approaches. This chapter originated in an earlier essay written by Horkheimer in response to a series of articles by Sidney Hook, Dewey, and Ernest Nagel in the *Partisan Review*.[64] These two revisions resulted in a work that opened not with a lament for the lost cause of European socialism but with a critique of recent trends in U.S. philosophy. While the changes meant that the book would engage U.S. philosophy in a way that the lectures had not, they would also result in significant difficulties both for Horkheimer and for the book's reception.

Horkheimer's response to Hook, Dewey, and Nagel was originally written in German, and the English translation was assigned to Benjamin Nelson, whom the institute had engaged to perform various editorial tasks. Horkheimer's dissatisfaction with the pace and the results of the translation led to a bitter dispute during the spring and summer of 1944, with Horkheimer attributing the problem to Nelson's sympathy for Hook's position. "After all," Horkheimer explained to Lowenthal in one of his milder assessments of the situation, "he is deeply rooted in the tradition in which he was brought up."[65] The material on pragmatism in the first chapter was added in response to a request by one of the readers of the manuscript for Oxford: a young Columbia sociologist named C. Wright Mills.[66]

Horkheimer, however, knew rather little about pragmatism when he first delivered the lectures.[67] The extended discussion of Dewey at the start of the second lecture was prompted by the suggestion (which would have been hardly surprising from an audience at Columbia) that Dewey's philosophy offered an alternative to the impasse sketched in the opening lecture (*SR*, 5–6). Giving little indication that he was aware of the broader tradition with which Dewey was associated, Horkheimer focused on Dewey's "philosophy of experience," which he argued was similar to Bergson's philosophy, thus allowing Horkheimer to repeat criticisms that, he informed his audience, "once brought me Bergson's personal acknowledgement that although he could not agree with me, he felt that it was the most lively and pertinent objection which he had yet encountered" (*SR*, 8). The material on pragmatism was among the last additions to *Eclipse of Reason*, and when Horkheimer sent the revisions to Lowenthal, he noted, "You can see from my quotes that I read not a few of these native products and I have now the feeling to be an expert on it." Yet he persisted in interpreting pragmatism in light of European philosophical traditions with which he had long been familiar: "The whole thing belongs definitely into the period before the first World War and is somehow on the line of empirico-criticism."[68]

As the date for delivering the manuscript approached, a host of editorial decisions remained unresolved. As late as a month before the due date, the book still lacked a title: *The Agony of Reason, Subjectivization of Reason,* and *Objective and Subjective Reason* were considered and found wanting. *Twilight of Reason* was provisionally adopted, although by February, Horkheimer had misgivings: it was too close to the title of "The End of Reason," it reminded him of Götterdämmerung, it was "too pessimistic," "'twilights' and 'of reason' are legion," and "the book does not correspond to it."[69] When a form arrived from Oxford in March requesting information from Horkheimer for its files, he had still not picked a title.[70] In the end Philip Vaudrin, an Oxford editor, suggested the final title.[71] A decision also had to be reached about what to do about the preface: Horkheimer had written one but was dissatisfied with it and requested that Guterman draft an alternative. In the end Horkheimer wrote a new preface in January after reviewing the manuscript.[72] Suggestions from Adorno for additions and alterations in the manuscript were being sent to Lowenthal by Horkheimer throughout January 1946, as an increasingly desperate Horkheimer complained of his deteriorating physical condition: "During the nights I have arterial cramps in the arms and legs and uncomfortable headaches; during the day, at least with the slightest exertion, there are the well-known heart-pains."[73] He had also begun to have serious reservations about the concluding chapter: "The book, as it is, opposes the concept of nature so directly to that of spirit, and the idea of object to that of subject, that our philosophy appears as much too static and dogmatic. We have accused the others, both Neo-Thomists and Positivists, of stopping thought at isolated and therefore contradictory concepts and, as it is, it would be only too easy for them to accuse us of doing the same thing. . . . I do not feel any doubt that in the last chapter this gap should be filled."[74] At almost the last moment, parts of a manuscript written years earlier, "Sociology of Class Relations," were inserted into the book's discussion of the decline of the individual, and—after incorporating the editorial changes that Horkheimer transmitted in a massive telegram—Lowenthal delivered the manuscript to Oxford at the end of January.[75]

For the moment Horkheimer seemed satisfied with the work. When Margaret Nicholson, his copy editor at Oxford, suggested a few stylistic revisions, he resisted, explaining to Lowenthal that "this book is antagonistic to present-day literary habits in philosophy as well as related subjects. Therefore its form cannot be 'adjusted' to this kind of stuff. For instance there is no point in 'leading up to my thesis' as she states . . . for there is no 'thesis' in dialectical reflections like ours. The book should now be published as it is and she will be surprised how much response it will have."[76] But the arrival of proofs at summer's end sparked further anxieties from Horkheimer about the book's style, and Lowenthal sought to ameliorate them by suggesting that he would have the proofs read by "Harold Rosenberg or one of the other members of the literary avant-garde."[77] In November 1946, with the book now three months from its initially scheduled publication date, Horkheimer inquired whether it might be possible to insert subtitles in the margins, prompting an exasperated Lowenthal to point out that Oxford would surely reject such a proposal since it would involve resetting the entire book; he requested that Horkheimer "please do me the favor and enjoy the completion of this work."[78]

The Reception of *Eclipse of Reason*

Whatever contentment Horkheimer might have taken from the publication of *Eclipse of Reason* was fleeting.[79] Shortly after receiving a copy, he wrote to Lowenthal expressing concern about what he saw as a "distorting error" in the summary of the book's argument on its inside cover, observing that the mistake "gives me the idea that advertisement and plugging are not handled too well with regard to the book."[80] He went on to urge Lowenthal to have Guterman "see to it that we get prominent reviews in the *New York Times Book Magazine* and at other prominent places," a request he would repeat in subsequent letters.[81] The notion that book reviews could be arranged by applying influence was consistent with the account of the culture industry in *Dialectic of Enlightenment*. Horkheimer and Adorno had argued that the idea that independent entrepreneurs brought goods to the market, where they succeeded or failed on their own merits, was a quaint illusion of a long-lost world. Modern monopoly capitalism was a world of "rackets," where power and influence were the keys to success.[82] In one of his contributions to Lazarsfeld's radio research project, Adorno had concluded that radio stations do not play what listeners want to hear; they play what has been plugged. As Horkheimer brought the fruits of his labor to market, he was not about to forget how the culture industry worked.

Over the next several months he continued to press Lowenthal to make sure that Oxford was doing whatever it could to ensure that *Eclipse of Reason* would find an audience. "I have the definite feeling," he wrote to Lowenthal about Oxford's efforts to secure reviews, "that they are utterly neglecting this matter which, for us, is vital indeed."[83] When the press failed to send copies of the book to an additional list of names that Horkheimer had supplied, he informed Lowenthal that he himself would buy copies and send them to those on the list who were "particularly important."[84] He followed the advertising of the book closely and, at the end of July, expressed dismay to Lowenthal that he had yet to see an ad in the *Saturday Review*, "where, in my opinion, it belongs."[85] When a review of a book by their fellow exile Ludwig Marcuse appeared in the *New York Times,* Horkheimer was quick to note its appearance and to observe, "His Plato has certainly more affinity for this medium than my Hegel."[86] Unsure whether it would be appropriate to send Oxford some of the letters he had received praising the book, he suggested that Lowenthal should have the press contact the individuals directly.[87] He mused about the possibility of having his friend Ruth Nanda Anshen, a prominent New York writer and editor, organize "a miniature fan-mail for me," explaining that "she is enthusiastic without reserve."[88]

Lowenthal did his best to alleviate Horkheimer's anxieties. He urged him not to overestimate Guterman's influence on journals and noted that Oxford had an "excellent publicity director" and that it would be "awkward to put pressure behind such a large organization as the press."[89] He kept Horkheimer informed about the progress of reviews, though, as it turned out, there was rather little to report. By September, Lowenthal was reduced to clutching at straws: a passing reference to the book in an article by Helen Lynd in the *Nation* was enough to warrant notice.[90] Nevertheless he held out hope that the book might draw more attention in professional journals and informed Horkheimer that he had been contacted by Herbert Schneider, the editor of the *Journal of Philosophy*, about a possible reviewer and had suggested the historian Charles Trinkaus, who, as Lowenthal explained to Horkheimer, is "a great admirer of yours, and a former collaborator of the *Zeitschrift*."[91]

Horkheimer received the first of the reviews—which, as it turned out, would be by far the most favorable—several months prior to its publication. It was written by Arthur E. Murphy and appeared in the *Philosophical Review*.[92] Though he is not well known today, Murphy was one of the leading U.S. philosophers of the time. He had been one of the editors of George Herbert Mead's posthumously published works and, while generally sympathetic to pragmatism, had argued in his 1943 book *The Uses of Reason* that the movement's leading figures had never been able to overcome their "early fright of metaphysics" and, leery of making claims about "reality," wound up weakening their theory of truth in ways that left them open to the charge of skepticism and relativism.[93] Horkheimer learned of Murphy's book only after the publication of his own and, expressing admiration for Murphy's work, sent him a copy of *Eclipse of Reason*.[94] In his response Murphy noted that, by "an interesting coincidence," he had already read the book; he enclosed a copy of his forthcoming review.[95]

The review hailed the book as "a remarkably penetrating study" and found it particularly "striking and valuable" in its attempt to "trace the social background and implications of the philosophical theories in which this merely subjective use of reason is justified or exemplified" (190–91). While granting that the "positivistic and instrumentalist philosophers" criticized by Horkheimer would be likely to regard the book as "just another misinterpretation of their doctrine," Murphy found Horkheimer's claim that such approaches reduced philosophy to "social engineering" compelling and characterized Horkheimer's description of the "cultural consequences of this self-liquidation of reason" as "brilliantly sketched" (191). Murphy was also impressed that, having criticized the reduction of reason to technology, Horkheimer did not—as was "the fashion of the times"—make "an appeal to the irrational" but instead recognized that "the cure for the limitations of reason is to be found not in the rejection of reason but in a more just and comprehensive understanding of its meaning and use" (192). Indeed this had been the central point of Murphy's own work. In a contribution to a symposium in the *Philosophical Review* on the last hundred years of U.S. philosophy that appeared at about the time of his response to Horkheimer, Murphy offered an interpretation of philosophical developments from 1917 to 1947 that converged in significant ways with Horkheimer's diagnosis.[96]

In his survey Murphy argued that over the last quarter century philosophical ideas have "lost their status as reasons addressed to a community and maintained by a process within which their claims make sense and have a social function" and instead have been transformed into tools and "weapons in a world-wide struggle for power" ("Ideas," 378). In a contrast that paralleled Horkheimer's discussion of the "conflicting panaceas" of empiricist and traditionalist approaches, Murphy argued that what he termed "critical philosophy" had reached a point where "in a properly selected language we can say with logical impunity almost anything we please so long as we do not attempt to give a philosophical reason for it," while "speculative philosophy" had become "increasingly dubious in its rational foundations and increasingly ready to turn to uncriticizable intuition and traditional authoritarian support for the confirmation of its claims" ("Ideas," 381).[97] Against attempts to recast liberalism as one more "ideology," one in need of support through appeals to "eternal verities," Murphy insisted that liberal societies regard their central ideas as reasons that have the capacity "to justify themselves in the open, to the common sense and purpose of co-operative life" ("Ideas," 388). For Murphy this central ideal sustained the work of Charles S. Peirce, Josiah Royce, and Dewey at the start of the century, and it remained for him "the highest point of self-understanding that American philosophy has so far reached" ("Ideas," 388).

Murphy faulted *Eclipse of Reason* on only one point. He remained puzzled about the alternative Horkheimer was proposing: "Where . . . are we to find a rational basis for the objective evaluation of social ends?" Citing a "difficult sentence" from *Eclipse of Reason*—"Philosophy confronts the existent, in its historical context, with the claim of its conceptual principles, in order to criticize the two and thus transcend them" (*ER*, 192)—Murphy confessed, "I wish I could see quite specifically what this means, for I think it means something important" (review, 192). The sentence might have suggested "something important" to Murphy because he may have sensed an affinity to his own work. In his conception of philosophy as an attempt to engage in public reasoning about the "sense and purpose of co-operative life," Murphy echoed Kant's famous definition of enlightenment as the "public use of reason" and raised a set of concerns that would eventually be taken up by Jürgen Habermas several decades later in his own attempt to reformulate Horkheimer's conception of critical social theory. The review closed with the hope that Horkheimer might explore such issues more fully in a future work: "If it were as good a book on the constructive side as *Eclipse of Reason* is on the critical, it would be a valuable contribution to contemporary philosophy" (review, 192). But the "constructive" sequel to *Eclipse of Reason* remained unwritten, and later reviewers of Horkheimer's book would be a good deal less generous than Murphy.[98]

The most scathing review, by the Duke University philosopher Glenn Negley, appeared in *Ethics*.[99] It began by noting that during the war the "analytical differences" between philosophers had been overshadowed by their "moral and emotional agreement." Negley expressed the hope that, should this spirit of cooperation continue, it might aid in "clarifying for our predominantly individualistic philosophy the fundamental concepts of corporate value." Such an effort, as Negley understood it, would involve translating the concepts of "corporate analysis" into the context of democratic philosophy, a process that would require "forbearance toward that which is culturally different" and a "sincere effort to understand and to be understood despite confusions of terminology." Negley closed his opening paragraph with the observation that Horkheimer's book, "like so many others, evidences none of these essential characteristics." And then, for the rest of the review, he trashed the book.

The argument of Horkheimer's book struck Negley as yet another example of "an all too familiar pattern": "Western civilization is vulgar materialism, subjectivization of reason is rushing men to madness, positivistic instrumentalism has no regard for truth and reality, and philosophy has become the unwitting tool of practical science or the witless perpetrator of traditional mythology" (review, 75). Arguing that, in the face of such criticisms, it would be advisable to "examine the use of reason by the person who proclaims the absence of reason in others," Negley offered a few quotations from the book's opening chapter and then cited at length a passage in which Horkheimer—paraphrasing arguments that Adorno had articulated at greater length in his essays on musical listening—argued that the "average concertgoer" has lost all sense of the "objective meaning" of Beethoven's *Eroica* symphony. To this Negley responded, "It is only a surfeit of the pretentious insolence of such remarks that prompts consideration of them. I personally resent being told that I am not capable of listening to Beethoven. It seems to me a very questionable analysis of fact to assume that, because concert-goers today are so numerous as to constitute what can be called a 'mass,' this must imply that the concert-goer today cannot achieve the sophisticated appreciation of the relatively small elite of Beethoven's audience" (75).

He also took issue with book's treatment of pragmatism, suggesting that here too Horkheimer was repeating familiar criticisms with his attacks on this "devilish kind of philosophy" but had failed to distinguish between "the activity of scientific research, the analysis of scientific research, scientific methodology, the analysis of scientific method, and the material products of scientific investigation" (75–76). But, having made these distinctions, Negley did nothing with them and instead criticized Horkheimer's claim that, because of its neutrality with regard to ends, formal reason could not be prevented from serving "the most diabolical social forces." He confidently cited a *New Yorker* article that quoted a report on scientific research in the Third Reich as counterevidence and noted that it "found no studies of even the most routine interest that were based on reprehensible or unethical methods."[100]

Negley's attacks on Horkheimer became more shrill as the review proceeded. He characterized Horkheimer's use of the term *cultural commodity* to refer to the products of the culture industry as an example of "uncritical name-calling" that "cheapens the analysis, not the art" (review, 77). Observing that Horkheimer had criticized the modern insensitivity to nature and had expressed concern for the treatment of animals yet nevertheless thought "rather highly of the Platonic philosophy," he suggested that Horkheimer "ought to be reminded that Plato advised that the testimony of slaves should be accepted only when they are subjected to torture" (77). And while he purported to share Horkheimer's concern that, in the face of starvation in much of the world, a large part of its machinery nevertheless stands idle and hours are devoted to "moronic advertisements and to the production of instruments of destruction" (quoted from *ER,* 143), he confessed that "I can more easily stomach the sight of idle kilns than the stench of human bodies burning twenty-four hours a day" (review, 77), thus implying that Horkheimer's arguments ultimately lent support to the same forces that had driven the institute into exile. He concluded that Horkheimer's book itself must be regarded as a prime example of that "eclipse of reason" that "occurs whenever methods of inquiry are enforced which are contrary to known fact," and while he seemed to grant Horkheimer's argument that the task of philosophy is to foster a "mutual critique" of philosophical systems, he was adamant that such a mutual critique could "be based only upon a body of fact acceptable because arrived at by reasonable methods of inquiry" (review, 77). On the question of just what might constitute a reasonable method of inquiry, Negley was silent.

The review of *Eclipse of Reason* in the *Journal of Philosophy* was written not, as Lowenthal had hoped, by Horkheimer's admirer Trinkaus but by a Columbia philosopher named John R. Everett.[101] While more temperate than Negley's, in the end the review was no less critical. It is apparent that Everett was already familiar with Horkheimer's general position, and he began by observing that "Professor Horkheimer has written a book which states more clearly than he had done previously his fundamental thesis regarding the decline of the West. His avowed purpose is to show how the condition of Western philosophy indicates the disintegration of meaningful society. True to his dialectical heritage he sometimes blames philosophy for the social collapse, and at other times charges commercialized capitalism with responsibility for bad philosophy" (603). Everett took issue with the way Horkheimer had treated naturalistic approaches in the second chapter, arguing that he "appears ignorant of some of the most important work done by contemporary naturalistic philosophers. . . . His own rather thinly disguised left-wing Hegelianism allows him to lump all who disagree into categories called either positivism or neo-positivism" (605).

20   James Schmidt

While Everett was willing to grant that it might be "possible to criticize contemporary naturalism fairly by saying that it has not yet developed theories of value which satisfy the crying needs of our time," he found Horkheimer's treatment of Dewey "particularly inappropriate," since it failed to take note of Dewey's "forthright social philosophy, based on an ethic of self-realization, and issuing in his concept of a 'new individualism'" (605). He closed the review by noting that, despite the excesses of the book's "attacks upon naturalism," Horkheimer attempted to "achieve a balance" in his conclusion by expressing reservations about potentially reactionary aspects of "objective reason." Everett was, however, unimpressed by the attempt, observing that what Horkheimer was seeking was nothing more than what "most balanced philosophers" have always sought: "A mutual critique which takes the best from rationalism and the best from empiricism" (605). He doubted that Horkheimer's work contributed much to this reconciliation. "To place all the ills of the present world on the doorstep of empiricism," Everett concluded, "is a rather jaundiced peace-offering" (605).

The reception of *Eclipse of Reason* could not have been very heartening for Horkheimer. Murphy's willingness to engage the book's arguments was lacking in the other reviewers. Everett appeared to be settling old scores—Lowenthal indicates in one of his letters that the Columbia philosophy department viewed Horkheimer with some suspicion—and Negley's nasty polemic was hardly an invitation to dialogue.[102] It must have been particularly troubling that the reviewers had taken aim at what Horkheimer himself recognized as the book's weakest part: its failure to elaborate a compelling alternative to the opposition between substantive and formal reason that had been sketched in the opening chapters. Worse still, the additions Horkheimer had made to the manuscript to engage recent trends in U.S. philosophy only exposed him to the charge that he had at best a superficial understanding of the traditions he criticized. Even Murphy's generous review bore no fruit: Horkheimer made no use of Murphy's work in any of his later writings, nor did Murphy ever speak of Horkheimer's work again.

Horkheimer's attempt to present a summary of his philosophy to a U.S. audience thus fell almost entirely on deaf ears. Ultimately, however, this failure became, at most, a footnote in the story of the U.S. exile of the Frankfurt School. Since the end of the war, Horkheimer had been exploring the possibility of reopening a branch of the institute at Frankfurt.[103] With negotiations over affiliations between the institute and U.S. universities stalled, the prospect of a move to Frankfurt looked quite appealing. Horkheimer returned, bringing Adorno and Pollock with him; Lowenthal, Marcuse, and Neumann remained behind.

Epilogue: The Culture Industry Cuts Its Losses

On July 27, 1952, the *New York Times* carried an advertisement from Gimbels department store that asked, "Ever see 49 TONS of books?" It went on to explain,

"A book weighs about 1 pound. . . . thrifty Gimbels sells 98,000 pounds, all originally published at $1 to $6." Lest patrons of the store that promised "Nobody but Nobody Undersells Gimbels" suspect that the place was going highbrow, the ad continued: "Does Gimbels have 49 tons of books because we're bookish? Not at all—even if our copy writers do use Phi Beta keys to open their lockers. We've got lots of books because we can sell lots of books. Big things just naturally come to Gimbels (take our famous table sales!) If you can't read, there are picture books. If you can't cook, there are cook books. If your who-dun-it fan is yearning for fresh blood and gore, find enough mysteries to bury him to the ears in clues."[104] Stretching down the page in three columns was a list of what could be had for the bargain price of two books for one dollar (single titles were fifty-nine cents) along with brief descriptions.

The list offers a snapshot of what Americans in the early 1950s could grab at bargain-basement prices. Under the heading "Current Events," customers could pick up Vannevar Bush's *Modern Arms and Free Men*—an account of "modern scientific warfare"—or John Fischer's *Why They Behave Like Russians* (described as "an informed account"). The section labeled "Economics—Sociology—Law" included Ashley Montagu's *Statement on Race* and Robert Payne's *Zero—The Story of Terrorism*. Under "Sports—Hobbies—Humor" one could find books on how to play canasta and checkers as well as Frederick van de Water's *In Defense of Worms* (which, it turns out, was a book about fishing). There were biographies, some expected (an illustrated life of Franklin Roosevelt), some surprising (Esther Meynell's *Portrait of William Morris*). Finally there was a section on religion and philosophy, where—along with *Christ in You* ("Automatic Writing of a Psychic") and C. F. Ramuz's *What Is Man?* ("A Christian answer to Communism")—the following item was listed: "*Eclipse of Reason*. By Max Horkheimer. Decline of traditional values in modern life . . . Pub. at 2.75."

And so Horkheimer's attempt to present "in epitome" the dark account of the modern world that he and Adorno had conceived under sunny California skies wound up with "49 TONS of books" on the bargain tables of a New York department store. Some New Yorkers, interested in learning something about the "decline of traditional values in modern life," may have paid their money and taken their chances. One wonders what they made of it. Perhaps a few of those who shopped at Gimbels in the summer of 1952 discovered that the bag of books they purchased included a message in a bottle, bearing tidings from "unknown spiritual friends" who now lived an ocean away.

Notes

1. Lowenthal to Horkheimer, May 22, 1947, folder 36, Leo Lowenthal Papers, Houghton Library, Harvard University. Unless otherwise indicated, citations of Lowenthal's correspondence refer to this collection, discussed in note 24 below. The

587 letters to Horkheimer dating from 1934 to 1966 are contained in forty-seven folders cataloged as bMS Ger 185 (78). The 684 letters from Horkheimer to Lowenthal are cataloged as bMS Ger 185 (47). I cite the letters by date and folder number and have silently corrected minor errors in spelling and punctuation.

2. Max Horkheimer, *Eclipse of Reason* (New York: Oxford University Press, 1947), vi–vii. Hereafter cited as *ER*.

3. Lowenthal to Horkheimer, May 22, 1947, folder 36.

4. Lowenthal to Horkheimer, April 19, 1947, folder 35.

5. Lazarsfeld to Horkheimer, July 19, 1947, in Max Horkheimer, *Gesammelte Schriften*, ed. Gunzelin Schmid Noerr (Frankfurt am Main: Fischer, 1996), 17:846. Hereafter cited as *GS*. See also Hans-Georg Gadamer's praise for the book in his letter to Horkheimer of March 15, 1950, in *GS*, 18:122–23.

6. Lowenthal to Horkheimer, January 17, 1946, folder 29.

7. Rolf Wiggershaus, *The Frankfurt School: Its Histories, Theories, and Political Significance* (Cambridge, Mass.: MIT Press, 1994), 344.

8. Horkheimer to Pollock, January 7, 1944, in *GS*, 17:539.

9. Horkheimer to Pollock, December 18, 1945, in *GS*, 17:687–88.

10. Jay notes that his "access to the extremely valuable Horkheimer-Lowenthal correspondence was qualified by an understandable reluctance on the part of the correspondents to embarrass people who might still be alive" (*The Dialectical Imagination* [Boston: Little, Brown, 1973], xvii). The terms of the deposit stipulated that the papers would remain restricted until December 31, 1998.

11. On the image of the "message in a bottle," see Theodor W. Adorno, *Minima Moralia: Reflections from Damaged Life*, trans. E. F. N. Jephcott (London: Verso, 1974), 210; and Martin Jay, ed., *An Unmastered Past: The Autobiographical Reflections of Leo Lowenthal* (Berkeley: University of California Press, 1987), 63, 148, 237.

12. Max Horkheimer, "Art and Mass Culture," in *Critical Theory* (New York: Herder and Herder, 1972), 290.

13. Anson Rabinbach, *In the Shadow of Catastrophe: German Intellectuals between Apocalypse and Enlightenment* (Berkeley: University of California Press, 1997), 196.

14. For a discussion of the meeting see Horkheimer to Lowenthal, November 1, 1946, folder 30.

15. Horkheimer to Lowenthal, October 28, 1946, folder 29.

16. See Horkheimer to Frank D. Fackenthal, president of Columbia University, June 12, 1946, in *GS*, 17:736–37.

17. These efforts are discussed in Horkheimer to Lowenthal, November 1, 1946, folder 30. As late as March 3, 1948 (folder 37), Horkheimer telegrammed Lowenthal that the attitude of the sociology department at UCLA was "very favorable."

18. Horkheimer to Juliette Favez, February 17, 1939, in *GS*, 16:561. For a discussion of his plans for this work, see James Schmidt, "Language, Mythology, and Enlightenment: Historical Notes on Horkheimer and Adorno's Dialectic of Enlightenment," *Social Research* 65 (1998): 807–38.

19. On this period see Wiggershaus, *Frankfurt School*, 291–302.

20. Lowenthal to Horkheimer, September 19, 1941, folder 12; Lowenthal to Horkheimer, May 1, 1941, in *GS,* 17:32.

21. Horkheimer to Lowenthal, January 20, 1942, folder 9; Horkheimer, summary of telephone conversation with Lowenthal, November 8, 1942, folder 13.

22. For discussions of Pollock's difficulties in dealing with other members of the institute see Lowenthal to Horkheimer, September 23, 1941, folder 13; January 21, 1942, folder 16; and October 29, 1942, folder 21.

23. Most of the documentation of the financial side of Lowenthal's activities is contained in his letters to Pollock, bMS Ger 185 (82). For reports of visits to brokerage firms, see the letters in folder 2. For the real estate venture, see Lowenthal to Pollock, July 1, 1942, folder 5; August 7, 1942, folder 6; and August 17, 1942, folder 6; and the series of letters to Pollock from 1944 and 1945 in folder 7.

24. Lowenthal preserved carbon copies of his letters to Horkheimer as well as copies of Horkheimer's responses. It should be noted that Lowenthal's letters to Horkheimer were in German at first, but he switched to English in January 1942. Although there is no explanation for the alteration in the letters themselves, the change probably stems from a desire to avoid communication in what, after December 8, 1941, would have been the language of a nation with which the United States was at war.

25. For an exhaustive and insightful discussion based on archival sources in Frankfurt and at Columbia, see Thomas Wheatland, "The Frankfurt School's Invitation from Columbia University: How the Horkheimer Circle Settled on Morningside Heights," *German Politics and Society* 22, no. 3 (2004): 1–32.

26. See ibid., 11–13.

27. On Lynd's interest in Fromm's work, see ibid., 23–26.

28. See Thomas Wheatland, "Isolation, Assimilation, and Opposition: A Reception History of the Horkheimer Circle in the United States, 1934–1979" (Ph.D. diss., Boston College, 2002), 141–43.

29. See Thomas Wheatland, "Paul Lazarsfeld, the Horkheimer Circle, and Columbia University" (paper presented at the conference "Contested Legacies," Bard College, August 2002); and Paul Lazarsfeld, "An Essay in the History of Social Research: A Memoir," in *The Intellectual Migration: Europe and America, 1930–1960,* ed. Donald Fleming and Bernard Bailyn (Cambridge, Mass.: Harvard University Press, 1969), 274–75, 289. Lazarsfeld also served, along with Adorno and Benjamin, as a representative of the institute in a private discussion—with a group of thinkers associated with the Vienna Circle—of Horkheimer's article "The Latest Attack on Metaphysics." For a brief mention of this rather curious event, held in Paris in the summer of 1937, see Adorno to Horkheimer, August 7, 1937, in *GS,* 16:210.

30. Wiggershaus, *Frankfurt School,* 223–9.

31. Since 1936 the institute had offered a course, listed in the sociology department, in the extension division. See Wheatland, "Isolation, Assimilation, and Opposition," 126–27.

32. Lowenthal to Horkheimer, January 23, 1942 (first letter), folder 16.

33. Horkheimer to Lowenthal, January 20, 1942, folder 9.
34. Lowenthal to Horkheimer, January 23, 1942 (second letter), folder 16.
35. Ibid.
36. Postscript dated January 25, 1942, in Horkheimer to Lowenthal, January 20, 1942, in *GS*, 17:247–48.
37. Ibid., 248.
38. Horkheimer to Lowenthal, October 31, 1942, in *GS*, 17:367.
39. Horkheimer to Lowenthal, August 16, 1942, folder 12.
40. Horkheimer to Adorno, September 17, 1942, in *GS*, 17:331.
41. A version of the proposal, written in 1939, was published as "Research Project on Anti-Semitism," *Studies in Philosophy and Social Science* 9 (1941): 124–43. See also Horkheimer to Edward S. Greenbaum, inquiring about the status of the proposal, June 18, 1940, in *GS*, 16:719–25.
42. Wiggershaus, Frankfurt School, 350–57.
43. Horkheimer to Lowenthal, March 26, 1943, in *GS*, 17:438–39.
44. For a progress report see Horkheimer to Lowenthal, September 29, 1943, folder 16.
45. Horkheimer to Lowenthal, January 3, 1944, folder 16.
46. Lowenthal to Horkheimer, August 10, 1944, folder 26. The same file contains a proposal from Lowenthal, dated August 24, to rearrange the book's table of contents, a suggestion that corresponds to the version that was published. I have not been able to determine the original order of the chapters.
47. Horkheimer to Lowenthal, June 14, 1944, folder 17.
48. I discuss the unfinished character of *Dialectic of Enlightenment* in "Language, Mythology, and Enlightenment."
49. Horkheimer to Lowenthal, February 5, 1943, folder 15, refers to "Tillich's demands" for titles for the lectures.
50. This material was sent in February and March 1943. See Horkheimer to Lowenthal, February 24, 1943; March 3, 1943; and March 13, 1943 (all folder 15).
51. Several versions of this outline exist in the Lowenthal papers (see folder 14). One includes penciled annotations of the dates for the lectures.
52. Max Horkheimer, "The End of Reason," *Studies in Philosophy and Social Science* 9 (1941): 366–88.
53. Lowenthal to Horkheimer, October 11, 1943, folder 24; the letter also contains other information about arrangements for the lectures.
54. Horkheimer to Pollock, January 7, 1944, in *GS*, 17:538–39.
55. Horkheimer to Lowenthal, January 3, 1944, folder 16.
56. In a telegram to Lowenthal sent on January 13, 1944, folder 16, Horkheimer wrote that he would "prefer an American instead of Guterman but Freeman unknown to me." Guterman nevertheless contributed much to preparing the lectures for publication.
57. Horkheimer to MacIver, August 9, 1944, in *GS*, 17:591.

58. See Max Horkheimer, "Society and Reason: Five Public Lectures Delivered at the Department of Philosophy of Columbia University" (February–March 1944), Max Horkheimer Archive, Frankfurt, LIX, 36, 6a, lecture 2, 5–12. Hereafter cited as *SR*. After the discussion of Dewey, Horkheimer notes, "The objections which I had expected to be raised against my analysis last time were different from those which I have just noted."

59. See the printed card announcing Horkheimer's lectures in Horkheimer's letters to Lowenthal, folder 17. The topics are repeated on the front page of the lecture manuscript.

60. Horkheimer seems to have planned to discuss romanticism in his third lecture and as a result prefaced the lecture with discussions of German idealism that were dropped from the book, as were the lecture's apologies about not discussing romanticism and also its concluding discussion of Hegel (see *SR*, 25–28).

61. The lecture ends twelve pages later. Some of the points raised in the last part, including a brief discussion of culture's role in enforcing conformity, later found a home in the third and fourth chapters of *Eclipse of Reason*.

62. Horkheimer to MacIver, August 9, 1944, in *GS*, 17:591.

63. Lowenthal to Horkheimer, September 25, 1944, folder 26.

64. Horkheimer first mentioned the article in his letter to Herbert Marcuse of September 11, 1943, in *GS*, 17:471.

65. Horkheimer to Lowenthal, March 28, 1944, folder 17. Lowenthal defended Nelson in his letter of August 4, 1944, in *GS*, 17:585–86.

66. Lowenthal informed Horkheimer that Mills was one of the book's readers in his letter of November 13, 1945, folder 28.

67. He appears, for example, to have been completely unfamiliar with the work of George Herbert Mead. In an October 4, 1943, letter to Horkheimer about a young woman being hired by the institute, Lowenthal wrote, "Her favorite reading in college was George H. Mead and if you look it up in the *Encyclopedia of Social Science* you will find that this Mead apparently was a philosopher and sociologist with genuine problems," folder 23.

68. Horkheimer to Lowenthal, December 21, 1944, folder 20.

69. Ibid.; Horkheimer to Lowenthal, January 17, 1946, folder 20; February 5, 1946, folder 21.

70. Horkheimer to Lowenthal, March 20, 1946, folder 23.

71. Lowenthal to Horkheimer, March 20, 1946, folder 31. At this point Lowenthal and Guterman seemed to favor *The Shadow of Progress*.

72. See Horkheimer to Lowenthal, December 28, 1945, and January 10, 1946, folder 20.

73. Horkheimer to Lowenthal, December 28, 1945, folder 20.

74. Horkheimer to Lowenthal, January 10, 1946, folder 20.

75. Horkheimer sent Lowenthal a letter to Margaret Nicholson, his editor at Oxford, dated January 30, 1946, which was to be included with the manuscript when delivered, folder 22.

76. Horkheimer to Lowenthal, March 6, 1946, folder 23.

77. Lowenthal to Horkheimer, August 23, 1946, folder 27.

78. Horkheimer to Lowenthal, November 4, 1946, folder 30; Lowenthal to Horkheimer, November 8, 1946, folder 34.

79. The publication of the book was announced in the *New York Times,* May 8, 1947, though copies were circulating among Horkheimer's friends and associates for about a month prior to this date. The publication note in the *New York Times* offered the following summary: "An analysis of 'the disintegration of the basic concepts of Western civilization.'"

80. Horkheimer to Lowenthal, April 23, 1947, folder 31. Horkheimer was displeased with "the beginning of the second paragraph" on the inside jacket: "Industrial civilization, with its emphasis on practical means, has undermined the concepts designed to represent such an objective truth." While it is difficult to determine specifically what bothered Horkheimer about this, it is possible that he was troubled by the suggestion that the book was to be read simply as a defense of "objective reason."

81. See Horkheimer to Lowenthal, April 29, 1947, folder 31, and May 12, 1947, folder 32.

82. Horkheimer had hoped to incorporate an account of "rackets" into *Dialectic of Enlightenment,* but little was actually written beyond a 1943 manuscript, "On the Sociology of Class Relations," parts of which were imported into *Eclipse of Reason.* Originally written in English, the manuscript has been published as "Zur Soziologie der Klassenverhältnisse," in *GS,* 12:75–104.

83. Horkheimer to Lowenthal, May 12, 1947, folder 32.

84. Ibid.

85. Horkheimer to Lowenthal, July 30, 1947, folder 34. Oxford purchased at least one advertisement in the *New York Times Book Review* (June 8, 1947), where the book was one of six listed. There is no description of its contents beyond a blurb from the novelist, social historian, and political activist Waldo Frank: "A diagnosis, lucid and profound, of the basic disease of our civilization. . . . I hope that this significant, urgent essay will be read in the universities, churches, and progressive organizations of the country."

86. Horkheimer to Lowenthal, August 30, 1947, folder 34. The work in question was Ludwig Marcuse, *Plato and Dionysius: A Double Biography,* trans. Joel Ames (New York: Knopf, 1947).

87. Horkheimer to Lowenthal, July 30, 1947, folder 34.

88. Horkheimer to Lowenthal, August 8, 1947, folder 34.

89. Lowenthal to Horkheimer, May 10, 1947, folder 36.

90. Lowenthal to Horkheimer, September 26, 1947, folder 38. The reference appears in the *Nation,* September 27, 1947, 91. Lowenthal to Horkheimer, August 4, 1947, folder 37.

91. Lowenthal to Horkheimer, August 4, 1947, folder 37.

92. Arthur E. Murphy, review of Max Horkheimer, *Eclipse of Reason, Philosophical Review* 57 (March1948): 190–92.

93. On this point see Arthur E. Murphy, *The Uses of Reason* (New York: Macmillan, 1943), 88–91.

94. Horkheimer to Murphy, May 29, 1947, in *GS,* 17:816.

95. Murphy to Horkheimer, June 22, 1947, in *GS,* 17:822–23. Although it is possible that, given his anxiety about securing reviews of *Eclipse of Reason,* Horkheimer may have learned from other sources that Murphy was reviewing the book, the fact that Horkheimer sent his letter to the University of Illinois, where Murphy was teaching at the time of the publication of *The Uses of Reason,* rather than Cornell University, his current position, makes this doubtful.

96. Arthur E. Murphy, "Ideas and Ideologies: 1917–1947," *Philosophical Review* 56 (July 1947): 374–89. Hereafter cited as "Ideas." It is likely that this is the article to which Murphy alluded in his letter to Horkheimer of June 22, 1947, which promised to send "a reprint of a recent article of mine in which I think I have come somewhat closer to your views (though I had not seen them when the article was written)," in *GS,* 17:822.

97. On the latter point see Murphy, "Tradition and Traditionalists," in John Dewey, Sidney Hook, Arthur E. Murphy, Irwin Edman, et al., *The Authoritarian Attempt to Capture Education* (New York: King's Crown, 1945), 18–25.

98. The review by J. B. Mabbott in the British journal *Philosophy* 23 (1948): 368–69 confined itself to summarizing the book's argument; it concluded by noting the rather sketchy character of Horkheimer's proposed alternative (a complaint found in all reviews of the book) but nevertheless praised the book's argument as "impressive and convincing." While Mabbott found the book "not easy to read" and thought that it mixed philosophy and sociology in a way that "is difficult to disentangle," he judged it to be "written with great spirit and seriousness" and to contain "many stimulating and striking observations" (369). Charles Denecke's review in the Fordham University journal *Thought* 23 (1948): 348–49 also consisted for the most part of a summary, with a few comments at the end criticizing the book for misunderstanding Thomism.

99. Glenn Negley, review of Max Horkheimer, *Eclipse of Reason, Ethics* 58 (October 1947): 75–77. In his memorial notice on Negley in the *Proceedings of the American Philosophical Association* 56 (1982): 98–99, Peyton Richter described him as "a toughminded political and legal philosopher who took delight in defending normative ethics, metaphysics, and utopian speculation against their enemies." Negley received his doctorate from Chicago in 1939 and combined his graduate studies with work as a legislative assistant in the Illinois State Senate. He came to Duke in 1946 and, at the time of his review of Horkheimer, had published one book, *The Organization of Knowledge* (1942). He was later responsible for assembling a large collection of utopian literature at Duke.

100. The citation refers to Berton Rouché, "Zweckwissenschaft," *New Yorker* (August 9, 1947): 46.

101. John R. Everett, review of Max Horkheimer, *Eclipse of Reason, Journal of Philosophy* 45 (1948): 603–5. Everett did his graduate work at Columbia, obtaining an A.M. in economics in 1943 and a Ph.D. in religion in 1945 (with a dissertation titled "Religion

in Economics: A Study of John Bates Clark, Richard T. Ely [and] Simon N. Patten"). He also obtained a B.D. from Union Theological Seminary in 1944. He was a lecturer in philosophy at Columbia in 1943 and 1944 and was appointed assistant professor of philosophy in 1948; he resigned his position effective June 30, 1950, to become president of Hollins College in Roanoke, Virginia, and in 1964 returned to New York as president of the New School for Social Research.

102. In his letter to Horkheimer of January 4, 1943, Lowenthal reported that Tillich had told him that the department "minds two things. First, that both of you are living on much too large a scale while the assistants and collaborators have a very hard life and secondly, that terrible speculations have ruined the Institute's fortune," folder 22.

103. See, for example, Horkheimer to Lowenthal, July 29, 1946, folder 25, which reports that Horkheimer's friend and neighbor William Dieterle, a Hollywood director and member of the institute's board, who was about to depart for Europe in search of new talent for the producer David O. Selznick, had promised to raise the issue of a possible branch office with officials at the University of Frankfurt.

104. *New York Times,* July 27, 1952. An earlier version of the ad, with a similar listing of books but without the discussion of their weight, had appeared in the *Times* of May 18, 1952.

Richard Bodek

Max Horkheimer and "The Jews and Europe"
A Reevaluation

From Moses Mendelssohn's *Jerusalem; or, On Religious Power and Judaism* through the writings of members of the Frankfurt School in the 1930s and beyond into exile, the Enlightenment has had a profound effect on modern German-Jewish thought. One of the most prominent strands of that thought has been neo-Kantianism, with its emphasis on a rational understanding of the world and its central concern with ethics. Among the last of the Jewish neo-Kantians was Hermann Cohen, who taught and/or influenced such thinkers as Franz Rosenzweig, Martin Buber, and Walter Benjamin. Cohen's importance lay especially in his attempt to link academic philosophy to practical ethics and at the same time to Judaism. A story, told by Leo Lowenthal, a central member of the Frankfurt School, exemplifies this: "Franz Rosenzweig relates a conversation that took place in Marburg between Friedrich Albert Lange and Cohen. Lange asks, 'Do our views on Christianity differ?' Cohen replies, 'No, for what you call Christianity, I call prophetic Judaism." And to this conversation Cohen appends the remark, 'Thus, with one blow, did ethical socialism unite us beyond the bounds of our religions.' . . . But alongside Kant and socialism, there appears Judaism as a third term."[1]

    For Cohen, Judaism was a rational religion that would allow for a clear understanding of the world. In those terms Cohen was unquestionably a child of the Enlightenment and believed that Judaism was a kind of rational gift to the world. According to Lowenthal's understanding of Cohen's thought, Cohen believed that Jewish suffering was not tragic, nor did hatred truly exist.[2] This aspect of his thought did not have a great deal of influence, as most nineteenth- and early-twentieth-century German Jewish thinkers were interested in the problem of anti-Semitism. One tenet of most Jewish neo-Kantianism was that more enlightenment would help to alleviate this fundamental problem. Yet, in the wake of the First World War, revolutionary activity in Germany, and the rise of Nazism, this once-firm belief lost much of its luster. Both the rise of National Socialism in Germany and the NSDAP's policy of anti-Semitism led some of the twentieth century's German-Jewish thinkers to reconsider the nature of the Enlightenment, the Haskalah

(Jewish Enlightenment), and the role of Jews in the modern world. Among these thinkers were many of the members of the Institut für Sozialforschung, later known as the Frankfurt School. A continuing research project in which I am engaged will examine the Frankfurt School's views of enlightenment and modernity, concentrating both on intra-school debates and on dialogues, which members of the school conducted with other German-Jewish thinkers. This article represents one fragment of this larger project, an analysis of Max Horkheimer's 1939 article "Europe and the Jews," placing it into the context of much German-Jewish thought, both that which influenced it, and that which it influenced. In short, I would like to rehabilitate a much-maligned article, one that has not received much respect from later critics. I will argue that "Europe and the Jews" was both in the mainstream of previous works of German-Jewish thought, and fundamental to other, more widely respected works that came later.

The Institut für Sozialforschung, founded in 1923, was an interdisciplinary, largely Marxist faculty, dedicated to investigating contemporary and historical phenomena. Among its more prominent thinkers were two philosophers, Max Horkheimer and Theodor Adorno, both of whom studied under Hans Cornelius, an important neo-Kantian thinker. After the Nazi *Machtergreifung*, the institute moved to New York, where it undertook studies of fascism, of the Enlightenment, and of anti-Semitism. These questions were conjoined in the 1947 book *Dialectic of Enlightenment*, which questions the emancipatory role of the Enlightenment, seeing it instead as a return to mythology. Central to its argument was the nature of anti-Semitism in the modern world. Adorno and Horkheimer claimed that anti-Semitism was both one of the most important intellectual forces in modernity and a natural consequence of the Enlightenment.

This work found its origins in 1944, when Max Horkheimer and Theodor Adorno wrote "Philosophische Fragmente," the first draft of what was to become *Dialectic of Enlightenment*. This latter work was quite possibly the most important to come out of the Frankfurt School, a group of expatriate German (mostly Jewish) philosophers and social scientists. It was an attempt to discover why "mankind, instead of entering into a truly human condition, is sinking into a new kind of barbarism."[3] *Dialectic of Enlightenment* raised questions and put forward theses about the nature of modernity, mythology, the Enlightenment, fascism, and monopoly capitalism, culminating in a theory of anti-Semitism.

They maintained that although enlightenment would bring rationality, such rationality was instrumental, searching for means to achieve the goals of whoever employed it. In addition rationality is a totalizing force. Its purveyors assume that all would be persuaded that reason's totality is irrefutable. Europe's Jews did not fulfill this assumption, as they did not shed their cultural distinctiveness in the process of assimilation. Therefore, Horkheimer and Adorno posited, total rationality necessitated total violence, its natural tool.

Horkheimer and Adorno's theory of anti-Semitism is multifaceted, befitting a book originally titled a fragment. Among their ideas are the following. Nationalist views of Jews are in fact a self-portrait. "They long for total possession and unlimited power at any price."[4] Anti-Semitism in its Nazi form (economic aryanization) brings no real economic benefits, rather it "panders to [their] urge to destroy."[5] For bourgeois anti-Semites, Jews were hateful because of their position in the capitalist sphere of circulation. As merchants they would take the hatred that belonged to others onto themselves.[6]

The authors also argued that there were characteristics that all anti-Semites shared. Anti-Semites all wanted to imitate their mental image of the Jew. The fascist love for "ritual discipline, the uniforms, and the whole apparatus, which is at first sight irrational, was to allow mimetic behavior."[7] This is one reason that they accused Jews of "participating in forbidden magic and bloody ritual."[8] The irony of this, according to Horkheimer and Adorno, was that Jews in fact abandoned magic for duty [the commandments]. In short anti-Semitism was a kind of false projection. "Mimesis imitates the environment, but false projection makes the environment like itself."[9] This and other similar insights in *Dialectic of Enlightenment* owe an important debt to Sigmund Freud's work on the uncanny, in which he argued that the "uncanny" was that class of the terrifying that led back to something long known to us, once very familiar.[10] Later generations of readers have questioned whether these ideas were or could constitute a unified whole. Nevertheless the literature on the Frankfurt School finds them to be both subtle and interesting, at least in their (seeming) attempt to unify various paradigms in the search for a unified theory of anti-Semitism.

Such praise is decidedly not the case for Max Horkheimer's 1939 article "The Jews and Europe," an essay for which posterity has roundly criticized him. In brief many historians have reduced Horkheimer's argument to the following: Jews provided (at least the most prominent) face of the sphere of circulation, which at that historical juncture was losing economic importance—thus, Nazi anti-Semitism. Commenting on the piece, Martin Jay claims that Horkheimer's early thoughts on anti-Semitism consisted of a "facile dismissal of specifically Jewish problems."[11] Anson Rabinbach claimed that by 1943, "little remained of the central argument of Horkheimer's 'the Jews and Europe.'"[12] Dan Diner, albeit with more sympathy for Horkheimer, finds himself in general agreement, mounting the relatively weak defense that "to judge Horkheimer's position on anti-Semitism in this way is to take up a critical position outside history, outside the times, experiences and the sense of life crucial not only for Horkheimer and the original Frankfurt School but for German Jews in general."[13] One sees points of congruence between Horkheimer's critics and defenders—namely that Horkheimer erred in "The Jews and Europe" but corrected his mistakes, or at least altered his view, in *Dialectic of Enlightenment*.

"The Jews and Europe" was Horkheimer's first essay on fascism, and it represented a general political statement.[14] It was in this piece that Horkheimer, having claimed that "countries turn totalitarian faster than the books can find publishers,"[15] argued that the seeds of National Socialism were already present in the French Revolution.[16] Criticism of Horkheimer has concerned itself with his tone and with his supposed unyielding economism. For example, Horkheimer took German Jewish refugees to task for abrogating their responsibilities by not criticizing the political situation in the United States.[17] Furthermore he included the apparently unforgivable lines: "Whoever is not willing to talk about capitalism should also keep quiet about Fascism."[18] and "The transition from liberalism has occurred logically enough, and less brutally than from the mercantile system into that of the nineteenth century."[19] Contra Diner, one can posit that Horkheimer showed a remarkable prescience about the horrors of Nazi Germany in particular and the twentieth century in general. The reader can look at "The Jews and Europe" less as a monolithic statement and more as a series of ideas, ideas that may or may not be in internal harmony. But it is also worth being familiar with others involved in the Frankfurt School so that the tug and pull of various influences can be understood.

Franz Neumann

At one level it is easy to construct a relatively straightforward typology of Frankfurt School thinkers, at least before the appearance of *Dialectic of Enlightenment*. Franz Neumann, for example, occupies the role of arch–economistic thinker.

Neumann (born 1900) was a lawyer for the German trade unions and the Social Democratic Party until 1933, becoming a full-time academic only in exile. He has come to be thought of as one of the most economistic thinkers of the school, one having little patience for questions of culture. Neumann, as he enters the stage in Anson Rabinbach's "Why Were the Jews Sacrificed?," is represented by the quote, "I can imagine, and I have done this in my book, that one can represent National Socialism without attributing to the Jewish problem a central role."[20] Yet Rabinbach ought to have known better than to take this bit of Marxist posturing at face value. For in "the book," *Behemoth*—written in 1941 and arguably still one of the best analyses of the National Socialist state—Neumann made a number of statements that cast this claim into doubt. Examples include his contention that within Nazism, racism and anti-Semitism substitute for class struggle. Thus anti-Semitism was a crucial tool to integrate Aryan society into a whole. Furthermore the Third Reich used anti-Semitism to justify eastern expansion.[21] He also argued that anti-Semitism operated as a rejection of Christianity.[22] More interesting, though, is his typology of anti-Semitism into totalitarian and nontotalitarian forms. "For the totalitarian Anti-Semite, the Jew has long ceased to be a human being. He has become the incarnation of evil in Germany, nay, in the entire world. In other words, totalitarian Anti-Semitism is magic and beyond discussion."[23]

Magic? Beyond discussion? Here is a language that explodes classical Marxism and forces the "Jewish Question" to the center of discussion. For Horkheimer and Adorno, magic was "milieu bound," as opposed to myth, which, like the Enlightenment, would provide a series of rules that could be generalized.[24] If he used magic in the same sense as did Horkheimer and Adorno, then the usual descriptions of Neumann seem to be far too flat. This ought not be too surprising, though, for the author of a work entitled *Behemoth,* consciously invoking not only Hobbes but Jewish eschatology as well.

Anson Rabinbach's claim that Horkheimer and Adorno needed to satisfy their more dogmatic colleagues evaporates when faced with this admission of Marxism's defeat on the part of one of its most adamant defenders. Horkheimer's agenda was sophisticated from the outset. In "The Jews and Europe," he invoked the so-called dark writers of the bourgeoisie, dark writers—in this case the Marquis de Sade—in that they made explicit what was hidden by liberal theories of the Enlightenment in a discussion of terror that seems to provide their defense of instrumental reason. For Horkheimer instrumental reason was reason at the point of its self-destruction, when only self-preservation was left in its wake. It is thus post moral.[25] For his example of how this works, he quoted de Sade, for him a paradigmatic figure:

> The wild animal called the people necessarily requires iron leadership; you will be lost immediately if you allow it to become aware of its strength. . . . The ruled individual needs no other virtue than patience and subordination; mind, talents, sciences belong on the side of the government. The greatest misfortune results from the overthrow of these principles. The real authority of the government will cease to exist, if everyone feels called to share in it; the horror of anarchy comes from such extravagance. The only means to avoid these dangers is to tighten the chain as much as possible, to pass the strictest laws, to avoid the enlightenment of the people, above all to resist the fatal freedom of the press, which is the source of all the knowledge that emancipates the people, and finally to terrify them by means of severe and frequent punishments. . . . Do not delude yourself that I understand by "people" the venal and corrupt class that, thrown upon our earth like the scum of Nature, is only able to exist in the sweat of its brow. What the National Socialists know was already known a hundred years ago. "One should only assemble people in church or in arms; then they don't think, they only listen and obey." The place of St. Peter's is taken by the Berlin Sport Palace [where Nazi rallies were staged].[26]

Horkheimer later marshaled Kant to the dark writers' side in what is seemingly a validation of Jay's reading of the text:

> The later Kant is not so much more convinced of the lower classes' right to freedom than Sade and de Bonald. According to practical reason, the

people must obey as if in prison, only with the difference that it also should have its own conscience as warden and overseer, alongside the agents of the regime in power. "The origin of the highest power is for practical purposes inscrutable for the people which is subject to it, i.e. the subjects should not practically reason . . . about its origin; for if the subject who had pondered out the ultimate origin were to resist that now prevailing authority, then by the laws of the latter, i.e., with complete justification, he would be punished, destroyed, or (outlawed, *exlex*) expelled." Kant embraces the theory that "whoever is in possession of the supreme ruling and legislating power over a people, must be obeyed, and so juridically-absolutely, that even to research the title to this acquisition in public, that is, to doubt it, in order to resist it in case of some failing, is itself punishable; that it is a categorical imperative: Obey authority that has power over you (in everything which does not contradict the inwardly moral). But the scholar of Kant knows: the inwardly moral can never protest against an onerous task ordered by the respective authority."[27]

But, for Horkheimer, like Neumann, such terror has its limits. He claims that the so-called totalitarian states could still "dissolve overnight into a chaos of gangster battles."[28] Here the simplistic framework imposed on Horkheimer begins to break down. Horkheimer segued to a discussion of atomization in a fascist regime. "Fear of unemployment is supplanted by fear of the state. Fear atomizes."[29] Furthermore,

> Like work under the dictates of the state, the belief in Führer and community propagated by the state appears to be an escape from a bleak existence. Everyone knows what he has to do and more or less what tomorrow will be like. One is no longer a beggar, and if there is war, one won't die alone. The "folk community" continues the ideology of 1914. National outbursts are the approved substitute for the revolution. Unconsciously, the workers realize the horror of their existence, which they are nevertheless unable to change. Salvation must come from above. Insincere as may be the belief in the insignificance of the individual, the survival of the "folk," or the leaders as personalities, it at least expresses an experience, in contrast to apathetic Christianity. The society is abandoned by the idolized leaders, but not quite as abandoned as it always was by the True God.[30]

Here the contention that Horkheimer was merely interested in circulation breaks down. However briefly, Horkheimer addressed a series of issues with which classical Marxism was ill equipped to deal:

bleak existence versus community
the question of salvation in a post-Christian world

idealized leadership which, although it has abandoned society,
  is still more present than is God

Here is a space that a psychoanalytically informed model could, and did, illuminate. There are ideas and attitudes here which gesture toward Freud's notion of the uncanny, a theory that posits that the horrible achieves its horror precisely because of its familiarity. In order to understand some of the framework that underpins "The Jews and Europe," it is important to acquaint oneself with some of the arguments in Sigmund Freud's "The 'Uncanny.'" For Freud, "the 'uncanny' is that class of the terrifying which leads back to something long known to us, once very familiar."[31] Buried in this idea of the uncanny (*unheimlich* in German) is the known (or *heimlich*), the meaning of the one crossing over into the other.[32] To illustrate this claim, Freud retells and analyzes the story of the Sandman, one of E. T. A. Hoffmann's tales of the macabre.[33] Without retelling the tale itself, it is important to note that for Freud its significance lies in the shift of certain characters and feelings from the known to the unknown and back. This is especially evident in his discussion of doubles (*Doppelgänger*).

The Jews, once thoroughly known and familiar because of their role in financial circulation, have according to Horkheimer become "unfamiliar" as that role has diminished. Admittedly nowhere does Horkheimer refer explicitly to Freud's argument. It nevertheless models an argument about familiarization and defamiliarization that runs through "The Jews and Europe" like a red thread. Freud's thoughts on the uncanny must at least have been common enough currency to become part of Horkheimer's intellectual arsenal.

Indeed this space left open in "The Jews and Europe" questions the model of the sphere of circulation. This questioning, in fact, is where the Frankfurt School's trajectory is leading it. Their Anti-Semitism Project (the research plan for which was written in 1941 and which eventually produced *The Authoritarian Personality*) was decided on in 1940. The research plan claimed that anti-Semitism was inherent in contemporary culture. In quite blunt language, it called for a reading of Voltaire rather than Julius Streicher—Nazi pornographer and publicist—to support this point. Furthermore it claimed that the antiaristocratic language of the French Revolution—which referred to aristocrats as parasites, living in luxury, with international connections bore "a resemblance to anti-Semitism in modern Germany."[34]

"The Jews and Europe" also presages Hannah Arendt's notion of the banality of evil and its centrality to fascism. Certainly some of the themes and analyses that emerged in "Europe and the Jews" return in Hannah Arendt's *Origins of Totalitarianism*. Indeed the latter—a classic work—is inconceivable without the theoretical claims of the former. Arendt, in a discussion of the French population's hatred of aristocrats, borrowed the argument that this hatred was a result of "their rapid loss of real power [not being] accompanied by any considerable decline in their fortunes . . . ; wealth without visible function is much more intolerable because nobody can understand why it should be tolerated."[35] She then echoes Horkheimer when she claims that "Antisemitism reached its climax when Jews had similarly lost their public functions and their influence, and were left with nothing but their wealth."[36] She contends that Nazism employed terror against the Jews, a perfectly innocent group, in order to ensure the continued obedience of the "perfectly obedient"[37] Her analysis of modern anti-Semitism is rooted in the development of nation-states rather than in theology.[38] Jews' important exceptionalism was rooted in their peculiar class status, or perhaps lack thereof, rather than in their beliefs. This was because their wealth, which would suggest middle-class status, was not tied to capitalist development.[39] Even this wealth had disintegrated in the decades preceding the outbreak of World War I.[40] Finally, she claimed that "Antisemitism, having lost its ground in the special conditions that had influenced its development during the nineteenth century, could be freely elaborated by charlatans and crackpots into that weird mixture of half-truths and wild superstitions which emerged in Europe after 1914, the ideology of all frustrated and resentful elements."[41] With this final point, Arendt, like Horkheimer, borrows some ideas and analyses from Freud's work on the uncanny.

"The Jews and Europe" is also complementary with the view of Judaism posited by the Frankfurt Lehrhaus of Franz Rosenzweig, which meant to establish a new model of community based on the study of shared texts. In the language of the Frankfurt School, this was the difference between nature (the Jews) and fascist mimesis.

Stronger evidence follows:

> Anti-Semitism will come to a natural end in the totalitarian order *when nothing humane remains, although a few Jews might* [emphasis added]. The hatred of Jews belongs to the ascendant phase of fascism. At most, anti-Semitism in Germany is a safety valve for the younger members of the SA. It serves to intimidate the populace by showing that the system will stop at nothing. The pogroms are aimed politically more at the spectators than the Jews. Will anyone react? There is nothing more to be gained. The great anti-Semitic propaganda is addressed to foreign countries. Prominent Aryans in business and other areas may express all the outrage they wish, especially if their countries are far from the action; their respectively fascist masses do not take it very seriously. People can secretly appreciate the cruelty by which they are so outraged. In continents from whose produce all of humanity could live, every beggar fears that the Jewish émigré might deprive him of his living. Reserve armies of the unemployed and the petty bourgeoisie love Hitler all over the world for his Anti-Semitism, and the core of the ruling class agrees with that love. By increasing cruelty to the

level of absurdity, its horror is mollified. That the offended divine power leaves the evildoers unpunished proves once again that it does not exist at all. In the reproduction of inhumanity, people confirm to themselves that the old humanity and religion along with the entire liberal ideology no longer have any value. Pity is really the last sin.[42]

One must again question this text. Diner and Jay both seem quite flat in the face of a passage, which conveys (understated) horror. "Nothing humane remains, although a few Jews might." A few? What does he envision? "By increasing cruelty to the level of absurdity its horror is mollified." "People can secretly appreciate the cruelty by which they are so outraged." Again Horkheimer broke the chains of classical Marxism within which his critics seek to bind him.

Horkheimer provides a prescient read of the twentieth century in which absurd levels of cruelty grow progressively less noticeable. In short, although this is as much a thought experiment as it is an article, much of what makes the final chapter of *Dialectic of Enlightenment* so interesting is touched on in this oft-neglected piece. Certainly it is part of the nineteenth- and twentieth-century discussion of enlightenment and anti-Semitism that was so central to the thought of so many German-Jewish intellectuals. This is a trajectory that begins with Mendelssohn's unselfconscious adoption of the Enlightenment, through Gershom Scholem's belief, implicit in his research on Kabbalah and Jewish mysticism, that much anti-Semitism is based on the idea that Jews were too modern, to Hannah Arendt's theory of the banality of evil, which saw anti-Semitism as empty, its importance lying in its use as an organizing principle.

Notes

1. Leo Lowenthal, "Hermann Cohen," in Lowenthal, *Critical Theory and Frankfurt Theorists: Lectures—Correspondence—Conversations* (New Brunswick, N.J.: Transaction Publishers, 1989), 36.

2. Leo Lowenthal, "Hermann Cohen," 39.

3. Max Horkheimer and Theodor Adorno, *Dialectic of Enlightenment,* trans. John Cumming (New York: Continuum, 1990), xi.

4. Ibid., 168–69.

5. Ibid., 170.

6. Ibid., 173–74.

7. Ibid., 184.

8. Max Horkheimer and Theodor Adorno, *Dialectic of Enlightenment,* 186.

9. Ibid., 187.

10. Sigmund Freud, "The 'Uncanny," *Collected Papers,* vol. 4, trans. Joan Riviere (London: Hogarth Press, 1924–1950), 369–70.

11. Martin Jay, "The Jews and the Frankfurt School: Critical Theory's analysis of Anti-Semitism," in Jay, *Permanent Exiles: Essays on the Intellectual Migration from Germany to America* (New York: Columbia University Press, 1985), 90.

12. Anson Rabinbach, *In the Shadow of Catastrophe: German Intellectuals between Apocalypse and Enlightenment* (Berkeley: University of California Press, 1997), 187.

13. Dan Diner, "Reason and the 'Other': Horkheimer's Reflections on Anti-Semitism and Mass Annihilation," in Seyla Benhabib et al., eds., *On Max Horkheimer: New Perspectives* (Cambridge, Mass.: MIT Press, 1993), 335.

14. Rolf Wiggershaus, *The Frankfurt School: Its History, Theories, and Political Significance*, trans. Michael Roberts (Cambridge, Mass.: MIT Press, 1994), 257.

15. Max Horkheimer, "The Jews and Europe," trans. Mark Ritter, in Stephen Eric Bronner and Douglas MacKay Kellner, eds., *Critical Theory and Society: A Reader.* (New York and London: Routledge, 1989), 78. The essay was originally published as "Die Juden und Europa," *Zeitschrift für Sozialforschung* 8, no. 1/2 (1939): 115–37.

16. Horkheimer, "Jews and Europe," 88.

17. Ibid., 78

18. Ibid.

19. Ibid.

20. Letter from Franz Neumann to Theodor Adorno, August 14, 1940, Max Horkheimer Correspondence. Max Horkheimer–Archiv, Stadt und Universitatsbibliothek, Frankfurt/Main. Quoted in Anson Rabinbach, "Why Were the Jews Sacrificed? The Place of Anti-Semitism in Dialectic of Enlightenment," *New German Critique* 81 (Autumn 2000): 6.

21. Franz Neumann, *Behemoth: The Structure and Practice of National Socialism 1933–1944* (London, New York: Oxford University Press, 1944), 125.

22. Ibid., 127.

23. Ibid., 121–22.

24. An interesting discussion of this is in James Schmidt, "Language, Mythology, and Enlightenment: Historical Notes on Horkheimer and Adorno's Dialectic of Enlightenment," *Social Research* 65 (Winter 1998): 13.

25. Wiggershaus, *The Frankfurt School*, 313.

26. Horkheimer, "Jews and Europe," 84.

27. Ibid., 85.

28. Ibid., 85.

29. Ibid., 86.

30. Ibid., 87.

31. Sigmund Freud, "The Uncanny," 369–70.

32. Ibid., 375.

33. Ibid., 379–86.

34. "Research Project on Anti-Semitism," *Studies in Philosophy and Social Science* 9 (1941): 129.

35. Hannah Arendt, *Origins of Totalitarianism* (New York: Harvest Books, 1973), 4.

36. Ibid., 4.

37. Ibid., 6.

38. Ibid., 9–10.

39. Ibid., 13.
40. Ibid., 15.
41. Ibid., 53.
42. Horkheimer, "Jews and Europe," 92.

Jeremy Telman

Selective Affinities
On U.S. Reception of Hans Kelsen's Legal Theory

H. Stuart Hughes noted that Thomas Mann's readers remained faithful to him despite the difficulty of his prose. More generally he observed "in other realms of thought what the Germans call *Wahlverwandtschaften*. Some styles of thinking prospered, and others withered or barely held their own in the new American setting."[1] Theodor Adorno was not interested in adapting to a new setting. In his *Minima Moralia,* he remarked "Wer keine Heimat mehr hat, / dem wird wohl gar das Schreiben zum Wohnen" (for those who lose their homeland / writing itself becomes a place to live).[2]

Some European émigrés were notoriously ungracious in acknowledging the nations that took them in and saved them from the concentration camps. Theodor Adorno estimated that 90 percent of his German publications were written during his eleven-year exile in the United States,[3] but Adorno nonetheless complained that his U.S. editors characterized his writing as "poorly organized," an indignity that Adorno claimed no German editor would have inflicted on him.[4] In his unsurpassingly unguarded memoir, *Rückblicke,* Hans-Joachim Schoeps proudly related his efforts to return to Germany as soon as the war ended.[5] Like Adorno, Schoeps was not reluctant to speak dismissively of the Swedes who saved him from extermination, noting that the "normal" Swede gets by with an unbelievably small vocabulary and relies so heavily on stereotypical expressions that one can predict with great certitude what the common Swede will say when confronted with certain situations.[6]

Schoeps was a historian of ideas and religion. His contributions to the social sciences were significant, but he was not a foundational thinker.[7] Adorno, on the other hand, became a U.S. academic cultural hero. His critique of the U.S. culture industry only contributed to the industry in cultural criticism—poorly organized or otherwise—in the U.S. markets and elsewhere.[8] Adorno scorned the United States, but the U.S. academy adores Adorno.[9]

The experience of Hans Kelsen (1881–1973) in the United States has been the reverse of Adorno's. Apparently Kelsen was one of those émigré intellectuals whose "style of thinking," as Hughes put it, "withered or barely held [its] own in the new American setting."[10] Kelsen's relative obscurity continues despite a recent revival of interest in German legal theory among U.S. academics. Oddly enough, that revival of interest, which has been spearheaded by self-described post-Marxists and other progressives seeking to develop a new critique of liberalism, has not focused on Kelsen and his social-democratic critics, instead latching onto the writings of Kelsen's Nazi nemesis, Carl Schmitt.[11] Interest in Schmitt has continued to grow, as reflected in the recent writings of the leading U.S. economics and law theorist and practitioner, Judge Richard Posner.[12] Still one finds surprisingly little U.S. legal scholarship addressing Kelsen's writings.[13] It is worth examining the reasons underlying the rejection by the U.S. legal academy of Kelsen's brand of legal positivism, and there are aspects of U.S. jurisprudence where a Kelsenian intervention might be welcome. If we are going to look to German theory to help us address the conundrums of liberal jurisprudence, it would be nice if we could rely on a German who was not a Nazi.[14]

Kelsen's Life and Reputation

Kelsen was born in Prague in 1881. His father was a skilled artisan who worked with lighting fixtures and eventually opened his own shops, first in Prague and later, a few years after Kelsen's birth, in Vienna.[15] Kelsen originally wanted to study philosophy, but he had not been an outstanding student and so admission to the philosophical faculty would have been a challenge. Recognizing that hurdle and the additional difficulties of finding a career as a philosopher, Kelsen chose to study law.[16] He received his doctorate in 1906 and completed his *Habilitationsschrift*, which was the first book-length articulation of his legal theory, in 1911.[17] That same year Kelsen received his first appointment at the University of Vienna as a lecturer (*Privatdozent*) in the fields of public law and legal philosophy (*Staatsrecht und Rechtsphilosophie*).[18] In addition to his position at the University of Vienna, Kelsen also taught constitutional and administrative law as well as trade and exchange law for an academy operated by the Austrian Trade Ministry.[19]

During World War I, while continuing his scholarly research and publication, Kelsen served in the military and began work on drafting what eventually became the constitution of the new Austrian Republic.[20] In 1918 the law faculty at the University of Vienna named him assistant professor (*Extraordinarius*) and in 1919 full professor (*Ordinarius*) of public and administrative law (*Staats- und Verwaltungsrecht*).[21] In addition to being one of the framers of Austria's 1919 constitution, he set up Austria's Constitutional Court, on which he also sat from 1921 until 1930.[22] The sheer volume of Kelsen's scholarly output during this period is simply overwhelming, comprising approximately two hundred books and articles published while Kelsen was studying and teaching in Vienna.[23]

By 1930 Vienna's fabled gemütlichkeit had worn thin for Professor Kelsen. He ran afoul of the ruling Christian Social Party, in large part because of his role in a lengthy series of legal disputes relating to Austria's policy of permitting Catholics to remarry.[24] In connection with his involvement with these cases, Kelsen was subjected to withering attacks.[25] His position at the university became increasingly uncomfortable when two of his colleagues joined in these attacks.[26] It was time for Kelsen to move on, and so he took up a position on the law faculty at the University of Cologne. Karl Renner, the Austrian politician and jurist who had invited Kelsen to participate in drafting the Austrian constitution, regretted that political forces had made Vienna inhospitable to Kelsen and hailed Kelsen in the *Wiener Allgemeine Zeitung* as "the most original teacher of law of our time."[27]

At the time of the Nazi seizure of power, Kelsen, an Austrian Jew who had converted to Catholicism in 1905,[28] was Germany's leading legal theorist and the dean of the Faculty of Law at the University of Cologne.[29] Forced from his university post because of his Jewish ancestry, Kelsen fled to Geneva in 1933 and to the United States in 1940.[30] When Kelsen left Cologne, six of his seven colleagues on the law faculty (Carl Schmitt was the exception) protested the removal of Kelsen from the faculty and characterized his departure as "not only a painful loss to the University of Cologne, but also a blow to the reputation of German scholarship."[31] In 1934 the U.S. legal theorist and dean of Harvard Law School, Roscoe Pound, characterized Kelsen as "undoubtedly the leading jurist of the time."[32] A generation later, the leading English positivist theorist, H. L. A. Hart, considered Kelsen "the most stimulating writer on analytical jurisprudence of our day."[33]

Kelsen seems to have taken to his place of refuge, as he remained here and died in Berkeley in 1973.[34] Kelsen thus spent thirty years actively engaged in scholarship and teaching in the United States and at visiting professorships abroad,[35] but his approach to legal theory never found a following in the United States, even as his reputation grew internationally. Karl Llewellyn, a leading practitioner of the realist school of jurisprudence, regarded "Kelsen's work as utterly sterile," although he acknowledged Kelsen's intellect.[36] Echoing Oliver Wendell Holmes's famous dictum that the life of the law is not logic but experience, Harold Laski denounced Kelsen's legal theory as a sterile "exercise in logic and not in life."[37] To this day, outside of the area of public international law, where his influence is unavoidable,[38] Kelsen and his ideas are rarely considered in the U.S. legal academy.

Elements of Kelsen's Pure Theory of Law

Kelsen arrived in the United States just as legal realism was establishing itself as the dominant paradigm for legal scholarship and teaching in the United States.[39] The twin hallmarks of realism are two forms of rule-skepticism: the view that legal rules are a myth because law consists only of the decisions of courts, and the view that statutes and other legislative creations are too indeterminate to constrain judges or govern their decisions.[40] Kelsen's legal theory could not have been more different from the realism that the U.S. legal academy had adopted as its new orthodoxy.

Natural and Positive Law

Before the advent of realism, theories of jurisprudence generally could be divided into natural law theories and positivist theories. Natural law theorists believe that there can be an objective justification for law—that is, there can be good laws and bad laws—and that such objective standards are available because all law derives from universal principles, which themselves derive either from God's law or from rules of reason.[41] Positivists believe that laws are simply posited and are valid for their society if they are properly derived from the sovereign and are backed up by the threat of sanction.[42] The German tradition of statutory positivism, in which Kelsen was trained and to which his pure theory of law is a response, thus sought to justify even the authoritarian acts of the Bismarckian *Reich* as lawful because they had been issued by or in the name of a legitimate sovereign.[43]

In most circumstances, in modern legal systems—and certainly in international law—the positivist position wins out because as a practical matter one's certainty that one's conduct is just (either as a matter of God's law or by whatever other measure one uses to establish absolute truth) is of no consequence if the law says otherwise. Moreover, however much we would like to think of the law as a moral or ethical code, our experience of the lobbying, logrolling, special-interest politics and voter manipulation that is at the heart of contemporary legislative politics tells us that, whatever else the law might be, it is not a reflection of a universal consensus regarding ethical conduct. However, the tension between natural law principles and positivist principles becomes of great consequence on every occasion when a lawmaker—either a legislator or a judge facing an issue of first impression—has to formulate a new rule of law. In that context doctrines of principle have a distinct advantage over the relativism that positivism engenders. However, as discussed below, the challenge for liberal jurisprudence is to articulate the means by which a principled approach to the law can be constrained so that it reflects not merely the moral preferences of the lawgiver or of the majority but also protects the fundamental rights of disadvantaged classes, the poor, or those who otherwise seek protection through consistent and equitable enforcement of laws of general applicability.

Elements of the Pure Theory of Law

Kelsen's approach to legal theory was a significant departure from both legal positivist and natural law theory in that Kelsen "undertook to develop . . . a legal theory purified of all political ideology."[44] His neo-Kantian theory sought to establish the a priori categories underlying law that made legal norms present to cognition.[45] These categories are distinct from analogous categories underlying theories of ethics, psychology, biology and theology, the concepts of which in Kelsen's view had come to dominate legal theory and thus block the realization of a pure theory of law.[46] Kelsen's theory of law is thus "pure" in two senses. First, it purports to be free from any ideological considerations, and it makes no value judgments concerning the comparative advantages of different legal systems. Second, Kelsen thus seeks to create a science of law as an autonomous field, divorced from politics and morality but subject to objective rules.[47]

Kelsen distinguishes his science of law from the natural sciences in that mere observation does not tell us anything about how the law operates. For example, to a neutral observer, a jury sentencing a criminal defendant to death might look a lot like a criminal syndicate ordering a hit. The two events cannot be distinguished in terms of their outward appearances, but only by reference to norms that provide a scheme of interpretation of the events.[48] The notion that only certain conduct is legally cognizable is familiar to any legal practitioner who has ever struggled to find a cause of action that will afford his client a remedy. We might, for example, find it morally reprehensible to force one person to witness the torture of another. For the most part, however, the common law provides that the person forced to witness the torture of another has a legally cognizable claim against the torturer only if the witness suffers bodily harm as a result or if the torture victim is a member of the witness's "immediate family."[49] Similarly we might think it immoral to breach one's contracts, but the law will only take cognizance of a breach—and grant a remedy to the nonbreaching party—if that party has suffered some economic harm as a result of the breach.[50] While this mode of thinking about law as divorced from morality is wholly alien to natural law theory, it can be reconciled with the American realist school. One thinks, for example, of Holmes's characterization of contract as an agreement either to perform or to pay damages in case of breach.[51]

Kelsen envisions law as a normative science. Because of its normative character, law has certain formal resemblances to ethics or morality. The structure of legal systems, according to Kelsen, is that they consist of certain normative rules that instruct the subjects of law how they *ought* to behave. Law differs from ethics or morality, however, in that it is indifferent to the substance of those rules and in that the consequence of violating a legal norm is legal sanction rather than moral or ethical sanction.[52] However, by limiting his pure theory of the law to the study of legal norms, Kelsen did not mean to rule out the possibility of moral, ethical, or political critiques of law. On the contrary, Kelsen considered what he called "legal sociology" to be a worthwhile endeavor, but one distinguishable from the pure theory of law: "It asks, say, what prompts a legislator to decide on exactly these norms and to issue no others, and it asks what effects his regulations have had. It asks how religious imagination, say, or economic data influence the activity of the courts, and what motivates people to behave or to fail to behave in conformity with the legal system."[53]

Similarly, with respect to the relationship between law and morality, Kelsen rejects not "the dictate that the law ought to be moral and good; that goes without saying.... Rather, what is rejected is the view that the law as such is part of morality, and that therefore every law, as law, is in some sense and to some degree moral."[54] Nonetheless the most common critique of positivist systems of law such as Kelsen's is that they lead to moral relativism and provide no basis for a principled opposition to an unjust legal system.[55]

Reception of Kelsen in the United States

While Kelsen was alive and actively engaged in scholarly research and publication, his writings were reviewed in the country's leading legal periodicals, but the reviews were short discussions, only a few pages in length, of often lengthy and always complex works, and the reviewers tended to be partisans who announced their programmatic allegiance or opposition to Kelsen's approach.[56] Although Kelsen's new works, which originally appeared in English while he lived in the United States, were reviewed, translations of his main works published in English for the first time while he lived in the United States were largely ignored.[57] Kelsen's *General Theory of Law and State* was selected as the first volume of the American Academy of Legal Scholars' Twentieth Century Legal Philosophy Series.[58] However, the U.S. legal academy produced no significant or lengthy responses to this work or to Kelsen's other writings.[59] The Columbia Law Review assigned the task of reviewing Kelsen's critique of the United Nations to the director of that organization's legal department.[60] Not surprisingly the review was less than enthusiastic. In the preface to his book, Kelsen specified that the work would deal "with the law of the Organization, not with its actual or desired role in the international play of powers."[61] The review expressly rejected Kelsen's approach, noting that "the Charter is not just a legal text ...; it is a political document designed to embody statements of ideals, of principles, and of moral sentiment."[62]

Kelsen's highly theoretical and largely deductive approach to the law was easy prey for U.S. pragmatists, whose attention to the fine details of legal doctrine focused on Kelsen's many empirical errors. Thus Oscar Shachter took Kelsen to task for failing to give effect to the principles he espoused in his 1950 work *The Law of the United Nations*.[63] In the book Kelsen claimed to have entertained "all possible interpretations" of law relevant to the law of the United Nations.[64] Schachter's review was devoted to enumerating some of the significant—even leading—interpretations that Kelsen ignored, and Schachter wondered whether Kelsen's "'purely juristic' analysis has not actually been influenced by ideological (or shall we say, crypto-political) considerations," from which Schachter infers "that Kelsen's underlying objective is a revision of the Charter ... and a building of a new organization closer to his own heart's desire."[65] Louis Sohn, like Schachter, a leading light of the U.S. international legal community, similarly faults Kelsen for showing "his preference for one interpretation, ordinarily the most inadequate one from the point of view of organizational progress, with complete disregard of alternatives."[66]

More generally politics doubly doomed Kelsen to failure in the United States. U.S. jurisprudence in the twentieth century and to this day has prided itself on its hard-headed realism, or pragmatism.[67] While Kelsen is a towering figure in the field of public international law, even in the U.S., his insistence that law must be treated separately and differently from politics renders him unpalatable even to U.S. practitioners of international law. The first sentence in a leading casebook on public international law runs as follows: "First, law is politics."[68] The author of that sentence, Louis Henkin, is one of the editors of the casebook and, as the chief reporter for the American Law Institute's *Third Restatement of the Foreign Relations Law of the United States*, one of the most influential scholars in the field of public international law.[69] Kelsen's approach is simply antithetical to the dominant approach to law in the United States, and his reception here reflects that fact. Most Americans cannot make any sense of his work or find it not worth the bother because his premises contradict the fundamental tenets of the U.S. approach to law. Kelsen was largely dismissed as a formalist, an approach that legal realism sought to overcome.[70]

A second political reason for Kelsen's failure to reach a U.S. audience has to do with the substantive politics of the U.S. academy in the postwar era. Kelsen's theory failed political litmus tests because, although Kelsen personally supported parliamentary democracy, his desire to produce a pure theory of law required him to avoid connecting the system of law to any substantive political theory.[71] Unable to reconcile the privileging of a particular political perspective with the relativism that informs the positivist tradition, Kelsen created a system in which the legal constraints on state action are purely formal. Any action by a state official is valid, from the perspective of the pure theory of law, so long as the official was authorized to take that action.[72] Of course, such action can still be subjected to external normative critique, but at a time when fascism and totalitarianism posed genuine threats to the ascendancy of democracy as the global model for governance, Kelsen's theory did not seem to U.S. legal theorists to provide a sufficiently robust defense of democracy or for sufficient safeguards against abuses of the law by fascist or totalitarian governments.

Kelsen's theory and legal positivism generally are thus susceptible to attack on the ground that they provide no principled opposition to unlawful governments. Although a government may come into power through illegal means, the legal order established by such a usurping government may nonetheless be legitimate according to positivist theory. And Kelsen's theory has indeed been exploited by criminal governments in court cases in which the legitimacy of the legal order established by those governments has been challenged.[73]

The criticism is based on a fundamental misconception not only regarding the aims of Kelsen's legal science but also regarding the capabilities of legal theory per se. It is certainly the case that Kelsen's theory recognizes that legal rules promulgated by a usurping government are law to the extent that the usurping government can enforce its laws. Within Kelsen's system the question is simply one of efficacy. However, Kelsen's theory in no way equates technical legality with moral legitimacy. Indeed the purpose of his system is to identify the qualities of legal norms as distinct from moral or social norms. And Kelsen recognizes that a regime's lack of moral legitimacy can have a negative impact on its attempt to establish its legal system. To the extent that a government lacks political legitimacy, it may not be able to maintain its monopoly on the use of force, and that in turn will undermine the efficacy of its rules and deprive those rules from being recognizable as law.

But the larger point is that all ways of thinking about the law can be manipulated to suit the purposes of usurping governments. We should recall that nearly all governments come into being through unlawful processes, and the more sophisticated of such governments come to power armed with political, moral, and legal arguments justifying their claim to power. Jurists who resist such power will not be jurists for long, and those who remain behind will ultimately recognize, one way or the other, that the usurping power has full legal authority. Kelsen at least recognizes that judicial officers are limited in their powers—they can only enforce rules that are legal norms—that is, rules that can be enforced by the governing power. It is for this reason that Richard Posner recognizes in Kelsen a fellow pragmatist.[74]

The political critique of Kelsen ignores his monistic approach to the law. That is, for Kelsen, there is only one law—the law consists of one system of norms arranged hierarchically. Each norm derives its authority from a superior norm within the system. And for Kelsen the norms of international law are superior to those of national law, as national law derives its authority through recognition of national governments by foreign governments and perhaps also by international (or multinational) organizations and institutions.[75] Thus no country would be able to establish the efficacy of its rule over its own territory unless it could satisfy foreign governments that they ought to recognize the legitimacy of that rule. Kelsen's monistic theory can accommodate—in a way that is both theoretically satisfying and attentive to the reality of international relations—extralegal critiques of national legal systems. But such extralegal critiques need not be based on any universal moral rules; they are simply a product of communal consensus—the sort of normative theory based on intersubjective interactions that provide the underlying structure for the normative theory of Jürgen Habermas.[76]

In addition to the political hurdles to a positive reception of Kelsen in the United States, there were also stylistic issues. Kelsen's writing style, heavily larded with neo-Kantian jargon, demands a reader familiar with the neo-Kantian tradition and with the European style of legal reasoning, which is based far less on case precedent than are common law systems of legal reasoning and thus is far less grounded in empiricism and includes few discussions of concrete, actual or hypothetical scenarios.[77]

Finally, Kelsen continued to refine and revise his legal theory throughout his lifetime, periodically revisiting, supplementing, replacing, or abandoning positions that were central to his earlier thought. Stanley Paulson, one of the leading North American explicators of Kelsen's work, divides his thought into three distinct periods—a "constructivist" phase, associated with Kelsen's *Habilitationsschrift* of 1911; a neo-Kantian phase that culminated in the 1934 *Reine Rechtslehre*, and finally a volitional phase associated with the 1960 edition of the *Reine Rechtslehre*.[78] In addition Kelsen published lengthy treatises in 1945, the *General Theory of Law and State*, and posthumously in the *General Theory of Norms*. In each of these systematic treatments, Kelsen altered his theory in response to new critical impulses and challenges to his pure theory of law. In short Kelsen is hard to read without a solid grounding in Continental philosophy, he is susceptible to the charge of lacking empirical rigor, and he is a moving target.

In any case many U.S. critics of Kelsen focus exclusively on the alleged political shortcomings of his approach to law and thus ignore a vast corpus of legal thought that touches on a vast array of topics. Kelsen published more than four hundred works during his lifetime, covering not only topics in the field of jurisprudence but also in constitutional law, international law, the history of law and philosophy, contemporary politics and political theory.[79] Although there have been some collections of scholarly essays on Kelsen's work, there has yet to be a scholarly monograph on Kelsen's legal theory as a whole published in the United States.[80]

Kelsen and the Problem of Indeterminacy

One key problem that liberal theories of adjudication have tried to address runs as follows: liberals value laws that are of general applicability, clear, widely disseminated, prospective in nature, and consistent both in substance and in application. Inevitably, however, there are gaps in the law that administrators and judges have to fill on a case-by-case basis.[81] Consequently the law is underdetermined, and contemporary legal theorists debate both the extent and the consequences of this underdetermination or indeterminacy of the law. Formalists are the group of legal theorists least concerned with indeterminacy. Such thinkers generally believe that the problem of indeterminacy arises only in the rare "hard case" that falls outside of the clear guidance of existing law.[82] But the dominant approach to law in the United States, realism, generally views legal rules as providing inadequate guidance to legal decision-makers.[83] From this perspective thinkers as diverse as Richard Posner and Ronald Dworkin are really no different from the realists, but they look to external sources of objectivity and uniformity in order to regularize legal decision-making processes. For Posner the laws of economics guide legal reasoning; for Dworkin judges apply the law coherently when they interpret the law to accord with the political morality of the community.[84] Critical legal theorists are so suspicious of the discretion exercised by the government that they find legal indeterminacy to be the inescapable rule, and critical legal theorists despair of finding the means to resolve the problem of indeterminacy.[85] For critical legal theorists, judges and legislators simply exercise their power in realms where the law is indeterminate.[86]

Because Kelsen's approach to the law is so different from that of U.S. legal theorists, his notions concerning legal indeterminacy defamiliarize this familiar conundrum, thus offering the possibility of a new perspective and new insights. In Kelsen's view the legal norm is always incomplete until it has been individualized through application to a particular case.[87] As Kelsen puts it, "the higher-level norm cannot be binding with respect to every detail of the act putting it into practice. There must always remain a range of discretion . . . so that the higher-level norm, in relation to the act applying it (an act of norm creation or of pure implementation) has simply the character of a frame to be filled in by way of the act."[88] Thus, on the issue of indeterminacy, Kelsen does not distinguish between easy cases (cases of "pure implementation" of an existing norm) and hard cases (acts of norm creation). He does not see any difference between what a judge does when she applies an existing norm to a particular case and when she creates a new legal norm in order to address a case of first impression.

Kelsen notes that indeterminacy is not only inevitable but it is often also intended.[89] Our legislators know, when they create laws, that the laws will be subject to interpretation and implementation by courts or by administrative agencies, and they entrust those courts and administrative agencies with discretion to act within the indeterminate realm. Kelsen thus does not regard the discretion exercised by courts and administrative bodies as a threat to the integrity of his norm-based legal system. On the contrary his system is flexible enough to permit a range of possibilities for gap filling, all of which remain governed by the system of norms as interpretive frame.[90] But Kelsen flatly rejects the notion that there is only one proper way of interpreting the law or filling in the gaps between legal norms. As he succinctly puts it, "From the standpoint of the positive law, however, there is no criterion on the basis of which one of the possibilities given within the frame of the norm to be applied could be favoured over the other possibilities."[91] Bowing to the inevitable, Kelsen concedes that norms established through judicial decision are no different from legislative acts—they are acts of will.[92]

On the one hand, this reasoning seems to put Kelsen in the critical legal studies or radical realist camp—indeterminacy is everywhere, and judges make decisions according to their possibly idiosyncratic predilections. But Kelsen concludes that, because the system is one that assumes that norms are realized only when applied in an individual case, there are in fact no gaps in the law and no problem of filling them.[93]

Kelsen's solution to the problem of indeterminacy seems to return us, by sleight of hand, to the formalist position. In theory an effective legislature lays down normative rules that judges apply in accordance with a subsidiary set of rules for the implementation of legal norms, thus producing a gapless legal system in which indeterminacy is tamed through the will of lawmakers. But Kelsen's system, despite its theoretical and abstract character, is resolutely realist, as Posner has noted. Like other realist approaches, it calls on academics to awake from their theoretical reveries and address the world as it exists. In particular Kelsen suggests that the problem of indeterminacy or of gaps is best addressed at the constitutional level and not through a critique of adjudication. That is, once we have recognized that there is no way around indeterminacy, it becomes incumbent on us—to the extent that we are concerned that courts and administrative agencies might act in an arbitrary and capricious manner—to design a system of government that provides maximal guidance to those courts and agencies and ensures to the greatest extent possible that there is recourse in the event of an unconscionable outcome.

Kelsen's solution to the adjudicatory conundrum also points us to a new starting point—democratic theory. We have to accept that, regardless of how painstakingly legislators set forth legal norms based on a democratic mandate, some body—perhaps a court, perhaps an administrative agency—will have to implement those norms in individual cases. If we are concerned that such bodies are not accountable to the electorate through democratic processes, then perhaps we ought to consider means of making them so. But the fact that we have, at least at the federal level, not done so suggests that our concern with indeterminacy is, on the whole, trumped by our concern with having laws implemented by individuals and bodies that have developed the legal expertise to do so in accordance with the legal norms established by the legislature.

Conclusion

The foregoing discussion sets forth the academic and political context for the U.S. legal academy's rejection of Hans Kelsen's legal theory. There was no affinity between the highly abstract pure theory of law and the legal realism that dominated U.S. jurisprudence during Kelsen's thirty-year sojourn in the United States. Today, however, as Richard Posner has noted, it is clear that the political climate in the U.S. legal academy in the postwar era obscured the similarities in approach linking Kelsen's pure theory with U.S. pragmatism. As U.S. jurisprudence is looking to Continental theorists to help them address the issue of legal indeterminacy, the time has come for Kelsen to make his belated contribution to the "sea change" in the U.S. human sciences that H. Stuart Hughes so insightfully described thirty years ago.

Notes

1. H. Stuart Hughes, *The Sea Change: The Migration of Social Thought, 1930–1965* (New York: Harper & Row, 1975), 27.

2. Theodor Adorno, *Minima Moralia: Reflexionen aus dem beschädigten Leben* (Frankfurt: Suhrkamp, 1951), 152.

3. Tom Huhn, introduction, in Tom Huhn, ed., *The Cambridge Companion to Adorno* (Cambridge: Cambridge University Press, 2004), 2.

4. Theodor Adorno, "On the Question: 'What Is German?'" *New German Critique* 36 (Fall 1985): 121–31. Adorno, "On the Question," 121, 127. Adorno's response to being told by his editor that his manuscript was "badly organized": "In Germany, I said to myself, despite everything that had happened there, at least I would be spared this." After recounting another such incident, Adorno concludes, "I do not mention these examples in order to complain about the country where I found refuge but rather to explain why I did not stay" (128). One can only wonder how Adorno could square this claim with his own estimation of his productivity while in the United States. See Huhn, introduction, *The Cambridge Companion*, 2. In any case Hughes offers a different view on the subject of U.S. editors. Speaking of the émigrés, he writes, "Those whose native languages were German or Italian or Magyar were forced to write in an idiom that was ungracious, narrow in range, and merely serviceable. Yet the Americans were polite about it, far more polite that the British would have been. The editors at the publishing houses did what they could to turn Teutonic English into a passable imitation of the literary language, and the public, accustomed to the slipshod writing of so many U.S.-born authors, did not protest" (Hughes, *The Sea Change*, 29).

5. Hans-Joachim Schoeps, *Rückblicke: Die letzten dreißig Jahre (1925–1955) und danach*, 2nd ed. Berlin: Haude & Spenersche Verlagsbuchhandlung, 1963. 136–37. Schoeps writes of a "magnetic power" (135) that pulled him back toward Germany. Although Schoeps first approached the U.S. embassy in Sweden in May 1945, the occupying powers refused his requests to return to Germany until fall 1946 (136–37).

6. Schoeps, *Rückblicke*, 119 ("Der 'normale' Schwede kommt mit einem unwahrscheinlich geringen Vokabelschatz aus, da er sich immer der gleichen stereotypen Redewendungen bedient und man so mit erheblicher Sicherheit voraussagen kann, wie wohl Mendelsvenssons Kommentar auf diese oder jene Situation lauten wird.").

7. For a recent estimation of Schoeps's significance, see Marc A. Krell, *Intersecting Pathways: Modern Jewish Theologians in Conversation with Christianity* (New York: Oxford University Press, 2003), 43–67.

8. Adorno is one of only sixteen twentieth-century philosophers to whom the Cambridge University Press has thus far devoted a "companion" volume. Of the sixteen scholars who contributed to the Adorno volume, seven, including the editor, are teaching at U.S. universities. See Huhn, introduction, *The Cambridge Companion*, xi–xiv.

9. Huhn, *Cambridge Companion*, 397–420, provides a seven-page list of English-language editions of Adorno's writings and a fifteen-page select bibliography of books and articles on Adorno and critical theory.

10. Hughes, *The Sea Change*, 27. As Albert Calsamiglia has put it, "Kelsen's emigration to North America separated him from the world he knew and, though he made efforts to offer versions of the Pure Theory of Law that had U.S. legal thought as a point of reference, he never enjoyed any significant influence. The atmosphere of

empiricism that dominated the Anglo-Saxon world did not appreciate the contribution of the Central European jurist"(198–99). Albert Calsamiglia, "For Kelsen," *Ratio Juris* 13 (June 2000): 196–215.

11. Chantal Mouffe, ed., *The Challenge of Carl Schmitt* (London: Verso, 1999); David Dyzenhaus, ed., *Law as Politics: Carl Schmitt's Critique of Liberalism*. (Durham, N.C., and London: Duke University Press, 1998); John P. McCormick, *Carl Schmitt's Critique of Liberalism: Against Politics as Technology* (Cambridge: Cambridge University Press, 1997). Significant exceptions include David Dyzenhaus, *Legality and Legitimacy: Carl Schmitt, Hans Kelsen and Hermann Heller in Weimar* (Oxford: Clarendon Press, 1997); and Peter C. Caldwell, *Popular Sovereignty and the Crisis of German Constitutional Law: The Theory & Practice of Weimar Constitutionalism*. (Durham, N.C., and London: Duke University Press, 1997).

12. Richard A. Posner, *Law, Pragmatism, and Democracy* (Cambridge, Mass.: Harvard University Press, 2003), 174–80, 352. Posner discusses Schmitt's approach to the problem of indeterminacy, which is the very issue on which contemporary theorists have sought his counsel (352). William Scheuerman notes that Schmitt's "reflections on legal indeterminacy raise provocative questions for contemporary political and legal theory." William E. Scheuerman, *Carl Schmitt: The End of Law* (Lanham, Md.: Rowman & Littlefield, 1999).

13. As Calsamiglia put it, "At present, in North America, Kelsen is practically unknown, and with only a few exceptions . . . American jurisprudence has totally ignored his contribution." "For Kelsen," 199. Posner admits that until recently he had never read Kelsen. Posner, *Law, Pragmatism*, 250. Having remedied that *Bildungslücke*, Posner, in a strikingly assimilative reading, discovers in Kelsen a fellow practitioner of the pragmatic approach to adjudication (250–91).

14. Jeremy Telman, "Should We Read Carl Schmitt Today?" *Berkeley Journal of International Law* 19, no.1 (2001): 129–60.

15. Rudolf Aladár Métall, *Hans Kelsen: Leben und Werk* (Vienna: Franz Deuticke, 1969), 2. Métall's book is still treated as the definitive Kelsen biography, and it is a rich source of factual information and partisan gossip. However, it was written by one of Kelsen's students whose touching devotion to the man precludes any critical engagement with Kelsen's thought or his life.

16. Ibid., 4–5.
17. Ibid., 8, 14.
18. Ibid., 15.
19. Ibid., 19.
20. Ibid., 18–28.
21. Ibid., 28, 38.
22. Ibid., 34, 47–57; Wayne Morrison, *Jurisprudence: From the Greeks to Post-Modernism* (London: Cavendish, 1997), 323n1.
23. Métall provides a chronological listing of Kelsen's publications. *Hans Kelsen,* 124–34
24. Ibid., 54–57.

25. Ibid., 55–56.

26. Ibid., 56.

27. Quoted in ibid., 57 ("der originellste Rechtslehrer unserer Zeit überhaupt").

28. Ibid., 11.

29. Ibid., 57–63.

30. Ibid., 63–64, 76–77.

31. Ibid., 61 ("nicht nur ein empfindlicher Verlust für die Universität Köln, sondern auch eine Schädigung des Ansehens der deutschen Wissenschaft" [not only a deep loss for the University of Cologne, but a blow to the reputation of German scholarship]).

32. Roscoe Pound, "Law and the Science of Law in Recent Theories," *Yale Law Journal* 43 (February 1934): 525–36. 525, 532.

33. H. L. A. Hart, "Kelsen Visited," in *Essays in Jurisprudence and Philosophy* (Oxford: Clarendon Press, 1983), 287–308, 308.

34. Nicoletta Bersier Ladavac, "Bibliographical Note and Biography," *European Journal of International Law* 9, no. 2 (1998): 391–400, 391, 392.

35. During the time that he was living in the United States, Kelsen taught and/or held visiting professorships in Geneva, Newport, the Hague, Vienna, Copenhagen, Stockholm, Helsingfors, Edinburgh, and Chicago. He received honorary doctorates from Utrecht, Harvard, Chicago, Mexico, Berkeley, Salamanca, Berlin, Vienna, New York, Paris, and Salzburg (see Ladavac). I am grateful to Professor Oscar Sarlo for informing me that Kelsen also made important lecture tours in Latin America, including Cuba (1941); Buenos Aires, Montevideo, and Rio de Janiero (1949); and Mexico (1960).

36. Karl N. Llewellyn, *Jurisprudence: Realism in Theory and Practice* (Chicago: University of Chicago Press, 1962), 356n6.

37. Harold Laski, *A Grammar of Politics,* 4th ed. (London: Allen & Unwin, 1938), vi.

38. Anthony Carty contends that Kelsen's influence is responsible for the inability of international lawyers to raise fundamental challenges to the principle of state sovereignty and to account for the effects of politics on law. Anthony Carty, "The Continuing Influence of Kelsen on the General Perception of the Discipline of International Law," *European Journal of International Law* 9, no. 2 (1998): 344–54, 344.

39. Laura Kalman provides a detailed discussion of the institutional struggles that accompanied the rise of legal realism in *Legal Realism at Yale, 1927–1960* (Chapel Hill: University of North Carolina Press, 1986).

40. Michael Steven Green, "Legal Realism as a Theory of Law," *William and Mary Law Review* 46 (April, 2005): 1915–2000, 1917–18.

41. *Black's Law Dictionary* defines natural law as "A philosophical system of legal and moral principles purportedly deriving from a universalized conception of human nature or divine justice rather than from legislative or judicial action: moral law embodied in principles of right and wrong." Bryan A. Garner, ed., *Black's Law Dictionary,* 8th ed. (St. Paul, Minn.: West Group, 2004), 1055. In his *Dictionary of Modern Legal Usage,* Garner cites Leo Strauss's definition of natural law as "law that determines

what is right and wrong and that has power or is valid by nature, inherently, hence everywhere and always." Bryan A. Garner, *A Dictionary of Modern Legal Usage*, 2nd ed. (Oxford: Oxford University Press, 1995), 561–62.

42. John L. Austin, *The Province of Jurisprudence Determined* (Cambridge: Cambridge University Press, 1995), 166. The book is a modern edition of Austin's lectures on jurisprudence which date from 1830. Austin is often referred to as the father of modern English jurisprudence. For example, in Morrison, *Jurisprudence*, 218.

43. Caldwell, *Popular Sovereignty*, 13–39. Calsamiglia sets out Kelsen's indebtedness to and dissatisfaction with the German positivist approach to law dating back to Savigny's German historical school. "For Kelsen." 200–04.

44. Hans Kelsen, *Introduction to the Problems of Legal Theory*. Bonnie L. Paulsen and Stanley L. Paulsen, trans. (Oxford: Clarendon Press, 2002), 1.

45. "The idea was to develop those tendencies of jurisprudence that focus solely on cognition of the law rather than on the shaping of it, and to bring the results of this cognition as close as possible to the highest values of all science: objectivity and exactitude" (ibid).

46. Ibid., 7–8

47. As Kelsen put it, "The purity of the theory is to be secured against the claims of a so-called *'sociological'* point of view, which employs causal, scientific methods to appropriate the law as a part of natural reality. And it is to be secured against the *natural law theory*, which, by ignoring the fundamental referent found exclusively in the positive law, takes legal theory out of the realm of positive legal norms and into that ethico-political postulates." Kelsen, Hans, "Foreword to the Second Printing of *Main Problems in the Theory of Public Law*," in Stanley L. Paulson, ed., *Normativity and Norms: Essays on Kelsen* (Oxford, U.K.: Clarendon Press, 1998), 3–20, 3–4.

48. Ibid., 9–10.

49. American Law Institute, *Restatement (2nd) of the Law of Torts* (St. Paul, Minn.: American Law Institute, 1965), ¶46, vol. 1: 71–72. The leading legal treatise on torts notes that the law was slow to recognize a tort for intentional infliction of emotional distress and has narrowly circumscribed the conditions under which the intentional infliction of emotional distress is compensable. W. Page Keeton et al., *Prosser and Keeton on the Law of Torts*, 5th ed. (St. Paul, Minn.: West, 1984), 54–66.

50. American Law Institute, *Restatement (2nd) of the Law of Contracts*. St Paul, Minn.: American Law Institute, 1981. ¶¶344–45, 102–9; Lord, Richard A., ed., *Williston on Contracts*. 4th ed. St. Paul, Minn.: West, 2002. §64.1.

51. Oliver Wendell Holmes Jr., "The Path of the Law," *Harvard Law Review* 10 (March 1897): 457–78, 462.

52. Kelsen, *Introduction to the Problems*, 15–19.

53. Ibid., 14.

54. Ibid., 15. As the natural law theorist John Finnis puts it, Kelsen's position was that "there may be moral truths, but if so they are completely outside the field of vision of legal science or legal philosophy." John Finnis, "On the Incoherence of Legal Positivism," *Notre Dame Law Review* 75 (August, 2000): 1597–1611, 1598.

55. Stanley L. Paulson, "Lon L. Fuller, Gustav Radbruch and the 'Positivist' Theses," *Law and Philosophy* 13 (1994): 313–59, 313.

56. J. P. Haesaert concluded that Kelsen's *Principles of International Law* was "speculation in the disguise and semblance of law." J. P. Haesaert, review of Hans Kelsen, *Principles of International Law, American Journal of Comparative Law* 2 (Autumn 1953): 576–79, 576. Louis B. Sohn, reviewing Kelsen's *The Law of the United Nations*, criticized Kelsen's "ivory tower" approach to the evolution of law and observed that "human destiny cannot be always guided by pure law and clear logic." Louis B. Sohn, review of Hans Kelsen, *The Law of the United Nations, Harvard Law Review* 64 (January 1951): 517–19, 518. Thomas I. Cook pronounced Kelsen's *General Theory of Law and State* "doomed to failure" because "an ethically nonnormative legal positivism undoubtedly does end up either by introducing the norms of ethics covertly or by going back to the fact of political power and turning it into an ethical norm which is then assumed to be the only proper norm for law." Thomas I. Cook, review of *General Theory of Law and State, California Law Review* 34 (September 1946): 617–20, 618. There were also positive evaluations of Kelsen's work, but these were written by some of the few North American partisans of legal positivism. Indeed many such reviewers were German-trained legal theorists steeped in positivist dogma. Stanley Paulson notes that the best discussions of Kelsen's work to appear in U.S. law reviews were written by fellow émigrés who had undertaken a thorough study of the pure theory of law in Europe before coming to the United States. Stanley L. Paulson, "Die Rezeption Kelsens in Amerika," in Ota Weinberger and Werner Krawietz, eds., *Reine Rechtslehre im Spiegel ihrer Fortsetzer und Kritiker* (Vienna: Springer Verlag, 1988), 179–202, 180. For example, in his review of Kelsen's *General Theory of Law and the State*, R. K. Gooch asserts that "Kelsen's doctrines are probably the most influential of their kind in modern times," and he goes on to praise Kelsen's reasoning as clear, consistent, and often brilliant. R. K. Gooch, review of Kelsen, *General Theory of Law and State, Virginia Law Review* 32 (December 1945): 212–15, 213, 214. Josef L. Kunz, who had been a student of Kelsen's in Vienna, contributed an extremely learned review of Kelsen's *General Theory of Law and the State* in which he placed that work in the context of Kelsen's earlier theoretical works and lamented only the ways in which Kelsen had weakened his position in comparison with that put forward in Kelsen's 1911 statement of his pure theory of law. Josef L. Kunz, review of Kelsen, *General Theory of Law and State, University of Chicago Law Review* 13 (February 1946): 221–25, 224. The *North Carolina Law Review* entrusted the review of Kelsen's *Law and Peace in International Relations* to another Kelsen disciple, the political scientist Ervin Hexner, who expressed regret that he did not have adequate space in which to discuss all of Kelsen's interesting ideas. Ervin Hexner, review of Hans Kelsen, *Law and Peace in International Relations, North Carolina Law Review* 21, no. 1 (1942): 113–17, 117.

57. Paulson, "Die Rezeption Kelsens," 181.

58. Hans Kelsen, *General Theory of Law and State* (Cambridge, Mass.: Harvard University Press, 1945); Gooch, review, 213.

59. The problem is not simply one of accommodating Kelsen's approach to common law theory. Leading philosophers of law in England wrote at length on Kelsen. Hart, "Kelsen Visited" and "Kelsen's Doctrine," 286–342; Joseph Raz, *The Concept of a Legal System: An Introduction to the Theory of Legal System* (Oxford: Clarendon Press, 1980), 93–120.

60. A. H. Feller, "Review of Kelsen, *The Law of the United Nations*," *Columbia Law Review* 51 (April 1951): 537–39, 537.

61. Hans Kelsen, *The Law of the United Nations: A Critical Analysis of Its Fundamental Problems* (New York: Praeger, 1950), xiii.

62. Ibid., 538. Indeed reviews of Kelsen's works in U.S. law reviews are replete with dogmatic position statements that overdetermine the general tenor of the pieces. Reginald Parker, for example, confidently asserts that "law is either positive law or it is not law at all." Reginald Parker, review of Kelsen, *The Law of the United Nations*, *Illinois Law Review* 45 (January/February 1951): 822–24, 150. Gerhart Niemeyer counters that "rational law in all societies is not the origin, but a result of social solidarity and common experiences." Gerhart Niemeyer, review of Hans Kelsen, *Peace through Law*, *Harvard Law Review* 58 (December 1944): 304–7, 305. Parker's review of Kelsen's book on the U.N. Charter is completely uncritical. Parker, review of Kelsen, 822. Judicious treatments of Kelsen's work often came from nonlawyers. For example C. Wright Mills reviewed Kelsen's work with sympathy and intelligence. C. Wright Mills, review of Kelsen, *Society and Nature: A Sociological Inquiry*, *Political Science Quarterly* 59 (March 1944): 102–4, 102.

63. Oscar Schachter, review of Kelsen, *The Law of the United Nations*, *Yale Law Journal* 60 (January 1951): 189–93, 189.

64. Ibid., 190 (citing Kelsen, *United Nations*, at xvi).

65. Ibid., 193 (citing Kelsen, *United Nations*, at xvii).

66. Sohn, review of Hans Kelsen, 517, 518.

67. Stanley Paulson notes that U.S. Legal Realism reached its high water mark in the 1930s, just before Kelsen's arrival. "Die Rezeption Kelsens," 179.

68. Lori Damrosch et al., *International Law: Cases and Materials*, 4th ed. (St. Paul, Minn.: West, 2001), 1.

69. The purpose of restatements is to summarize the existing state of the law. They are a persuasive source of law often relied on by courts in the absence of clear statutory or case law authority from the relevant jurisdiction. In the case of international law, however, because the law is so inchoate and there is little case law or statutory authority available, the Restatement of U.S. Foreign Relations Law has a special status. It may be the only authority of any kind available to the courts, and the extent to which a court finds such authority persuasive often turns on the individual judge's sympathy toward the substantive position taken in the restatement or his or her openness to having the law determined by a group of legal scholars.

70. Paulson, "Die Rezeption Kelsens," 179–80.

71. "One of the objections most frequently raised against the Pure Theory is that by remaining entirely free of all politics, it stands apart from the ebb and flow of life

and is therefore worthless in terms of science. No less frequently, however, it is said that the Pure Theory of Law is not in a position to fulfill its own basic methodological requirement, and is itself merely the expression of a certain political value. But which political value?" Kelsen, *Introduction to the Problems,* 3.

72. Dyzenhaus, introduction, in Dyzenhaus, ed., *Law as Politics,* at 1, 11.

73. See, for example, *Madzimbamuto v. Lardner-Burke,* Judgment No. 6D/CIV/23/66 (High Court of Rhodesia, 1966); *Uganda v. Commissioner of Prisons (Ex parte Motovu),* 1966 E.A. 514; *Lakanmi v. Attorney General,* S.C. 58/59 (Supreme Court of Nigeria, 1970).

74. Posner, *Law, Pragmatism,* 270.

75. Ian Brownlie provides a good introduction to the concept of monism, along with useful references to more detailed discussions. Ian Brownlie, *Principles of Public International Law,* 5th ed. (Oxford: Oxford University Press, 1998), 31–33.

76. The fullest articulation of Habermas's normative theory can be found in his *Theory of Communicative Action,* 2 vols. (Boston, Mass: Beacon Press, 1985). His most comprehensive attempt to link that normative theory to legal theory is *Between Facts and Norms: Contributions to a Discourse Theory of Law and Democracy* (Cambridge, Mass: MIT Press, 1996).

77. Even some of Kelsen's supporters acknowledge that "his theory cannot be used to provide criteria for solving practical problems." Calsamiglia, "For Kelsen," 213. Given that Kelsen's approach to the law undoubtedly influenced his decision-making process when he was a judge on Austria's constitutional court, this seems like an overstatement.

78. Stanley L. Paulson, "Introduction: On Kelsen's Place in Jurisprudence," in Kelsen, *Introduction to the Problems of Legal Theory,* v.

79. Calsamiglia, "For Kelsen," 197. Métall provides a listing of more than six hundred works that Kelsen published up to 1966, but the list includes translations and book reviews. Some of the more surprising titles include a one-hundred-page essay on the idea of Platonic love, a forty-page essay on war crimes tribunals, and numerous writings on achieving peace through law. Métall, 124–55.

80. Richard Tur and William Twining, eds., *Essays on Kelsen* (Oxford: Clarendon Press, 1986); Salo Engel, ed., *Law, State, and International Legal Order: Essays in Honor of Hans Kelsen* (Knoxville: University of Tennessee Press, 1964).

81. Scheuerman, *Carl Schmitt,* 4–5.

82. Ibid., 6.

83. Ibid., 6–7.

84. Ibid., 7.

85. Ibid., 7–8.

86. This view of adjudication explains why Carl Schmitt's political theory, which rejects the liberal, consensus-building approach to politics, might be attractive to that sector of the U.S. academy that finds critical legal theory satisfying. Carl Schmitt, *The Concept of the Political,* trans. George Schwab (Chicago: University of Chicago Press, 1996). Schmitt criticizes the liberal conception of politics for viewing political opponents as analogous to economic competitors or adversaries in a debating society (28).

For Schmitt political opponents are enemies with whom one engages in combat, complete with "the real possibility of physical killing"(33).

87. Kelsen, *Introduction to the Problems*, 11–12.
88. Ibid., 78.
89. Ibid., 78–79.
90. Ibid., 80.
91. Ibid., 81.
92. Ibid., 83.
93. Ibid., 84–87.

Colin Loader

From *Bildung* to Planning
Karl Mannheim as a Refugee

Exile was not kind to Karl Mannheim, at least not the second time he underwent it. The first time, in 1919, he left his native Hungary and settled in Germany after the failure of the Communist revolution with which he was loosely affiliated. His transition into the new culture proved to be fairly smooth. This was not the case when he was forced to immigrate to Britain following the Nazi seizure of power in 1933. In Germany he had begun to achieve a position of some significance in academic circles. In Britain he was never more than marginal. His critics have claimed that the primary reason for this failure was the marked deterioration of his ideas. They argue that in his new British setting he abandoned the richness of Georg Lukács and Max Weber for the simplification of Auguste Comte.[1] However, one can counter that charge by pointing to the continuity between his later German career and his early British one.

More than a decade after his arrival in Britain, Mannheim reflected on the role of refugees, stating that they typically find themselves in the position of being separated from one culture and not yet fully integrated into another. This situation demands orientation for which they can rely completely on neither culture but which offers them the opportunity for mediation between the two. The function of the refugee, then, is to promote those elements of the old culture that can benefit the new one. These elements cannot simply be transferred in their original form but have to be adapted to the new circumstances.[2] Mannheim himself attempted to serve in this mediating role, bringing two primary elements with him, one that had made his reputation in Germany (the sociology of knowledge) and the other that lay at the heart of his later German endeavors (the ideal of *Bildung,* or cultivation). The latter has not received the attention of the former.[3]

The origin of the principle of *Bildung* was the topic of a book published in 1930 in a series edited by Mannheim. Its author, Hans Weil, would become a lecturer in the Pedagogical Seminar at Frankfurt and later an exile scholar in New York.[4] Weil wrote that young people such as he who came of age in the youth movement just before World War I "answered the pressing question of 'what should we do' with the call for *Bildung* of the personality in the sense of the German classics. However, we gradually perceived that this call no longer had any power to arouse enthusiasm in us. We found that the reality of our existence demanded another organizational principle."[5]

In search of this principle, Weil examined classical *Bildung* to see what could be retained and what could not. He identified three primary elements that were complementary but not without some tension. The first was the traditional Pietist dichotomy that placed inwardness over worldliness and informed German idealism. This element was given new content in the late eighteenth century through two concepts, *Bildung* as "the making in an image" (*Zum-Bilde-machens*) and as the "cultivation of inherent potential" (*Ausbildung vorgegebener Anlagen*), that addressed the relationship of the individual to the larger cultural community. The former identified the community as a harmonious organic unity of values in whose image the individual would be shaped. The latter emphasized the development of the individual's unique potentiality.[6]

These elements—idealism, organicism, and individuality—supported an elitism that characterized the *Bildungsbürgertum* until the early twentieth century. The cultivated elite, nourished as individuals in the rich cultural soil of the organic community, would be in harmony with the culture's values, which they best articulated. As a cultural elite, they provided orientation for other members of the cultural community whose concerns were primarily worldly. In other words, there would be no contradiction in the three elements of the ideal of *Bildung*. As long as the imperial state provided them the freedom and institutional support to develop their individuality, they saw no problem with its authoritarian nature.[7] This relationship, which allowed for both the individuality of members of the cultivated elite and the unity of cultural values, was later described by Mannheim in British exile as the "organic public."[8]

In the late imperial era this public and the culture it supported began to fragment, a process that accelerated with the advent of the republic. The authoritarian imperial state was replaced by new parliamentary institutions that seemed to embody the breakup of the supposed organic unity. Mannheim referred to this situation as the "disintegrated public."[9] While the term *crisis* had been used before the war, it was in constant play afterward. Books appeared on the crisis of historicism, culture, theology, spirit, science, mathematics, physics, mechanics, causality, and, of course, *Bildung*.[10] A number of those within the university, including Mannheim's sponsor Alfred Weber, supported the new democracy but refused to abandon their organic view of culture. They believed that with the proper intellectual leadership a cultural community could be created that was compatible with the democratic sociopolitical divisions.

In 1924 Mannheim followed his sponsor and tried to adapt the classical model of *Bildung* to the new reality. He formulated the concept of *Bildungskultur,* which he depicted as an expansion of a more basic communal culture. The latter's members share a common experiential reality with definite limitations in time and space. Such a community is characterized by the predominance of knowledge that is bound to it. Although Mannheim allowed for a range of communal cultures and knowledge, in his pure type whatever limited reflexivity may be present is mythic.[11]

As members of the communal culture are exposed to outside influences, as social differentiation occurs within, the reflexivity of knowledge increases. Such tendencies foster the expansion of knowledge that escapes the community's limited perspective. Although this increased reflexivity characterizes the *Bildungskultur*, it is not "free-floating." It remains a part of the larger cultural unity, and hence its diversity does not replace the latter with something new but simply expands it.[12] In postulating the *Bildungskultur*, Mannheim tried to allow for social differentiation and intellectual diversity while preserving organic cultural unity, with the cultivated elite as the tie between the two.

By 1929 Mannheim had abandoned this emphasis on cultural unity. In *Ideology and Utopia*, he portrayed the political world as pluralistic, the scene of competing parties. Intellectuals, rather than being simply the expanders of a single cultural unity, became the mediators among different positions. The intelligentsia was now described as "relatively free-floating," a status denied the earlier *Bildungskultur*. As intermediaries between the aspirations of competing political parties, intellectuals promoted those aspirations while increasing their reflexivity. Mannheim anticipated some kind of synthesis in only the vaguest way and seems to have hoped that it would occur within the framework of the parliamentary give-and-take of the republic.

In 1930 *Ideology and Utopia* earned him the chair of sociology at the University of Frankfurt. At the same time, the hopes expressed in that book were dashed with the onset of the Depression and the growth of the parties on the extremes at the expense of the middle. The inability of any coalition of parties to achieve a majority in the parliament resulted in the de facto rule of a small coterie of authoritarians bent on further weakening democratic institutions. In this deteriorating atmosphere Mannheim did not retreat from the question of politics but from the political as it was embodied in the parliamentary party. As he did so, the concept of *Bildung*, in a revised form, began to assume a renewed importance. He wrote, "By cultivational knowledge [*Bildungswissen*] . . . we shall understand the tendency towards a coherent life-orientation, with a bearing upon the overall personality as well as the totality of the objective life-situation insofar as it can be surveyed at the time."[13] Although this sounds very much like the classical theory of humanistic *Bildung*, he argued that the traditional concept was simply one version and in fact was inadequate for modern times.

A new form of *Bildung* required the development of a "sociological attitude," whose central component was "distantiation."[14] To distance is to objectify, but not to the degree that one becomes a neutral observer removed from the situation.

Distantiation means self-reflexivity, that is, making facts out of one's norms, not simply accepting their validity as given but placing them in "brackets" to transcend them. "Bracketing" involves "the interweaving of the occurrences within human development" in order to make one's "way through the intermeshing weave of the actual situation." Only when the other stands in true antinomic relationship to oneself, when one realizes that one is an object to the other, when one begins to entertain the notion that "I" am also an "it," does self-reflexivity begin. One regards oneself ironically as something that could be something else. The creation of a certain distance to and expansion of perspective opens one to the idea of one's own transformation.[15]

But reflexivity can have its dangers, for it means the recognition of pluralism and thus could lead to a relativistic fatalism and loss of will. This Mannheim rejected. The sociological type had to remain politically engaged. Thus he cited Carl Schmitt's contention that "a bad decision [is] still more valuable than no decision at all."[16] At the same time, however, he rejected Schmitt's brand of political engagement, labeled "reprimitivization," which represented a conscious denial of the pluralism of modernity, a decision to regress to the unequivocal meaning of a communal culture, to become "primitive" in the face of the modern world. The prime example for this, for Mannheim, was fascism with its emphasis on the political myth.

The alternative that Mannheim proposed is modeled on Max Weber's ethic of responsibility—the engagement for an ideal but with a sense of proportion, the ability to distance oneself enough from the ideal to allow for contextualization but without falling into fatalism. To put it in Mannheim's terms, the sociological attitude should combine decision and expansion, so that they exist in a dialectical relationship to one another. Expansion without political engagement can lead to a sterile fatalism. Decision without sociological clarification assumes the form of utopian conviction.

Mannheim's advocacy of the sociological attitude as the central component of a modern *Bildung* necessitated a rethinking of the relationship between sociology as an academic discipline and the larger "disintegrated" public. This meant a modification of his earlier notion of *Bildungskultur,* which was based on the premise of an organic public. Previously expansion had been the role of the cultural elite; now he proposed that it should be a quality of all citizens. Faced with the growing irrationality of society, people's actual life situations were increasingly thrown into chaos. The overcoming of this disorientation and creation of a sense of direction required a sociological *Bildung,* not only for elites but also for everyone. Mannheim wrote, "The democratization of social life, in the widest sense, and especially the democratization of politics, in the sense of the potential co-participation of the broad masses, makes it imperative to subject the latter to sociological-civic schooling. . . . For this society cannot maintain itself in the long term if the individuals comprising it are unable to exercise rational foresight, if they do not learn to act responsibly on the basis of factual diagnoses."[17] The intellectual now became more important as teacher of the sociological attitude than as the mediator between political parties. He or she had to instill the ethic of responsibility in all citizens. Active analysis would replace passive adherence.

But it is one thing to advocate this new form of *Bildung* and another to articulate the manner by which it would be put into practice. At Frankfurt, Mannheim did not offer a clear alternative to conventional formal education, which had not proved up to the task.[18] He had been entertaining ideas at this time about planning as an alternative form of *Bildung* but had not yet begun to fully develop them. Planning, as Mannheim would envision it, required a basic stability, a certain amount of cohesion. When he reached Britain, he found that stability, or at least he thought he did, and proceeded to develop the planning strategy in his first major work in exile, *Man and Society in an Age of Reconstruction*. That book was written in German and dedicated to his German colleagues. He later described it as "an attempt at self-enlightenment, made for the benefit of those who have actually lived through these experiences."[19] The theory of planning represents not an abrupt departure from his German concerns, but a continuation and transformation of them, especially the ideal of *Bildung*. The blending of these two concepts was central to his refugee strategy for adapting his old culture to his new one.

In *Man and Society*, Mannheim assessed, if only indirectly, his former society and the sociology that had emerged from it. He distinguished between the "organic public" on which the ideal of *Bildung* was based and the "disintegrated public" that succeeded it. He also outlined the characteristics of the public that he sought to promote, the "organized public," and to assess the role of sociology in its creation. He reiterated his belief that the classical ideal of *Bildung* and its idealist perspective had outlived its usefulness with the dissolution of the organic public in modern society. It had to be replaced by a more sociological approach.

This conviction can be seen in a paper on the strengths and weaknesses of German sociology that he presented in the year between his arrival in Britain and the publication of *Man and Society*. Intended for a British audience, it discussed what he as a former German sociologist and current refugee could offer to his hosts. Above all he believed that the extreme dislocation of Weimar indicated basic weaknesses of modern Western culture in general and that these formed the context of German sociology.[20] He wrote, "German sociology is the product of one of the greatest social dissolutions and reorganizations, accompanied by the highest form of self–consciousness and of self-criticism. . . . In this context, then, sociology is seen to be not only the product of this process of dissolution but also a rational attempt to assist in the reorganization of human society, to help in the reorganization and readaptation of the individual himself."[21]

At the end of this paper he compared U.S., British, and German sociology. Despite noting major differences in all three societies, he emphasized the similarity of U.S. and British sociology. For different reasons both focused on the solution to specific social problems, which were empirically examined in great detail. Both were less interested in theory than was German sociology. As a result they were less concerned with the interconnections of social parts to one another in a larger whole, preferring to study problems in relative isolation. There was also much less interest in class divisions and their political ramifications. It was just these failings that Mannheim saw as the strength of German sociology. Living in a society wracked with social conflict, German sociologists appreciated the need to look for interconnections, especially those between classes, and to use theory to do so.[22]

As its title indicates, *Man and Society in an Age of Reconstruction* was an attempt to demonstrate how a theoretical grounding for the envisioned organized public might be established. Mannheim introduced the terms *substantial irrationality* and *substantial rationality,* both of which provide individuals with orientation to some larger totality of meaning. Conversely "functional rationality" is ideally a subordinate form that is directed toward arriving at a specific goal and not at providing any general orientation and thus is akin to Max Weber's instrumental rationality. According to this distinction, purely communal cultures operate with a high degree of substantial irrationality, the most important form being religion, combined with a certain amount of functional rationality.

As substantially irrational forms of orientation become less effective in the modern world, as that world becomes increasingly differentiated, the participants in society become increasingly focused on specific goals that demand functional rationality but develop no comprehension of where they fit into a larger scheme of things. Without this greater degree of intellectual and moral certainty, society becomes, in Mannheim's words, "functionally irrational."

Politically such a scenario was described as "negative democratization."[23] The latter is characterized by the lack of an integrated elite and with that the absence of the cultural coherence that the elite provides for the masses. Without this larger orientation, without a sense of shared values, democracy turns on itself. It becomes more susceptible to panic and to the demagoguery (reprimitivization, in the language of Frankfurt) that preys on this panic, potentially giving rise to dictatorship. Unlike the earlier *Bildungskultur*—which allowed for diversity among the elites while assuming that this diversity informed an organic cultural center that not only tied the elites to one another but also tied them to the rest of the community—in the state of negative democratization that center is lost as are the ties that emanate from it. Negative democratization means cultural crisis. Clearly Germany provided the model for Mannheim's discussion here.

In summary Mannheim believed the meaning and coherence of the organic public is provided by substantial irrationality—for example, tradition and religion. People often act in a functionally rational way when pursuing specific goals, but that functional rationality is informed by the larger substantial irrationality. The organic public, and Mannheim's earlier concept of *Bildungskultur,* allows for a certain amount of differentiation among the elites while preserving the largely substantially irrational community as a whole. But as the differentiation extends through the entire society and divisions appear along functionally rational lines, the ability of substantially irrational institutions to provide a larger meaning declines. Eventually the process reaches a crisis point where the organic public is replaced by the disintegrated public characterized by negative democratization.

Mannheim's answer to this cultural crisis was the creation of a "substantial rationality," the construction of a new center of orientation that is neither organic nor primarily irrational but rather the result of self-reflexive cognition. Substantial rationality then is essentially *Bildung* informed by the sociological attitude. He believed that this could be accomplished through planning, which he addressed at the more abstract level of "thought at the level of planning." Mannheim's description of "thinking that plans" (*planendes Denken*)[24] is quite similar to his descriptions of the sociological attitude and *Bildung* in his Frankfurt lectures: "This new attitude consists in the fact that . . . the individual is able to perceive not only all the relevant facts and all the relevant ways of looking at things (ultimately he must perceive them if he is to avoid destruction), but he also becomes capable of seeing his special position in the social process, and of understanding that his thought is shaped by his position. . . . The individual not only attains a knowledge of himself but he can learn to understand the factors that determine his conduct, and can thus even attempt to regulate them."[25]

From his last years in Germany to those in Britain, Mannheim sought to reformulate the ideal of *Bildung* in light of a fragmented society and culture. The planning strategy is the culmination of that reformulation. The idea of planning, like his version of *Bildung,* focused on the ability of the individual to develop substantial rationality. As one would expect, such thinking allowed one consciously to orient oneself to the larger world, to see the interdependence between one's own life and those of other subjects. The terms from the Frankfurt lectures, *distantiation, expansion, self–reflexivity,* could easily be inserted here. Planning differs from preceding versions by adding an activist element. The divide between the reflexive intellectual and the political actor was ideally to be eliminated.

In fact *Man and Society* did not offer any clear lines of demarcation between the thinking of the planners and the planned. "Planning for democracy" and "democratic planning" were the two sides of one reciprocal relationship. Individuals were not seen as objects to be manipulated by the planner but as subjects able to participate in planning themselves. Viewing individuals as subjects rather than as objects is what distinguished planning from dictatorship. The answer to Mannheim's question "who plans the planners?" was "the planned."[26] Remembering this reciprocal relationship prevents us from identifying Mannheim with another recently emphasized trait of both modernist Weimar and the Nazi regime, the belief that human beings are plastic objects that can be molded through some kind of social engineering.[27]

Nor did he call for the restoration of either the traditional elites or some version of the organic cultural community.[28] He did acknowledge that the planners would have to come from existing groups, for he did not believe that the planning mentality could spring from nothing. He hoped that certain traditional elites would see the value of the democratization of thinking at the level of planning and, in essence, transform themselves. This is why he attached himself to a group of Christian religious thinkers known as the "Moot"—not because he had gone over to a form of religiosity but because he hoped these thinkers would promote the complementing of the substantial irrationality of religion with a substantial rationality.[29]

One way to clarify further Mannheim's conception of modern *Bildung* through planning is to relate it to Hans Weil's three elements of the classical ideal. It clearly departed from the first element, the emphasis on inwardness over worldliness, by emphasizing the sociological attitude. But less obvious is that it revisited the relationship of the other two. If the earlier proponents of the ideal largely ignored the inherent tension between making the individual in an image (*Zum-Bilde-machens*) and the cultivation of the individual's inherent potential (*Ausbildung vorgegebener Anlagen*), Mannheim did not and emphasized the latter as more democratic. Individuals' potential to orient themselves in conjunction with others, that is, the active reflexivity of the subject, takes priority over the passive nonreflexivity of the object. And through the development of this potential for thinking at the level of planning, the second element, the image in which individuals are to be shaped is determined by those individuals themselves.[30]

Man and Society appeared in an expanded English edition in 1940 with World War II underway. There, following the above-cited depiction of the original German edition as written for himself and his fellow refugees, he added, "If this book appears in English, its function alters automatically. It is no longer an attempt at self–enlightenment, made for the benefit of those who have actually lived through these experiences; it attempts to explain the standpoint of these people to a world which has only hearsay knowledge of such changes and is still wrapped in an illusion of traditional stability."[31]

In the years leading up to the war, Mannheim had become increasingly convinced of five things: that his vision of sociological *Bildung* through planning was the correct one; that the British (and the U.S.) public was displaying the traits of disintegration and had not yet recognized this; that the old elites and what remained of the organic public could be transformed to provide for an organized public; that the urgency of this transformation was greater than ever; and that he was the person who could effectively deliver this message. While the correctness of the first four assertions remains open to debate, there is no question about the incorrectness of the fifth. Mannheim became estranged from important elements of his new host society including some of those who had initially sponsored him. His attempts to attain a position in America also came to naught.[32]

It seems to me that when Mannheim was viewed simply as a German theorist concerned primarily with abstract philosophical questions—what he considered to be the weakness of German sociology—he was admired in Britain. But when he tried to engage himself in actual policy matters, his "Germanness" was derided for being too abstract.[33] The very qualities that he believed were lacking in British sociology—an inquiry beyond specific problems and the presence of a larger theoretical overview—and that he had to offer his new society were the ones seen as too foreign. Even those who were sympathetic to his message were so in a qualified way and never became his standard bearers. Perhaps there is no better example of this than the words of his colleague Lord A. D. Lindsay. In a review of Mannheim's last, posthumously published work, *Freedom, Power and Democratic Planning,* Lindsay suggested that someone should bring out a short book on the "wisdom of Mannheim." At the same time he stated that Mannheim had too much faith in sociology and implied that Mannheim was more interested in "planning for democracy," or the role of the planning elite, than he was with "democratic planning," or the control of that elite by the citizenry.[34] On another occasion he wrote that Mannheim's "talk was so illuminating, so able and stimulating, that he was difficult to resist, and we gave up argument, silent but not convinced, and then went away to ask ourselves hard why we did not really agree."[35]

Notes

1. See, for example, Jean Floud, "Karl Mannheim," *New Society* 222 (December 29, 1966): 971.

2. Karl Mannheim. "The Function of the Refugee." *New English Weekly* 27 (April 19, 1945): 5–6.

3. In fact Mannheim always saw the sociology of knowledge as a tool of political *Bildung* and then planning. See Colin Loader and David Kettler, *Karl Mannheim's Sociology as Political Education* (New Brunswick: Transaction, 2002),

4. For Weil's career, see Hildegard Feidel-Mertz, "Pädagogen im Exil—zum Beispiel: Hans Weil (1898–1972)," in Edith Böhne and Wolfgang Motzkau-Valeton, eds., *Die Künste und die Wissenschaften im Exil, 1933–1945,* 379–99 (Gerlingen: Lambert Schneider, 1992).

5. Hans Weil. *Die Entstehung des deutschen Bildungsprinzips,* 2nd ed (Bonn: H. Bouvier, 1967), iii.

6. Weil, *Entstehung des deutschen Bildungsprinzips,* 4–9.

7. There is a considerable body of literature on this topic, building on Fritz K. Ringer's seminal book *The Decline of the German Mandarins: The German Academic Community, 1890–1933* (Cambridge: Harvard University Press, 1969).

8. Karl Mannheim, *Man and Society in an Age of Reconstruction,* trans. Edward Shils (New York: Harcourt, Brace & World, 1940), 96–97. Orig. published as *Mensch und Gesellschaft im Zeitalter des Umbaus* (Leiden: A. W. Sijthoff, 1935), 73–74.

9. Mannheim, *Man and Society*, 96–97 [73–74].

10. Charles R. Heidegger Bambach, *Dilthey and the Crisis of Historicism* (Ithaca: Cornell University Press, 1995), 37–38, 4.

11. Karl Mannheim, *Structures of Thinking*, eds. David Kettler, Volker Meja and Nico Stehr, trans. Jeremy J. Shapiro and Shierry Weber Nicholson (London: Routledge, 1982), 265, 269 Orig. published as *Struktures des Denkens*, eds. David Kettler, Volker Meja, and Nico Stehr (Frankfurt am Main: Suhrkamp, 1980), 297, 301.

12. Mannheim, *Structures of Thinking*, 265–67 [297–99].

13. Karl Mannheim, "An Introduction to Sociology," in David Kettler and Colin Loader, eds. and trans., *Sociology as Political Education* (New Brunswick: Transaction, 2001), 154. Orig. published in Karl Mannheim, *Analyse der Moderne*, eds. Martin Endreß and Ilja Srubar, 19–123 (Opladen: Leske & Budrich, 2000), 46. For the contextualization of these Frankfurt writings, see Loader and Kettler, *Karl Mannheim's Sociology*.

14. Mannheim's position here was more assertive than in earlier statements—for example, those he offered in his defense of sociology against the charges of "sociologism" by Ernst Robert Curtius, when he seemed to be saying that sociology should play the role of auxiliary science. See "Problems of Sociology in Germany" in *From Karl Mannheim*, ed. Kurt H. Wolff (New York: Oxford University Press, 1971), 262–70. Orig. published in *Wissenssoziologie*, ed. Kurt H. Wolff, 622–23 (Neuwied: Luchterhand, 1970).

For the background of this controversy, see Dirk Hoeges, *Kontroverse am Abgrund: Ernst Robert Curtius und Karl Mannheim. Intellektuelle und "freischwebende Intelligenz" in der Weimarer Republik* (Frankfurt am Main: Fischer, 1994),

15. Mannheim, *Sociology as Political Education*, 9–22, 48, 35, 74–75 [52–66, 90, 78, 116–7]; Karl Mannheim, *Die Gegegwartsaufgaben der Soziologie* (Tübingen: J. C. B. Mohr, 1932), 27–31.

16. Mannheim, "Introduction to Sociology," 34 [77].

17. Mannheim, "Introduction to Sociology," 150–51 [38–39, 41].

18. His attempt in *Ideology and Utopia* to persuade academics to make stronger ties to the contemporary political situation largely fell on deaf ears. This was true even for sociologists. See Dirk Käsler, *Die frühe deutsche Soziologie 1909 bis 1934 und ihre Entstehungs-Milieus* (Opladen: Westdeutscher Verlag, 1984), 91–93. Carl H. Becker's plea (1919) at the beginning of the republic for essentially the same thing drew a storm of criticism. See Käsler, *Die frühe deutsche Soziologie*, 80, and Erhard Stölting, *Akademische Soziologie in der Weimarer Republik* (Berlin: Duncker & Humblot, 1986), 90–95.

19. Mannheim, *Man and Society*, 3.

20. The argument has also been convincingly made recently in Detlev J. K Peukert, *The Weimar Republic. The Crisis of Classical Modernity*, trans. Richard Deveson (New York: Hill & Wang, 1993). Also see David Frisby, *Fragments of Modernity* (Cambridge: MIT Press, 1988); and Peter Fritzsche, "Did Weimar Fail?" *Journal of Modern History* 68 (1996): 629–56

21. Karl Mannheim, "German Sociology (1918–1933)," in Paul Kecskemeti, ed. and trans., *Essays on Sociology and Social Psychology*, 209–8 (London: Routledge & Kegan Paul, 1953), 210.

22. Mannheim, "German Sociology," 224–28.

23. Mannheim, *Man and Society,* 63 [40].

24. Mannheim, *Man and Society,* 210 [175]. In the English translation, this term is unfortunately rendered as "planned thinking," which can be read as making the thinking subject into simply an object of planning, something Mannheim did not intend.

25. Mannheim, *Man and Society,* 212–13 [177–78]. Two major elements of the planning approach are the "principia media" and the "key position." Principia media are general forces in a concrete "bracketing." (Here one also sees a continuation of this latter term from Frankfurt with the same meaning.) They can be either abstracted into general principles or dealt with in terms of their interaction in a unique constellation. Mannheim advocated the latter approach. The second term, "key position," added a new dimension. It was the organizing factor in a given constellation of principia media, not only for interpreting them but also for manipulating them. This return did not mean that Mannheim now renounced the value of change, as some have claimed. But he believed that such change had to be understood in terms of a larger context (153–54, 177–90 [99, 130–48]).

26. Mannheim, *Man and Society,* 108–9, 228–29, 75 [85–87, 197–98, 56].

27. It has been argued that this view of humanity informs both the altruistically intended social programs of modern democracies, which played such an important role in the Weimar Republic, and the sinister ones of National Socialism, with whose "fierce nationalist revivals" Carl Schmitt has been identified. See Fritzsche, "Did Weimar Fail?" 655–56; Peukert, *Weimar Republic*. Mannheim himself has sometimes been placed in this category. But to do so ignores the importance of self–reflexivity for him.

28. For an example of this latter hope, see Friedrich Meinecke, *The German Catastrophe,* trans. Sidney B. Fay (Boston: Beacon Press, 1964). Meinecke, a renowned historian and for forty years the editor of the prestigious *Historische Zeitschrift,* was in his early seventies when the Nazis came to power. He was dismissed from his editorship because of his liberal bent but was allowed to remain in "internal migration." He ended his short postwar book with the suggestion that "Goethe Communities" be established that could aid in the restoration of that older organic unity of culture and politics on which the classical ideal of *Bildung* was premised.

29. For Mannheim and the Moot, see David Kettler and Volker Meja, *Karl Mannheim and the Crisis of Liberalism* (New Brunswick: Transaction, 1995), 251–68, 282–86; Colin Loader, *The Intellectual Development of Karl Mannheim* (Cambridge: Cambridge University Press, 1985), 156–59; Sigrid Ziffus, "Karl Mannheim und der Moot-Kreis," in Exil, *Wissenschaft, Identität: Die Emigration deutscher Sozialwissenschaftler 1933–1945,* ed. Ilja Srubar, 206–3 (Frankfurt/Main: Suhrkamp, 1988).

30. Weil himself would draw similar conclusions at the end of his book. Weil, *Entstehung des Bildungsprinzips,* 265–69.

31. Mannheim, *Man and Society,* 3

32. See Kettler and Meja, *Mannheim and the Crisis of Liberalism,* 193–240.

33. The most extreme example of this was Montgomery Belgion et al., "The Germanization of Britain," *New English Weekly* 26 (February 15, 1945): 137–38; 20 (March

1, 1945), 155–56; 21 (March 8, 1945), 167–68; 22 (March 15, 1945), 176; 23 (March 22 1945), 184; 24 (March 29, 1945), 192; 27: 1 (April 19, 1945), 5–6; 3 (May 3, 1945), 27–28. Also see G. F. Bantock, "The Cultural Implications of Planning and Popularization," *Scrutiny* 14 (Spring 1947): 171–72.

34. A. D. Lindsay, review of Mannheim, *Freedom, Power and Democratic Planning*. *British Journal of Sociology* 3 (September 1952): 85–86.

35. Lindsay, typescript copy of a review of T. S. Eliot's *Notes towards the Definition of Culture*. Lindsay Papers, University of Keele, England.

Donald Wallace

The Obscure Sea Change
Hermann Broch, Fascism, and the United States

On January 27, 1944, Hermann Broch became a U.S. citizen.[1] It was a pragmatic acknowledgement of the trust he put in the United States as the last defense against the spread of fascism. Throughout his exile Broch examined the ideology of democracy in the United States. He found its ideological goals both admirable and flawed. They were admirable in their fundamental principles of human equality and freedom; they were flawed in their one-sided approach to regulating democratic life. That is, U.S. democracy focused on the power of individual freedom and not on the duty of individuals toward society and fellow citizens. From Broch's perspective U.S. democracy rested on the commitment of its citizens to curtail governmental abuse. It did not, however, have any mechanism to curtail the abuse of individuals by other individuals. U.S. democracy was not total. Broch's theory of "total democracy" is an important critique of the United States as the standard bearer for liberal democracy.

To gain a complete understanding of Broch's legacy and a wider view of the overall intellectual migration of the prewar period, one must look beyond Broch's novels and include his political theory and his views on democracy. The religious and humanist impulse in Broch's call for democracies to protect human life foreshadowed the claims and goals of the movement for social change in the 1950s and 1960s; furthermore both his embrace of and criticism of U.S. democratic tradition reverberate in the current debates on the role the United States as a force for spreading democracy and freedom. To date the connection between Broch and these later political debates has been obscured by Broch's marginalization within the historiography. The study of his political theory, however, suggests that Broch, even as a dilettante political theorist and a novelist, presaged an important intellectual development of the American mind—a development that took place in churches and in the counterculture worlds of American youth, not in the universities or in the halls of government.

One day after Hitler invaded Austria, Broch was arrested by the members of the local National Socialist Party and imprisoned in a provincial jail.[2] After two weeks officials released him and he left Vienna on July 20, 1938; he never returned, spending the last twelve years of his life in exile in the United States. Thus Hermann Broch joined the growing numbers of European Jews, socialists, artists, and intellectuals who fled fascist terror for the United States in what H. Stuart Hughes famously described as a "sea change" in Western intellectual history.[3]

This generation of intellectuals did not endure the years of exile in silence or isolation. The migration did not represent the wholesale exchange of European culture for that of the United States. It meant the creation of a new intellectual climate in the United States, a climate enlivened by the arrival of European scientific and social scientific thought. In his book *The Sea Change,* Hughes demonstrated the importance of this generation to the development of both sciences and social sciences in the United States. Hughes's story, however, was limited in scope and in its focus on universities and on the upper echelons of power in the United States. Because of this focus, Hughes's book has little to say about the contributions to U.S. culture by artists, writers, and creative minds whose exile experience appeared to Hughes to be a failure. As he says of Broch, "In this respect the creative writers and the social thinkers among the émigrés faced different problems. The former continued to use their own language and to depend on translators for their American public; the greater part of them, including men as eminent as the dramatist Carl Zuckmayer and the novelist Herman Broch, passed their years in the United States in almost total obscurity."[4] If one looks beyond notoriety and fame, the question of failure is much more difficult to judge. Broch's story is one of active participation in the intellectual community of New York and New England, as well as engagement with the intellectual tidal surge of problem solving in regard to fascism, modernism, and the future of liberal democracy. If one is to judge the success or failure of Broch's influence on U.S. culture, one must look beyond the context of his physical and emotional life and beyond his strictly literary work.

Although Broch was, like the members of the Frankfurt School, highly critical of U.S. culture, especially in terms of its race relations, he was at the same time much more assimilationist; he embraced the United States and its fundamental principles of freedom and equality as the starting point for reeducating Europe on how to build and maintain a free society. The challenge from Broch's perspective was not to survive a period of separation and await his return to European society, but to engage the battle against fascism from a U.S. perspective. In terms of political theory this equated to his grafting a Viennese notion of civic humanism onto the U.S. tradition of negative rights. Broch also offered a stern warning about the viability of U.S. democracy. He warned of an uneasy similarity between the myth of the American Dream and National Socialism's promotion of victory and superiority in terms of nation and race. Overall Broch embraced his exile as both an opportunity to clarify his understanding of democracy and as a duty to educate the United States about its potential to follow European democracy down the path of mass hysteria.

The exploration of Broch's theories on fascism and democracy also help expand the debate on mass society and modernity within exile community in the United States. H. Stuart Hughes and Martin Jay have exposed the important role of thinkers such as Franz Neumann, Theodor Adorno, and Max Horkheimer, as well as the influence of social science institutions such as the Frankfurt School.[5] Broch's theories suggest a separate European approach to the questions of totalitarianism and fascism; it was an approach that rejected both Marxism and capitalism as holistic solutions to the value vacuum of the modern world. Broch in fact rejected socioeconomic factors as the primary means for understanding mass hysteria.[6] As Almund Greiter and Anton Pelinka point out, this fact differentiated Broch from thinkers such as Adorno and Horkheimer; for "Broch's approach (to the question of mass hysteria) is the individual. All mass phenomena are explainable through processes, which take place in the individual. Moments of socialization, both primary and secondary, are to a large extent excluded from his analysis."[7] Broch's democratic theory was driven by the basic assumption that free, open societies are founded on the freedom and sanctity of the individual as a source for value production.[8] He saw the breakdown of individual value production as the sine qua non for the breakdown of the larger social value system.[9]

His theory of knowledge provided a phenomenological picture of the ego as a separate and eternal sphere vis-à-vis the external world of the nonego. The ego in its separateness from the world—and thus from any relationship to death—could serve as a production center for values that were transcendent in terms of the temporal states such as fear and panic; the ego could produce an absolute, transcendent, and universal human essence. Broch called this the "earthly absolute." The epistemological basis for the "earthly absolute" occupies the majority of Broch's writing in his unpublished work on mass psychology.[10]

His *Theory of Mass Hysteria* (*Massenwahntheorie*) was a massive treatise on the source and solution for mass hysteria in the modern age. Broch saw this work as a moral duty and as his contribution to defending democracy.[11] He thought he could epistemologically diagnose and cure the breakdown of values and the resulting outbreaks of mass hysteria. He linked this project to his ideas on democracy by arguing that U.S. democracy could defeat fascism only if it avoided its own descent into political irrationality. Broch wanted to prevent the metamorphosis of community into "the mass," what he referred to as hypertrophy of values. Such a metamorphosis occurred through both the loss of rationality, or commitment to universal values of equality and humane conduct, and the loss of positive irrationality, that is, aspects of humanity such as friendship, camaraderie, and so forth.

The starting point for understanding Broch's ideas of democracy is to understand his ideas on culture itself. Culture for Broch was the awakening of human initiative in the face of death.[12] Broch saw death as the ultimate nonvalue, yet it nonetheless played an important role in civilization, for it created the cultural goal of the universal, as seen in the mythological importance of words such as *infinity* and *eternity*. In the face of that absolute nonvalue, human creativity opened the possibility for challenging death with an earthly absolute, a willed absolute created by us—which we can call humankind's "will to value." The earthly absolute was not in reality an a priori universal, but it did allow for the foundation of value—it represented humankind's rational ability to relate openly to irrational fears and impulses. Rationality thus becomes for Broch the shedding of light onto the darkness of the irrational.

In terms of his political theory, humankind's will to value was important because it was out of the ethical process of value construction that social value systems built universal values. Aesthetics was for Broch the effect of ethical action in the cultural arena; politics was for Broch the regulation of these aesthetic effects. In a sense Broch saw politics as the superstructural reflection of an ethical substructure. Broch further argued, however, that the relationship between ethical action and value systems was not a one-way process. Humankind's will to value initiated the creation of value. Society, however, when it embraced a particular value as complete and unchanging—thus closing the value system—endangered value production. This was because individuals shifted their creative impulse from value production to the pursue of a goal. In a psychological sense, Broch saw such teleological activity as moving closer to death, not creatively challenging it.

Modern mass politics continually pressured the individual with closed value systems (business for business, nationalism, *l'art pour l'art*).[13] The result was a closing off of the creative mind—what he called the "twilight of consciousness"—and psychological insecurity.[14] Modern politics in this way created the possibility for mass hysteria and opened up many groups in society to physical, economic, and political oppression as well. Broch's political solution turned around one central idea: "The Law for the Protection of Human Dignity." The law involved, on the one hand, the detailed theory of knowledge discussed above. On the other, it needed formal legislation to regulate citizen-to-citizen relationships. The goal of the law was to secure the physical environment of individuals so that they could pursue their will to value from a psychologically secure space as citizens. Broch conceived of economic and political security as an extension of this law, but he did not believe that healthy, open social value systems could be created or sustained simply by economic or political action. It was only unhealthy, closed value systems of the fascists that tried to buy individual freedom through material security.

Open value systems were systems that pursued but never fully defined absolute values through constant activity of creative citizens, as opposed to closed value systems that defined an absolute value in simple national, economic, or racist forms. Concretely defined, absolute values existed only in hypertrophic systems, and they set the stage for the onset of mass aberration. A value system would become closed at the point when a crisis exposed its failure to secure an acceptable level of material and psychic security. A healthy society required the presence of a central value system that promoted the pursuit of maximum levels of material and emotional security. This is the democratic regulative principle of the "pursuit of happiness." The complete autonomy of the central value system, however, would initiate a stage of crisis or the closing of the system. In a state of complete autonomy the logic of the system would hypertrophy, that is, its logic would lose contact with the actual functioning of reality and begin to promote values that are not applicable to the material world in which the value system is supposed to operate. Broch used the historical example of witch trials to demonstrate such "hypertrophia." When a dominant value system, such as Christianity, promotes the truth that witches exist, the application of that truth to reality can and will result in the development of a mass aberration, such as the witch trials.

As Broch diagnosed the European phenomenon of fascism, he began to question the situation in the United States. He saw signs of hypertrophia in the country and argued that it had to recognize and overcome two traditions of mass politics in U.S. democracy that tended toward the hypertrophic value system of fascism. The first of these was connected to the myth of the American Dream and to U.S. industrialization. Broch believed that too great an emphasis on material success led to the devaluation of psychological security. In essence the United States had a tendency to rank material success above the inviolability of human life. The second tradition arose from the racial tensions within U.S. society. Broch associated racial conflict in the United States with his notion of fascist demonology or the singling out of a communal enemy. Fascist demonology entailed the creation of a devil whose activities and even existence in a society were viewed as a threat to the values of the majority. For Broch both the Jew in European society and the African American in the United States offered a minority identity that could play the role of devil. In a period of crisis this devil would fall victim to the need for exorcism, as the majority value system attempted to stabilize its feeling of panic. These two traditions, materialism and racism, threatened U.S. democracy by fostering psychological insecurity in a historical context of war and economic crisis.

In Broch's critique of the American Dream, he revealed a less than optimistic view about the ability of the United States to address these weaknesses in its democratic traditions. Broch states in an untitled manuscript from the late 1930s:

> The unemployed were approached with slogans denouncing the existing "plutocracy," for the middle class a picture of a future anti-Communist order was envisaged, an order promising an increased volume of business; Pacifists were won over with slogans about "Europe's internal affairs" which do not concern America; Communists were trapped with semi-Socialist slogans. In any event, the attempt was made, whenever possible, to denounce World Jewry as plutocratic, Communistic, war-mongering, reactionary, revolutionary—in short as World Enemy Number One. This propaganda,

operating on a large scale, is very successful, and every convert means one step toward the complete subjugation of humanity and human liberty. This is how it worked in Europe, and there is no reason to believe that the American people will react differently. Man protests against barbarism only until he has become used to it.[15]

Broch questioned whether these democratic traditions would value human dignity over material security in the context of indifference. Broch saw such indifference present even in the exile community of Europeans—even European Jews.

> The [Europeans] whose physical, psychic, and, above all, economic existence has not been directly affected and, then, victimized . . . they are helpless; the right moment for defense is gone. But let us complete the gloomy picture by adding the undeniable fact that even those who, suffering bodily themselves, went through the apocalyptic horrors of today's Europe, as soon as they have reached . . . apparently safe shores, immediately join again the bulk of *indifferents* and do not belong any more to the class of the directly "injured."[16]

For the United States to serve as defender of Western civilization, it must see beyond the prospects of "accepting a victorious Germany as a financially sound buyer."[17]

Policies of isolation and appeasement within Europe and the United States brought such a prospect into question. The policies reflected a greater concern for territorial integrity than for human suffering. The war was a "logical inconsequence"; it only took place when Hitler's seizures of territories became too egregious. The obligation to defend territory "proved strong enough to achieve what no act of barbarism, no provocation, no breach of treaties, no abuse of ideological values had been able to achieve."[18] The object lesson of earlier European appeasement was not for Broch a simple call to arms, but a more fundamental call to reconsider the foundations of democracy. "Whether the American people will be able to lift themselves out of the morass of such fatal conservatism depends on their ability to find their way back to the spiritual values inherent in their traditions."[19] The only way fascism would be turned back would be by a spirited effort that came from a defense of humanity and a not a defense of territory.[20]

In considering the traditions of democracy in the United States, Broch concluded that classical U.S. notions of liberalism, negative rights, and governmental checks were an insufficient basis for sustainable democracy. U.S. democracy's ultimate goal was complete individualism vis-à-vis the government. He regarded such unchecked individualism as a source of instability. For no matter how much the individual strove for complete separation from others, the nature of the world is that humans need other humans.[21] In the modern world, if individual success were to be held out as the ultimate goal of society, slavery would become a social necessity.[22] Industrial, capitalist society required more than individual effort for profit production. It required a community of laborers, managers, and even government officials. Broch claimed that the idea of the American Dream ignored the necessity of community and the impact of industrialization on community in the modern age. For these reasons any democratic system that defined individual success as its ultimate goal also carried the seeds for psychological insecurity of the masses. Democratic citizenship could not be totally enacted if it were defined only from the point of view of individual success. Another way of looking at this is that social values directed at individual material success would drive the majority of the people closer to an awareness of death, engendering psychological insecurity. Material success would thus impede the individual's will to value. Without value production in the form of creative individual will, citizens would turn to the immediate security of political, national, or racial ideologies.

U.S. democracy did create access for individual activity and individual success, but it did so mainly in economic terms. The American Dream "required the community to release the individual from all ethical obligations . . . the radical economic liberalism . . . meant nothing but the undisturbed pursuit of business."[23] Broch took U.S. politics at its word: the business of America was business. Indeed democracy characterized itself by a commitment to isolationism and to strict capitalistic profit motives. He states, "The country's miraculous security, its inexhaustible natural resources, the unlimited opportunities for work for its sky-rocketing population—all these facilitated the growth of a purely commercial political attitude able to do without any political content to such an extent that the two major parties today can hardly be distinguished from each other in their ideas and program."[24]

Within this tradition U.S. democracy constructed a rigid system of empty or purely rhetorical watchwords such as *pacifism, antiimperialism,* and *protection of civil liberties and commercial pursuits.* Broch asserted that a "democracy that has become rigid has lost its power of resistance." The American "self-made man" has created the unpolitical herd. Both fascist ideology and the American Dream contained the same underlying value, that is, "the idea of victory."[25] Thus Broch's political theory was a call for overcoming U.S. moral ambiguity, the call for a "victory over the idea of victory."[26]

In contrast to the material interpretation of the pursuit of happiness, Broch offered his concept of total democracy, which protected the individual as a value-creating citizen. He argued that the right of the pursuit of happiness equated to the guarantee of a secure space in which each individual could develop intellectually and spiritually. He saw all political action and all social action, including religion, as locked in "the world's commotion and bustle" and unable to transcend earthly limitation of time, that is, they were actions infused with the inevitability of death.[27] Broch thus suggested that social value systems needed to be regulated not by socio-economic factors, but by cultural and psychological ones. In a paradoxical way Broch supported the classical liberal notion of individualism, but the criterion for productive individualism was psychological, not material.

Starting with his work on a joint U.S. and European project, *The City of Man*,[28] Broch began to focus on the process of enslavement (*Versklavung*) in modern society, by which Broch meant not simply imprisonment or forced labor but psychological insecurity.[29] "The world is moved by *Realpolitik*. . . . everybody has to look after his own interests, and the man who doesn't want to become enslaved himself must try to enslave others; eat so as not be eaten. We must admit that enslavement will be or is already the genuine form of our modern industrial society."[30]

As a defense against the irrational impulse to view the world as a "man eat man" affair (in Broch's eyes this meant placing political man outside the realm of humanity), Broch put forth his concept of "total democracy." The term *total* used to modify democracy, as well as Broch's references to a democratic "dictatorship," struck many observers at the time as problematic and even authoritarian.[31] Broch, however, consciously contrasted a humane democratic totality to an inhumane fascist totality. In his U.S. exile Broch repeatedly stressed the thin line that divided most democracies from fascism. Democracy differentiated itself by its spirituality and its moral outlook, that is, democracy preferred what he called open value systems. In such there was no attempt to impose community defined absolutes. For Broch values defined by a communal set of standards were merely attempts at securing a goal—they were an attempt at conquest or victory. In a democracy the value system was design to foster individual awareness of an absolute human value, not communal.[32] "Fascisms are caricatures of the true totality of values—exactly as their dynamics are nothing but a cartoon of the genuine functional process. . . . If a total democracy were content with a simple aping of the super-gratifications of the fascist methods, it would not last, indeed." The difference between fascist totality and total democracy for Broch was that total democracy builds on the idea of creating communities for the promotion of ethical values and the avoidance of human suffering.

Total democracy pursues the moral goal of the victory of good over evil. Fascism was different because it based its formation of community on the idea and the reality of human suffering. It entailed the creation of an outsider, who deserved and required punishment, and the creation of a value system that was strictly external and material. Since humans are not strictly external, material beings, fascism could not create a truly total community or absolute ethical system.[33] Broch's point in the end was to prove that fascism lacked totality.

Democracy was not exempt from mass hysteria; it was, however, a form of social organization historically conditioned to promote ideas of freedom and equality. In terms of regulative principles of democratic societies, Broch supported, as Almund Greiter and Anton Pelinka state, the principles of "freedom, equality, justice, and humanity. Principles established in the idea of human rights. . . . Human rights, which are developing pacifically, are in the first instance the human rights of liberal democracies—human rights that guaranteed the freedom of the individual from the state. Broch postulated, however, an expansion of the tradition of liberal Natural Law."[34] This expansion refers to Broch's belief that the idea of natural rights should include the concrete relationship of individual humans. In the U.S. context these rights were limited to an abstract relationship of citizen and state.

Broch used Germany to demonstrate the weakness of natural rights based only on the regulation of citizen and state. The rise of Hitler clearly validated Germany's failure to balance democratic regulative principles with the abstract power of the state. The Weimar Republic's Law for the Protection of the Republic demonstrated the weakness of democracies that focus too much on regulating government and citizens and not enough on creating individual security.[35] "Democracy . . . cannot safeguard its own existence by means of an abstract 'Law for the Protection of the Republic.' . . . If there is a concrete danger for democracy, it must be encountered by concrete means."[36] Broch's point was that in regard to democracy the legal protection of democracy must depend on the legal regulation of "concrete partners."

In addressing the issue of regulative principles, Broch was highly influenced by nineteenth-century historicism; he argued that questions of democracy in the contemporary world were understandable only as a continuum of the democratic tradition in the West since the eighteenth century. Through the crucible of revolution, American and French, the foundational theories of state and citizenship had been forged. Broch referred to these foundational theories as "regulative principles." The operation of democracy was based on a tension between the regulative principles (created through a revolution and the throwing off of oppression) and the government as the organ by which democracy is administered and protected. In the historical philosophy of Broch, democracy in the West remained fragile because of its novelty.[37] Both the American and the French revolutions occurred during a period of historical transition from the hypertrophy of the late Middle Ages (the breakdown of the stable and absolute system of values under the "Universal Church") to a period of secular stability. Whereas the late Middle Ages and the Renaissance were periods of hypertrophy marked by mass hysteria in the form of witch trials and internecine struggles within Christianity, the nineteenth century was a period of general political stability and rising democracy. This meant in Broch's system that European and U.S. foundations for democracy, forged in the transitional period of the eighteenth century, were at once revolutionary and stabilizing. Much of the strength of democracy in the United States was in fact its continued revolutionary distrust of the government as a force for oppression. Such democratic awareness or defensiveness exposed, however, a democratic fatalism—a lack of awareness of any other dangers, outside of governmental abuse, to democracy, for example, racial conflict, economic disparity, or xenophobia.

Broch traced such democratic fatalism back to the founding of the United States. The founding fathers had set out the relationship between citizen and state; they did not, however, set out the relationship between citizen and citizen—in the context of the eighteenth century, they felt it unnecessary.

> The Founding Fathers of the United States had such a fear of tyranny that they felt obliged to embody their anti-tyrannical principles into the Declaration of Independence and the Bill of Rights, laws whose sole purpose is to protect the citizens against encroachment of the government; the basic principles of every-day civic life were so natural and self-evident to them—they felt them to be the very substance of life and democracy—that no one conceived their incorporation into a written law might be necessary, in order to protect state against encroachment on the part of the citizen or the citizen himself against evil conduct of his fellow citizen. It sufficed them if the regulative principles were effective as a negative source of law.[38]

After his experiences with National Socialism and his witnessing the racial tensions within the United States, Broch questioned whether the basic principles governing citizen interaction in daily life were self-evident any longer.[39] Broch's concerns were manifested in his investigations of fascist tendencies in U.S. democracy and in his push to expand the regulative principles of democracy to include duty as well as freedom.

It was through his discussion of regulative principles that Broch linked his critique of the American Dream to the other problem in the U.S. democratic tradition, the issue of demonology. Broch observed in Europe that the National Socialists owed their political triumph to the idea that the German people, panicked by the insecurity of economic depression and national defeat, no longer saw freedom as a social value. They promoted instead materially measured values such as security and glory. The protection of such values became connected to abstract conceptions such as nation or blood, leaving some members of the society, both citizen and noncitizen, exposed to attack. The central value for fascism became victory, and the ritual of victory depended not only on the creation of success, but also on the creation of an opponent. Broch referred to the opponent in religious terms as the devil in the system.[40] Fascism also relied on a system of magical justice, that is, justice that corresponds to the irrational fears of the dominant society. The identification of demonology and the return to magical justice are crucial to a significant portion of Broch's definition of fascism, and he openly identified such an ideology in the tradition of the American Dream and U.S. racism.[41]

Broch's concerns about U.S. race relations took a more central position in his theory of fascism as tensions turned into outright instances of mass hysteria, exemplified by the Detroit riots of 1943. From the early 1940s onward, the racial makeup of Detroit changed rapidly as the war industry ramped up and turned the city into the "arsenal of American democracy." African Americans in large numbers migrated from the South to work in the defense factories. The demographic shift was part of the great migration of African Americans from the South to the North between the First World War and the end of the Second World War.[42] In June 1943 the growing tensions between whites and blacks competing for housing in the city led to clashes in the streets. Fueled by rumors of black mothers and babies being thrown from bridges and white women being raped and murdered, groups of whites and blacks attacked bystanders and police for almost two days. In the end President Roosevelt had to send in federal troops to restore order. All told, thirty-four people were killed and almost two thousand arrested. The event exposed for Broch both the depth of the racial divide and the danger of mass hysteria in U.S. society.[43]

Broch used the event to consider the future of U.S. democracy.[44] As blood spilled and hatred swept across Detroit, Broch weighed these events against the claims of equality and freedom in the United States. He suggested two polemical readings of the events: "There are many people, who contend that America always had her lynchings, her assaults on labor and other unpleasant events, full of violence and corruption, and that, nevertheless, America remained the best democracy on earth. Don't worry, they say, therefore, about the happenings in Detroit." In contradiction, "there are others, who say that . . . America will now have to pay for century-old sins against her basic democratic principles: to them, the happenings in Detroit are a symptom for a U.S. repetition of the European development leading to fascism, are symptoms for the crumbling of democratic liberty, equality and fraternity, symptoms for the uprising of fascist intolerance and race hatred and the [victory] of the primitive right of the stronger."[45] Broch rejected the complacency of the first attitude, and he engaged the second attitude not as a reality but as a more-than-possible future for the United States.

The attack on minority groups was the most dangerous political manifestation of fascist ideology. Its violent tendencies not only endangered the immediate lives of local minorities; they also undercut the essential dignity of human life and reinforced a value system based on victory and violence. Influenced by the historicism of the nineteenth century, Broch portrayed the magical justice of fascism as a repaganization of the modern world. Throughout history civilizations had taken up the cause of humanity and fought to replace magical justice with humane justice.[46] In its encounter with modernity, however, Europe turned its back on humane justice. The "enlightened" invention of the guillotine highlighted the corruption of humanity with the false security of the technology and its ability to minimize suffering. Celerity and cleanliness in murder did not change the ultimate outcome, death. "Democracy must embrace humaneness without compromise, and the state can prove its humaneness only by overcoming the negativism of death-warrants and by convincing the masses of the inviolability of all human life. It must be made clear that no human soul, however vile, shall be excluded from that right, and none placed so high—not even in representing the state commonwealth—as to arrogate the power of breaking this supreme democratic principle of human dignity."[47]

For the German nation, any claim to a humane, democratic tradition was made illegitimate by the economic depressions and national humiliation following the First World War. The "volkish" religion of National Socialism and its creation of the devil in the form of the Jew marked the ultimate realization of such a violently hypertrophied closed system. In the United States the hypertrophy of the democratic tradition began with the defeat of the Confederate states and the reconstruction of the South; the economic and social insecurity produced a hypertrophy seen in the passing of the black codes and the expansion of lynching and Ku Klux Klan activity. In both cases demonology and an irrational impulse to victory were sparked by social panic. "The national-socialist propaganda ... is geared for stirring up anti-Semitism. Together with its extensions (as, for example, negrophobia), anti-Semitism is the very 'carrier' of contagion, the very contagion itself of the fascist lunacy—and this is the datum that has to direct the democratic fight against mass delusion and its propaganda. Certainly, as soon as the belief in the god of victory is smashed, the belief in his counterpart, the devil, is bound to collapse, too."[48]

Broch implies here that opposition to fascism in the United States must be seen as something more than a confrontation between political and nationalist ideologies; it must also become manifest in the protection of minority rights and the universal value of human equality. Broch's political, and even his literary, works called for pragmatic solutions to mass hysteria, such as the development of institutions for the protection of human life from individual murders, from state-sponsored murder, including the death penalty; from mob violence such as lynchings and pogroms; and eventually from economic and nutritional deprivation.

Though Broch found historical examples of the hypertrophy of the U.S. democratic tradition in its racism, especially in the political and cultural institutions of the southern United States, he saw the greater danger in the expansion of the fascist demonology to the arena of national politics and foreign policy. In this arena the figure of the African American slave would not serve as an effective devil. As the hypertrophy of U.S. values moved beyond the regional issues of blood purity, issues of political and economic relationships would rise to the fore. In this process the centrality of success in the U.S. democratic tradition took on more importance, as did nationalist rhetoric with the development of cold war. The expansion of the demonology of the African American would, in the historical context of fascism versus democracy, or communism versus democracy, be moved to the sidelines. In other historical contexts, for example, the relationship of U.S. democracy to the developing nations, such demonology would still play a significant role.

The parallels between the United States and Germany were not exact for Broch. He saw the moral superiority of democracy over fascism as a "given fact." The difference between the "god of victory" in National Socialism and the success of the American Dream was one of hypertrophy. In contrast to the continual evolution of the open system, there was the dogma of the closed system. The closed system made claims to the infinite and the absolute through dogmatic "theologies" whose force became the basis for the claims to justice and normal behavior within a social group. An open system lacks absolute values; open systems "endeavor to attain the desired absolute validity through the unrestricted development and expansion of the system. The 'open system' is aware of the infinity of the world; it, therefore, knows that absolute validity is an infinitely distant goal, and not a final state concretely to attain."[49] Broch saw this as the intention behind the pursuit of happiness. It was an intention that had been lost as the material definition of "happiness" gained ground in the late nineteenth and early twentieth centuries.

It was Broch's belief that we must understand the difference between open and closed value systems on the individual level, what he called in Freudian terms normal and abnormal systems, because the psychosis or neurosis of the individual when reflected into the group value system results in periods of mass aberrations such as ritual killings, world wars, and genocide. Such aberrations were generally directed at one group, who became the enemy or the bringer of death and insecurity. From the development of these models of personal and group value systems, Broch applied a historical perspective. The combination of value system modeling and history allowed Broch to predicate the cycles of aberrations and to construct historical models of value disintegration and hypertrophy, the two instances where mass aberrations develop.

Broch saw modernity as a period of disintegration that was open to mass aberration. The solution thus was historical. The examination of periods of conversion from a closed central value system, or from a period lacking a central value system, to an open central value system could provide a model for the conversion process. In this vein Broch chose the historical example of Christian conversion, and from that example set up a model for modern democratic conversion, that is, a method by which mass hysteria could be contained within an open value system that allowed for the release of sadistic impulses through sublimated release mechanisms. Through this process minority groups, who were often subject to persecution for being the "enemy" of the dominant value system, would be protected.

To Broch the ultimate danger of the closed system was the point at which the closed system's absolute theology no longer explained or ordered the world of reality. At this point the closed system had only two choices: die or carry through its dogma by force, that is, hypertrophy. In the end all Broch's political work strove to identify and overcome hypertrophic value systems such as fascism. Conceiving of fascism as a modern paganism, Broch called for a conversion to democracy. In place of the closed system, Broch promoted an open, democratic system of value: "The fight against this aberration [Fascism], the return of man into the open system of humanitarianism, is the task of democracy. It is a fight against the magic ideology of victory, a fight for the idea of 'human justice'; and this is why the democratic mission must be regarded as the continuation of the Christian one, though on a secular, scientific, and especially psychological, basis. And the pattern that can be applied to all religious conversions may, obviously, well be applied to their secular continuation, too."[50] The ultimate goal for Broch was the establishment of constitutions and laws that were based on an open value system whose underlying central value was protecting the dignity of human life.

Broch also strove to convince individuals that values other than materialistic ones should be the basis for democracy. In Europe he saw no solution: fascism was too deeply entrenched, and the Nazis had been very effective in alienating any prophets of a counter crusade by identifying them as alien in race and character: Jewish and highbrow. In the United States the effects of modernization also presented a roadblock to such a countercrusade; the United States had exchanged its ethical or religious foundation for democracy for the foundational principle of business. Business, however, was simply material and thus could not produce an open value system.[51] Paradoxically, however, Broch found the solution in early American democracy, because he saw its origins as deeply connected to the issues of spirituality, morality, and human dignity. Broch saw the basis of a humane democracy in the preindustrial United States, where it developed out of the religious communalism of the early settlers.[52] These communities contained a spiritual and social communion that "stood godfather to modern democracy";[53] it was a tradition that "by virtue of its ethical and religious tinge, demanded an attitude of obligation to the community which was truly political."[54]

Democracy, like any other institution of civilization, had to be supported by a fundamental value. In the case of democracy that value was originally freedom.[55] By the early 1930s, however, it was obvious to Broch that democratic freedom had lost its redemptive power. Broch claimed that value systems became visible in society through ritual, but the modern world had seen a fundamental change in the expression and location of ritual. Since the Reformation and the Enlightenment, ritual had become steadily more private and less institutional. The modern world preached a religion without God; but the secularization of the modern world had not ended the basic human need for ritual—it had only killed its major symbols. In this atmosphere of value disintegration, both capitalism and fascism had raised a new god to the center of their rituals. It was the god of success: "a Machiavellianism of success that entered, without exception, all the other spheres of value as well. In the end the old chivalrousness of the military ritual was displaced by the wretched ritualization of success.[56] Broch's discussion of fascism questioned how long U.S. democratic tradition could remain open and free under the central value of materialism.

Hermann Broch's appeal to people of the United States in the 1940s was an appeal to recognize the choices before them, to recognize that fascism was already attempting to turn the United States away from its position as leader of a free, democratic world. Broch did not see National Socialism as the culmination of a German tradition, but rather as the turning away from a civilized German tradition. The destruction of people and cities clearly signified that culture had lost its redemptive value.[57] What was needed was a means by which the individual could reconnect with these ethical sources. For Broch it was a matter of individual responsibility: "democratic conviction means democratic responsibility, and only in such personal responsibility can one find the will to defend democratic freedom."[58] In a sense Broch was arguing for a crisis of democracy in Europe, similar to a crisis of liberalism, but the root of this crisis was not liberalism's inability to come to terms with massification of politics, its restrictive franchise, and its concern for class preservation; it was the loss of democratic personal responsibility stemming from the disintegration of values. Democracy had become a matter of fact—there was no engaged relationship to its functioning. Citizens no longer asked where their personal responsibilities began or where the government's ended.

Broch viewed European democracy as a failure, and he saw little hope in the democratic tradition that developed in the United States during the nineteenth century—the democratic tradition implied in the American Dream. However, he did find hope in the notion of a new American Dream, conceived around the ancient notions of reason and truth and constructed by a new generation of Americans, what Broch termed the "American youth." "The great hope here is directed toward . . . overcoming of Pragmatism which can be regarded as the perfect expression of the non-political manner of thought in the last few decades. . . . It becomes the unbound duty of anyone concerned with the future of humanity to address his own efforts to this youth among which the will to believe in truth, to believe in political sacrifice and responsibility is again taking shape. What youth wants, what it needs and strives for, is the restoration of the democratic idea, in its platonic reasoning as well as realistic program."[59]

Here Broch foreshadowed the countercultural movement of 1960s. The importance of the youth and the separation of a younger generation from the material values of their parents were Broch's solution to the growing threat of fascist thought in the United States. Even though Broch died before the Beat Generation created a truly visible culture and well before the rise of the counterculture movement of the 1960s, the intellectual similarities between these movements and his critique on U.S. democracy in the 1930s and 1940s demonstrate that the intellectual immigration of the interwar years brought more to the United States than simply a positivistic science and a theoretical basis for new social science. They brought the possibility of conceiving of a society where religious thought and the idea of love (here Platonic in its truest sense) formed the fundamental social value.[60] Broch was not alone in this development. Herbert Marcuse and Karl Popper also promoted similar notions of conceptualizing Western society outside of a strict democratic/communist dichotomy or a strict democratic/totalitarian one.

Broch's solutions, however, were not simple calls to "love thy neighbor." His theory of mass hysteria was based on the epistemological notion that a transcendent and universal value could be accessible—an earthly absolute, around which the conversion process would turn. Since access to such an earthly absolute was through the cognitive process, the central position of the individual in Broch's democratic theory is a sine qua non. This translated in pragmatic terms to the creation of a new regulative principle based not just on the negative rights tradition of the United States, but also on the notion of an enforceable duty, in which all citizens would be forced to ensure their access to full development (ego-expansion) by enforcement of a law for the protection of human life and dignity. The enforcement would by necessity be backed up by force.[61] This was total democracy.

Notes

The complete sources for the notes to this essay follow the notes in a "works cited" section.

1. Lützeler, *Hermann Broch*, 302.
2. Broch was arrested on suspicions of being a political radical, not for being a Jew.
3. Hughes, *The Sea Change*, 1–34.
4. Ibid., 28.
5. See Jay, *The Dialectical Imagination and Permanent Exiles*.
6. Greiter and Pelinka, "Hermann Broch als Demokratietheoretiker," 25.
7. Ibid.
8. This was the basic assumption behind Broch's theory on human rights as well.
9. Since the problem existed in the ego, he formulated his solution in the realm of cognition.
10. See Hermann Broch, *Kommentierte Werkausgabe*, vol.12.
11. "The fight against Mass Hysteria, the enlistment of man into an open system of humanity is the task of democracy." Broch, *Kommentierte Werkausgabe*, vol. 12, 63.
12. For a discussion of Broch's idea on value creation, see Broch, "Das Böse im Wertsystem der Kunst," in *Kommentierte Werkausgabe*, vol. 9, part 2, 119–57.
13. For a discussion of closed value systems, see Broch, "The Disintegration of Values," in *The Sleepwalkers*, 343–648.
14. For a discussion of Broch's ideas on "twilight consciousness," see Broch, *Massenwahntheorie*, in *Kommentierte Werkausgabe*, vol. 12.
15. Broch, undated manuscript, Beinecke Rare Book and Manuscript Library MSS. For this essay I relied on the archival material in the Hermann Broch Archive at the Beinecke Rare Book and Manuscript Library at Yale University. The documents are by and large unpublished notes or drafts of manuscripts. They are often not titled and not organized by date or title. Many of the documents I am using are connected to

Broch's work on mass psychology and his work for the project *The City of Man*. Paul Michael Lützeler has redacted many documents, both these and others from the archive, and published them under the title *Massenwahntheorie. Beiträge zu einer Psychologie der Politik* and *Politische Schriften*. Broch, *Kommentierte Werkausgabe*, vols. 11 and 12.

16. Broch, undated draft manuscript, Beinecke Rare Book and Manuscript Library MSS.

17. Ibid.

18. Broch, undated draft manuscript, Beinecke Rare Book and Manuscript Library MSS.

19. Ibid.

20. This was especially the case for the United States, whose territorial isolation distanced it from the menace of Hitler. In point of fact, one can argue that the United States did not see the Second World War as an ethical war until after the Japanese attack on Pearl Harbor.

21. Arendt, *Men in Dark Times*, 135–36.

22. Broch repeatedly used the term "slavery" in his work, by which he meant not just chattel slavery but basic economic and political oppression.

23. Broch, undated draft manuscript, Beinecke Rare Book and Manuscript Library MSS.

24. Broch, undated draft manuscript, Beinecke Rare Book and Manuscript Library MSS.

25. Ibid.

26. Ibid.

27. Hermann Broch, "Die mythische Erbschaft," quoted in Hannah Arendt, *Men in Dark Times*, 136.

28. See Broch et al., *The City of Man: A Declaration on World Democracy*. Signatories included Thomas Mann, Lewis Mumford, Reinhold Niebur, G. A. Borgese, Hermann Broch, Herbert Agar, Frank Aydelotte, Van Wyck Brooks, Ada L. Comstock, William Yandell Elliott, Dorothy Canfield Fisher, Christian Gauss, Oscar Jászi, Alvin Johnson, Hans Kohn, William Allan Neilson, and Gaetano Salvemini.

29. See also Broch's discussion of enslavement, *Die Demokratie im Zeitalter der Versklavung* (Democracy in an Age of Enslavement), in Broch, *Kommentierte Werkausgabe*, vol. 11, 110–91.

30. Broch continues "All this is only sound and logical, it is sound Realpolitik, and Hitler is [its] most honest, most clever exponent." Broch, undated draft, Beinecke Rare Book and Manuscript Library MSS.

31. Broch, undated draft manuscript, Beinecke Rare Book and Manuscript Library MSS.

32. This is an idea that distances Broch's thought from both the French Revolutionaries and Jean-Jacques Rousseau. Broch, undated draft manuscript, Beinecke Rare Book and Manuscript Library MSS

33. Broch's anti-Marxist stance can be easily detected here. Broch, though educated in Vienna, the heart of logical positivism and scientific materialism, was strongly

influenced by German idealism and the classical humanism tradition. His philosophy of history is very much nineteenth century and Hegelian and thus related to Marxism. But he rejects both the materialism of Marxism and the exterminationist rhetoric of its ideology.

34. Greiter and Pelinka, "*Hermann Broch als Demokratietheoretiker,*" 31.

35. This was passed by the Reichstag in 1922 in response to the murder of Walter Rathenau.

36. Broch, undated draft manuscript, Beinecke Rare Book and Manuscript Library MSS.

37. England, where, "having almost forgotten her revolutionary origins . . . every governmental spokesman, conservative or liberal, with his election becomes the object of real confidence. For every Englishman knows that the governmental power will be used in defense of the regulative principles on which the British way of life is based" Broch, undated draft, Beinecke Rare Book and Manuscript Library MSS.

38. Broch, undated draft manuscript, Beinecke Rare Book and Manuscript Library MSS. Broch's logic can be applied today to the debates on gun control and the 2nd Amendment.

39. Even today the battles over the interpretation of the 14th Amendment amongst various members of the Supreme Court and between constitutional scholars demonstrate that the issue is still far from self-evident.

40. Broch, who worked very closely with Hannah Arendt during his U.S. exile, developed a theory on the use and necessity of an opponent for the fascist system. The theory was very close to Arendt's notion of "the other."

41. Broch maintained a keen interest in the question of race in the United States throughout his exile. He even took active steps to support the protection of rights of African Americans; an examination of Broch's banking record revealed that he made regular contributions to the NAACP throughout his exile. Broch, undated draft, Beinecke Rare Book and Manuscript Library MSS.

42. See Ernst and Hugg, *Black America.*

43. See Dominic and Wilkerson, *Layered Violence.*

44. The discussion of the Detroit riots is found in an unpublished manuscript (in English) attached to a pamphlet on "The Law for the Protection of Human Dignity," Broch, undated draft manuscript, Beinecke Rare Book and Manuscript Library MSS.

45. Ibid.

46. Broch claimed that the earliest notions of such a humane goal can be seen in the story of Abraham's substitution of a ram for Isaac. In terms of politics, democracy amounted to a similar rehumanizing and unpaganizing of the world, that is, respecting God's separation between paganism and humaneness. For this reason Broch calls on democracy to end capital punishment. The modern world's attempts at compromise with savagery in the form of new methods of execution and its removal from the public eye had not ended the antihumanity implied in the antinomian notion of justice that calls for an eye for an eye. Democracy must embrace humanness without compromise, and, even though Broch concedes that during a time of war such

measures cannot be taken, he calls for a resolution that would ensure the abolition of the death penalty in the future. Such a resolution would become the centerpiece of the democratic propaganda and tied directly to the peace aims of the democratic nations.

47. Broch, undated draft manuscript, Beinecke Rare Book and Manuscript Library MSS.

48. Ibid.

49. Broch, undated draft manuscript, Beinecke Rare Book and Manuscript Library MSS.

50. Broch, undated draft manuscript, Beinecke Rare Book and Manuscript Library MSS.

51. Broch developed his political theory by expanding his aesthetic value theory to the world of politics. In his aesthetic system, art is judged on the basis of whether it can provoke an ethical response in the viewer. Art that cannot provoke such a response is empty of value, or is kitsch. Fascism was, for Broch, the political kitsch of the twentieth century. In the United States, and after the rise of the Third Reich, Broch recognized that his theory of the disintegration of values could be applied not only to art, but also to the political context of his time.

52. Paradoxically Broch also argues that U.S. individualism and its political independence (what he terms anarchism) developed out its early religious communities.

53. Broch, undated draft manuscript, Beinecke Rare Book and Manuscript Library MSS.

54. Broch, undated draft manuscript, Beinecke Rare Book and Manuscript Library MSS.

55. In Broch's early political writing (from 1919 to 1920), where he argued for a democratic postwar government, it was his fear of the potential loss of individual freedom under the influence of mass hysteria or in the face of Soviet communism that compelled him toward a democratic solution. See his 1919 article, "Konstitutionelle Diktatur als demokratisches Rätesystem," in Broch, *Kommentierte Werkausgabe*, vol. 13, part 1, 11–23.

56. Broch, undated draft manuscript, Beinecke Rare Book and Manuscript Library MSS. The letter of Esch to Frau Hugenau in the final section of Broch's novel *The Sleepwalkers* vividly portrays this value vacuum, here as an example of the capitalistic Machiavellianism. Esch, rapist and murder, calmly asserts his right to an equitable settlement of his affairs with the Hugenau family, a right seemingly undeniably protected by the value of commerce and legal contracts.

57. Broch offered this idea in the form of a question that hints at some degree of pessimism and ambiguity toward the ultimate good in humanity: "Do the intrinsic human values—provided that they still exist—offer sufficient justification for the appeal to defend these values against the assault of the dictators?" Broch, undated draft manuscript, Beinecke Rare Book and Manuscript Library MSS.

58. Broch, undated draft manuscript, Beinecke Rare Book and Manuscript Library MSS.

59. Ibid.

60. Paul Michael Lützeler makes a similar argument for the importance of Broch's political thought and its relationship to later movements such as Amnesty International. See Lützeler, introduction and "Visionaries in Exile," in *Hermann Broch Visionary in Exile*, 1–10 and 67–88.

61. Greiter and Pelinka, *"Hermann Broch als Demokratietheoretiker,"* 25.

Works Cited

Arendt, Hannah. *Men in Dark Times*. New York: Harcourt, Brace, and World, 1968.

Broch, Hermann. *Kommentierte Werkausgabe*, 13 vols. Edited by Paul Michael Lützeler. Frankfurt am Main: Suhrkamp, 1974–81.

———. *The Sleepwalkers*. Translated by Willa and Edmund Muir. New York: Vantage Books, 1945.

Broch, Hermann, et al. *The City of Man: A Declaration on World Democracy*. New York: Viking, 1940.

Capeci, Dominic J., Jr., and Martha Wilkerson. *Layered Violence: The Detroit Riots of 1943*. Jackson: University Press of Mississippi, 1991.

Ernst, Robert T., and Lawrence Hugg, eds. *Black America: Geographic Perspective*. Garden City, N.Y.: Anchor, 1976.

Fermi, Laura. *Illustrious Immigrants: The Intellectual Migration from Europe, 1930–1941*. Chicago: University of Chicago Press, 1971.

Greiter, Almund and Anton Pelinka. "Hermann Broch als Demokratietheoretiker." In *Hermann Broch und Seine Zeit*, edited by Richard Thieberger. Bern: Peter Lang, 1980.

Hughes, H. Stuart. *The Sea Change: The Migration of Social Thought, 1930–1965*. New York: Harper & Row, 1975.

Jay, Martin. *Permanent Exiles: Essays on the Intellectual Migration from Germany to America*. New York: Columbia University Press, 1985.

———. *The Dialectical Imagination: A History of the Frankfurt School and the Institute of Social Research, 1923–50*. Boston: Little, Brown, 1973.

Lützeler, Paul Michael. *Hermann Broch: A Biography*. Translated by Janice Furness. London: Quartet Books, 1987.

Lützeler, Paul Michael, ed. *Hermann Broch Visionary in Exile: The 2001 Yale Symposium*. Rochester, N.Y.: Camden House, 2001.

Gudrun Brokoph-Mauch

Fighting Windmills on Broadway
Max Reinhardt's Exile in the United States

Reflecting on his seventieth birthday, Max Reinhardt wrote a letter to Franz Werfel expressing his own failure in his efforts to bring "the fire to the stage" that—as Werfel had shown in his play *Das Lied der Bernadette*—would combat the doom of mortality.[1] Why this tone of resignation from a man who in 1930 was called a genius who had raised the world stage to new heights and whose name awakened "the idea of a truly sovereign theater?"[2] Do these dispirited words of the septuagenarian reflect the sum experiences of an artist who spent his last years in exile?

Reinhardt's exile in the United States began with his last Atlantic crossing in October 1937. Although he immigrated to California in 1934 with his two sons and Helene Thimig—his second wife—we cannot call the first three years of his relocation exile, as he was free to return to Europe at any time. In fact he did so and made trips to Austria every summer to participate in the Salzburg Festivals.[3] Only his last departure from Europe bore the mark of the involuntary that characterizes the exile.

Six months after Hitler became Reichskanzler, Reinhardt—threatened by the propaganda machine as "Jew Goldmann"—left his theater in Berlin for Austria.[4] But since he was not safe from the persecutions of the National Socialists, he established a second residence in California soon afterward.[5] When Reinhardt took leave of Europe in 1937, six months before the Austrian *Anschluss*, the United States did not receive him as on previous occasions as a celebrated guest but as artist in exile.

This new relationship to this country with which he was well acquainted was to bring him difficulties in his artistic work that he could not have foreseen on the basis of his earlier experiences in the United States. His acquaintance with the country can be divided into three phases: guest productions between the years 1923 to 1928, while he was director of the *Deutsche Theater* and the *Kammerspiele* in Berlin; film and theater productions in the early thirties in Hollywood and in New York during his residence in Austria, 1934 to 1937; exile in the United States from 1937 until his death in 1943. If we compare the three different phases of Reinhardt's stay in America, we can see clearly that as long as he could work freely in the European style as was the case before his exile, success was assured. But as soon as he had to deal with the reality of the U.S. film and theater world, which forced him into hitherto unknown compromises, problems arose, and his usual success disappeared. Moreover it cannot be denied that his reputation in the United States, which had been founded on the work prior to his exile, did not open doors for him during his exile, as he had hoped, but on the contrary closed those doors in a economic environment that had meanwhile changed.

Reinhardt's first visit to the United States in 1923 was a result of his production of Friedrich Frekas's oriental fairytale pantomime *Sumurun,* which received much acclaim when it was performed on Broadway under the direction of his partner Richard Ordinsky. It acquainted the U.S. theater world for the first time with Reinhardt's unique style and talent. What the public admired in *Sumurun* was the modern impressionistic setting, the lighting, the dynamics of the whole—all in stark contrast to the reigning naturalism on the U.S. stage—and the exemplary teamwork of the actors. Reinhardt's renewal of the acting style of the Austrian baroque, which employs strong gesticulatory elements and rests on a choreography for dance—was particularly effective in the wordless musical drama.[6] Following this successful production, Reinhardt went to New York in 1923 to bring a second pantomime, Carl Vollmoeller's *Mirakel,* to the stage. It resulted in 298 performances from January 15 to November 8, 1924 (*Sumurun* had 62) and was the talk of the theater world in New York. From 1925 to 1930 *Mirakel* toured the country, giving Reinhardt the chance to show off his ensemble theater of the *Deutsche Theater* in Berlin with German-language productions.[7]

His reputation in the United States seemed secured for all times with this guest performance for an exclusive, literary, partially German-speaking audience. The original contract was extended twice, and the producer of the guest performance, Otto Kahn, sent out for architectural plans for a Max Reinhardt theater in New York. Those plans, however, were never realized.

Reinhardt's second, longer stay in the United States was devoted to the realization of long-held film plans that resulted in his production of Shakespeare's *A Midsummer Night's Dream* on October 9, 1934. He had produced the theater version a month before at the California festivals in the Hollywood Bowl. In addition to his film work, he also produced Franz Werfel's play *The Eternal Road,* which was staged on January 7, 1937, at the Manhattan Opera House. With this parable of the exodus and persecution of the Jewish people, the totally unpolitical director worked with a tendentious and up-to-the-minute topical theme of personal interest. But, because of extremely high production costs and in spite of its popularity with the audience, the production of the *Eternal Road* went bankrupt after only 153 performances.

The second phase of Reinhardt's work in the United States throws a foreboding light on his life in exile. Although he reached the pinnacle of international acclaim with his film and was even nominated for the Nobel Prize, he could not garner any further film offers. The reason was that high production costs made *A Midsummer Night's Dream* a financial disappointment for Warner Brothers even as it brought Reinhardt great financial success. This was similar what happened with *The Eternal Road,* whose astronomical production costs prevented a U.S. tour that might have prevented the financial catastrophe. When Reinhardt came to the United States a third and last time, the financial conditions of the film and theater industries had changed for the worse because of the worldwide war situation. Consequently producers shied away from a new cooperation with him, remembering the huge expenses for his extravagant designs.

Reinhardt's exile divided between two geographic regions: California and New York. He spent the first three years in Hollywood, and then in 1940 he went to New York. He justified his move to New York in a letter to Graf Ledebour with the following words: "Here it is more pleasant, freer and more beautiful to live at this time than anywhere else in the world, but on this vast continent there is, as you know, only one street in which the legitimate life of the theater is really pulsating: the Broadway in New York. Soon it will be the only place on this earth."[8] The regret about the geographic change is unmistakable. Very little remained of his enthusiasm for the fabulous "theater city" and "wonderful audience.[9] On the contrary the move to New York became for him the realization of a "horrifying thought."[10] Yet Hollywood had turned its back on him. As early as 1936 he was passed over for the directorship of an English-language production of Hofmannsthal's *Everyman* (*Jedermann*) for the California festivals. Instead a former student, Johannes Paulsen, together with Einar Nilson, was chosen.[11] When the lucrative film contract on which Reinhardt had firmly counted did not appear and Helene Thimig was forced to support the household with tiny film roles, Reinhardt had no other choice but to go to Broadway.

The three projects which Max Reinhardt wanted to realize while in exile show clearly that the United States did not mean for him a new beginning but rather the continuation of his life's work: California festivals along the lines of the Salzburg Festivals, a theater school like the Reinhardt Seminars in Germany and Austria, and the foundation of a more formal theater like that of the Deutsche Theater in Berlin and the Theater in the Josefstadt in Vienna. Those three bastions of his international reputation could no longer support him in a country that saw the theater as an arm of the entertainment industry. His life's work had matured on a different soil than the one he found in the United States. His dream to make California the Mecca of enthusiastic festival pilgrims from all over the world seems today especially idealistic when one considers that Disneyland was founded in 1955 and became the Mecca of the broad masses rather than of art seekers. The seminar for actors and directors did come into existence; however, lack of finances led to its closing in three years.

What was left was to establish the "legitimate" theater on Broadway. This plan brought Reinhardt to New York. However, because of financial difficulties, he had to interrupt the actualization of this goal twice with the production of plays that lay outside his efforts for a permanent theater. These were Thornton Wilder's *Merchant of Yonkers* in 1938, *Rosalinda*—a U.S. *Fledermaus*—in 1942, and after that the failure of the theater project *Helen Goes to Troy,* an Offenbach adaptation that Reinhardt could not complete. Thus his work in New York went in two directions: first came his efforts to found his own ensemble theater, which finally culminated in the performance of Irwin Shaw's *Sons and Soldiers* in 1942. Next came individual productions of plays during and after the negotiations for his own theater on Broadway.

Reinhardt wanted to bring to Broadway the European ensemble theater with firmly contracted actors and staff and with a repertoire of several plays per season. With this ensemble theater he wanted to counteract the reigning ad hoc operations of the U.S. star theater and the "wild speculation circus" of the producers.[12] The firm engagement of all members of the theater was a fundamental precondition for him guaranteeing the full commitment of the whole person, serious work, and the "joy of playing," the most important ingredient in all artistic creations.[13] Instead of the reigning star, he wanted confluence and subordination of all individual elements under the "Gesamtkunstwerk." "The theater is in its very nature an orchestral art."[14] He counted on the team spirit of the U.S. youth for the abolition of the star. The ideal repertoire consisted for him of approximately five plays, preferably written by renowned living authors or newly adapted plays from world literature. His ideal building would be an older house because of better acoustics and ambience. He opposed small intimate theater as a point of principle. He hoped to finance this project mainly by large subscriptions and television and film contracts. He wanted to be active only on the stage, while leaving all administrative duties to local experts.[15] This building should also house his ensemble workshops which were an essential part of his international reputation.

To attract potential investors, he planned and started a tour of his workshop ensembles on January 7, 1940, through several U.S. cities with the expected culmination and climax in New York. But this enterprise ended suddenly at the first stop in San Francisco, when his business manager ran off with the evening's gross. However, Reinhardt did not give up, and he founded a production company.[16] First he worked with the director Edgar Clurman and the actress Stella Adler, later with the architect Norman Bel Geddes, the manager Richard Myers, and the actor Eddie Dowling, who later resigned a second time.[17] All his efforts for his own theater were ill fated. His negotiations for a suitable building ended in failure, and he could neither find wealthy investors nor an interesting play. When Reinhardt finally decided on Irwin Shaw's *Sons and Soldiers*—which premiered on May 9, 1942—it was no ringing success and had only twenty-two performances. The material proved to be too tendentious. The war topic so soon after Pearl Harbor pointed its finger too blatantly at the warring generation, creating discomfort among the audience and resulting in rejection from the press. The critics, however, praised the actors and Reinhardt's direction enthusiastically, calling him a "theater genius"[18] and a "master of stage tricks."[19]

Irwin Shaw, who never saw the play in its entirety, took all blame on himself and in a letter to Reinhardt admired his "excellent production with an exquisite cast."[20] But in spite of the recognition for Reinhardt's abilities, the performance could not be saved, leaving this first attempt to establish an ensemble theater as the last.

In a letter in which Reinhardt explains his plans for a repertory theater he wrote, "I'm not a dreamer, in any case not more than a theater man has to be. Up to this point I have realized all my dreams. A dream without reality means just as little to me as a reality without a dream. And the theater does consist only of realistic dreams."[21] However the dream of his own theater on Broadway would remain just a dream. For this dream to become reality the most basic precondition was missing: the long-term financial security that would assure that the well-being of the theater need not depend on the success or failure of a single piece. This, however, depended again on an attractive start-up play to interest investors.[22]

The choice of the play was unfortunate not just because of the war theme but also for another reason: Reinhardt's disloyalty to himself. In the past he had garnered his biggest successes with plays that had been well established in the theater world rather than new plays. "In order to be successful here," Reinhardt wrote, "I have to go my own way for better or worse. That is I have to work with well known plays which I adapt in my fashion."[23] In her memoirs Helene Thimig wrote that the Broadway producers, called angels in theater jargon, had not permitted him a classical play but only a modern one.[24] The failure with the war piece was all the more unexpected as Metro Goldwyn Mayer had financed 40 percent of the production to secure the film rights.[25]

In retrospect it is amazing how many difficulties Reinhardt encountered looking for an appropriate play for the opening of his theater. All requests to various potential contributors ended in failure: Eugene O'Neill was bound by contract to the Theater Guild; William Saroyan wanted to produce himself; Reinhardt could not engage the shy Greta Garbo for Maeterlinck's *Beatrice;* and Konstantin Simonow's play *Russian People* was already sold to the Theater Guild, which performed it with great success. Reinhardt never found an enthusiastic producer for Thomas Wolfe's dramatic work.[26] His plan to perform Hofmannsthal's *Jedermann* with African American songs and spirituals failed because the producers refused to hire black actors for the "serious theater." Finally, the dramatization of a story by

Franz Werfel was not realized because Werfel received a lucrative offer from Hollywood.[27] When Werfel's play did reach the stage shortly after Reinhardt's death under the title of *Jacobowsky and the Colonel,* it became an international hit.

Next to his failed efforts to secure his own theater, Reinhardt produced several pieces on Broadway. It is interesting to observe that his recipe for success in Europe was not easily repeated in the United States. His choice of Thornton Wilder's adaptation of Nestroy's play *Einen Jux will er sich machen* uncovered cultural barriers that Reinhardt had not considered. Although at first it seemed that the choice of a Pulitzer Prize–winning U.S. author could not fail, it did. Wilder—although familiar with the Viennese folk comedy—was not rooted in the culture and society, essential for comic effect. He could therefore not transpose the farce convincingly into the U.S. idiom. Wilder's background broke through irrepressibly so that he constantly found himself sitting between two chairs.[28] It is unlikely therefore that he attempted a real adaptation; instead he went for a "smiling parody of an old fashioned play"[29] that did not reach the audience, which was unfamiliar with the folk comedy and who did not appreciate the predominately "literary humor . . . with the flavor of a joke in Latin."[30] There were the usual problems with trying to translate humor into another language, but, most important, the difficulties were within the differences between the German and Anglo-Saxon theater mentality. "The theater is much more national than the sophisticate would like to admit . . . in a symphony the differences in schooling may be submerged, in a chamber music performance, however, they become glaringly obvious."[31]

It is also probable that the much younger author—for whom the cooperation with Reinhardt meant the fulfillment of a dream—felt restrained in his creative autonomy by the closeness of the great Reinhardt.[32] Moreover it became obvious through a trial performance in Boston that the production at the time of the premiere was not really ready for the stage yet.[33] The hasty changes before the New York performance could not give the play the degree of perfection that characterized Reinhardt's productions in the past. *The Merchant of Yonkers* premiered December 28, 1938, in the Guild Theatre and ran only fifty-nine times. This negative result clearly points to the difficulties of an artist in exile, all the more so since this play was extremely attractive to the audience after revision by the author in 1954 under the title *The Matchmaker* and conquered Broadway after another adaptation by Michael Stewart and Jerry Herman in 1964 under the title *Hello, Dolly.*

Several elements contributed to the failure. For one Reinhardt's choice of an Austrian play makes it clear that he had not yet wiped off the dust from his shoes. For another the production of *The Merchant of Yonkers* clearly shows the frustrations with which a foreigner insufficiently familiar, or not in agreement with, the practices of the U.S. theater had to struggle. The rigor of these practices on the one hand and Reinhardt's lack of flexibility on the other contributed equally to the failure of the performance. The biggest obstacle that reduced Reinhardt's customary autonomy was the rigorous budget, precisely calculated and keenly watch over by producer Shumlin, "the Merchant of New York," as Reinhardt called him.[34] Since Shumlin did not allow the slightest expansion of the budget, a fact with which Reinhardt never had to deal in Europe or previously in the United States, he was denied his choice of the theater building and the stage setting, as well as his trusted assistant and interpreter. These unaccustomed restrictions must have undermined his self-confidence and affected the direction of the play, especially when we consider that, as a former theater owner and director, he was not accustomed to being treated like an employee. In addition he could not rely on his keen instinct in the selection of the actors since as a foreigner he knew only a small number of them personally. As the few actors he knew through his work in California could not free themselves from prior commitments, the casting of the roles fell into the hands of the producers and author who did not follow Reinhardt's urgent advice to choose comic actors for the roles. Already during the rehearsals Reinhardt predicted the result: "Nothing is comical with this cast . . . and it is very doubtful that a Nestroy farce without the comical can be successful."[35]

The merciless rules of the union were another establishment of the Broadway industry that seriously disturbed Reinhardt, especially the strict eight-hour day, which interrupted the momentum of restless and devoted work to which Reinhardt had been accustomed all his life. In his opinion these rules made for normal everyday work should not apply to artistic work since they dampened the "joy of playing," which inflamed the enthusiasm of the audience.[36]

Problems of this kind were typical for Reinhardt's work on Broadway and can be explained in large part by the fact that in Germany and Austria he had been able to work under conditions that were in stark contrast to those in the United States. But Reinhardt's exile did not end in total failure. In his last year he succeeded with a genre that had always been suspect to him, the operetta.[37] In his financial distress he accepted the offer of the New Opera Company to produce *Die Fledermaus* together with Wolfgang Erich Korngold, with whom he had produced this play years earlier in Berlin. Reinhardt cut the weak libretto down to a minimum, commissioned his son Gottfried with the adaptation of the English text, and placed the main emphasis on the musical arrangement, which he expanded with other Strauss melodies. He cast all roles except for Orlofsky with opera singers, swept the stage in strong colors, and made a "waltz orgy" out of the ball scenes in the second act.[38] The operetta premiered on October 28, 1942, in the Forty-Fourth Street Theater and was a huge success. It continued on Broadway beyond Reinhardt's death and, with 521 productions, exceeded the twelve previous Broadway presentations of the same operetta, all of which had been much less successful.

The antecedent preparations for *Rosalinda,* as *Die Fledermaus* was called on Broadway, make it clear how much pull the name Max Reinhardt had lost in U.S. theater circles. Not Reinhardt but Felix Weissberger was originally chosen as director.

Weissberger had made a name for himself with his 1929 production of *Die Fledermaus*, which was an imitation of Reinhardt's Berlin production. Only through the intervention of Korngold was the originator rather than the plagiarist contracted. The success which Reinhardt's *Rosalinda* achieved with the public and the press led to another contract from the New York Opera Company, this time with Offenbach's *Helen Goes to Troy*. Reinhardt had been working on an adaptation of this operetta since 1939, as it had brought him fame in Europe and he had preferred it to *Die Fledermaus*.[39] But at that time he had only been able to interest the press in this operetta, but not the theaters.[40] Reinhardt did not live to see *Helen Goes to Troy* on Broadway, but his son Gottfried introduced the Max Reinhardt version half a year after Reinhardt's death, to the applause of the New York audience.

Reinhardt's success with *Rosalinda* and *Helen Goes to Troy* permits the assumption that after a frustrating beginning he would have found his place on Broadway after all, albeit with a genre he did not value and on an artistic level that would not have brought him much renown. Whether he wanted to or not, he had to join in the "dance around the golden calf" to suspend his role as idol and educator for the theater world at the end of his life in order to secure his income.[41] To make a professional change such as Carl Zuckmayer's, who lived in the United States and earned his income as a farmer "because he could not make any compromises in his profession as a writer" was impossible for him.[42] He had to do what he was destined to do, which meant in his case go to Broadway and make compromises.[43] "To perform serious theater today is really a Donquichoterie. This means to fight for high artistic ideals against enormous windmills clattering in the storm of our time."[44]

On the "high stakes market of this theater of chance," all arguments that try to explain why Reinhardt was not successful on Broadway are really indefensible.[45] However, three elements seem to have played a major role: the contemporary situation and its influence on the U.S. stage, the commercial basis of the administrative syndicate of the theater in New York, and Reinhardt's personal and professional uprooting through the exile. The confluence of these unfavorable components developed a resistance against Reinhardt's efforts that can be likened to the power of windmills. First and foremost the war had a paralyzing influence on the artistic taste of the public that—as far as it was interested in theater at all—demanded the sentimental melodrama as diversion from the threatening events of the day.[46] Contemporary plays about the war or Nazis did exist but were only consumed on the lowest artistic level.[47] The general demand was for escapism, the "gas mask," and not for the intellectual literary drama with which Reinhardt had conquered the world prior to his exile.[48] It is interesting though that he himself was more involved in the aspect of staging and acting than the literary aspects.[49] In contrast to Jessner and Piscator, he was not fascinated by the political play, and when he tried his hand at it with *Sons and Soldiers,* it was exactly this lack of experience with this genre that denied him success. The unscrupulous business sense of the Broadway industry added to the unfavorable historical situation. A small number of men controlled almost all theaters in the United States from 1896 until 1950 until antitrust legislation was passed, this control subjugated any kind of artistic impulse to the demand for immediate profit.[50]

In addition, as mentioned before, since his mammoth productions in the twenties and early thirties, Reinhardt's name had acquired the reputation of a "director of expensive and untimely performances."[51] No doubt it had not been forgotten that he had lined his own pockets with his spectacular performances but—because of the high production costs—had not filled those of his investors. This was an oversight that he had been able to afford as a guest, but once he was in exile it impeded his entry into the film and theater business. Moreover Reinhardt's adaptability was not just severely tested in the professional realm but also in his personal life, pressures that the almost seventy year old could not withstand. The unaccustomed financial distress and the isolation from Europe in a country to which he knew only too soon that he could never adapt[52] threw him off his "psychological balance,"[53] which he had maintained before his exile by his annual voyages to Austria. It is understandable that he wanted to rescue a piece of his homeland by the founding of his theater on Broadway after the model of the Theater in der Josefstadt, at a time when it would have been better to find an entry to his new and strange environment.[54] Instead he spent his energy building a world that he knew and loved in a country that was not prepared for it.

Max Reinhardt died on October 31, 1943, in New York, shortly after his seventieth birthday, which he had celebrated among his friends in exile on September 9. The celebratory speeches could not deceive him about the fact that in the same country in which a few years earlier as a guest he had experienced the climax of his career, now as an immigrant he had reached the nadir. But his international reputation has not been diminished by the soft din of the cash registers on Broadway. Still today he is remembered as the innovator of the world stage who "founded a new generation of onlookers and talented actors, of directors . . . and of a large school, a whole culture."[55]

Notes

1. Letter, September 1943, Max Reinhardt Archive, State University of New York, Binghamton.

2. Heinz Kindermann, *Max Reinhardts Weltwirkung* (Vienna: Böhlau, 1969), 26.

3. Gottfried Reinhardt, *Der Liebhaber. Erinnerungen eines Sohnes* (Müchep-Zurich: Droemer Knaur, 1973), 32.

4. Reinhardt obtained official permission to change his name from Goldmann in 1904: Leonard M. Fiedler, *Max Reinhardt in Selbstzeugnissen und Bilddokumenten* (Reinbek: Rowohlt, 1975), 141.

5. Fiedler, *Max Reinhardt in Selbstzeugnissen*, 117–18, and Edward Harris and Max Reinhardt, *Deutsche Exilliteratur seit 1933*, vol. 1, *Kalifornien*, part 1, edited by John M. Spalek and Joseph Strelka (Bern and Munich: Francke, 1976), 790.

6. Heinz Kindermann, *Max Reinhardts Weltwirkung*, 23.

7. The repertoire consisted of *Sommernachtstraum, Jedermann, Dantons Tod, Kabale und Liebe, Peripherie, Diener zweier Herren, Der lebende Leichnam und Gespenster*.

8. Max Reinhardt, *Schriften, Briefe, Reden, Aufsätze, Auszüge aus Regiebüchern*, edited by Hugo Fetting (Berlin: Henschelverlag, 1974), 239.

9. Interview in the *Neuen Freien Presse* (Vienna), November 4, 1928, quoted from Fiedler, *Max Reinhardt in Selbstzeugnissen*, 124–25.

10. Gusti Adler, *Max Reinhardt. Sein Leben* (Salzburg: Festungsverlag, 1964), 270.

11. Ibid.; Fuhrich-Leisler and Gisela Prossnitz, *Max Reinhardt in Amerika* (Salzburg: O. Müller, 1976).

12. Max Reinhardt, *Schriften*, 240.

13. Ibid., 242.

14. Ibid., 240.

15. Ibid, 242–45.

16. Letter from Max Reinhardt to Franz Werfel, October 10, 1940, Max Reinhardt Archive, State University of New York, Binghamton.

17. Fuhrich/Prossnitz, *Max Reinhardt in Amerika*, 385.

18. Stark Young, "Jus Divinum: Sons and Soldiers, by Irwin Shaw," *New Republic* 108 (May 17, 1943): 669.

19. Fuhrich/Prossnitz, *Max Reinhardt in Amerika*, 394.

20. Ibid., 397.

21. Max Reinhardt, *Schriften*, 246.

22. Fuhrich/Prossnitz, *Max Reinhardt in Amerika*, 385.

23. Helene Thimig, *Wie Max Reinhardt lebte* (Percha am Starnberger See: Schultz, 1973), 356.

24. Ibid., 352.

25. Gottfried Reinhardt, *Der Liebhaber*, 76.

26. Max Reinhardt's letter to Franz Werfel, October 29, 1941, Max Reinhardt Archive, Binghamton.

27. Fuhrich/Prossnitz, *Max Reinhardt in Amerika*, 366.

28. Martin Blank, "When Farce Isn't Funny," *Players* (April–May 1975): 90.

29. Ibid.

30. Fuhrich/Prossnitz, *Max Reinhardt in Amerika*, 345.

31. Gottfried Reinhardt, *Der Liebhaber*, 141.

32. Martin Blank, 90.

33. Fuhrich/Prossnitz, *Max Reinhardt in Amerika*, 542.

34. Thimig, *Wie Max Reinhardt lebte*, 348.

35. Ibid., 331.

36. Max Reinhardt, *Schriften*, 242.

37. Gottfried Reinhardt, *Der Liebhaber*, 59.

38. Fuhrich/Prossnitz, *Max Reinhardt in Amerika*, 373, 542.
39. Thimig, *Wie Max Reinhardt lebte*, 359.
40. Max Reinhardt, letter to the *New York Herald Tribune*, Max Reinhardt Archive, Binghamton.
41. Heinrich Braulich, *Max Reinhardt, Theater zwischen Traum und Wirklichkeit* (Berlin: Henschelverlag, 1966), 246.
42. Thimig, *Wie Max Reinhardt lebte*, 350.
43. Ibid., 357.
44. Max Reinhardt, *Schriften*, S. 253.
45. Fuhrich/Prossnitz, *Max Reinhardt in Amerika*, 413.
46. Peter Bauland, *The Hooded Eagle* (Syracuse: Syracuse University Press, 1971), 155–57.
47. Ibid.
48. Max Reinhardt, *Schriften*, 254,
49. Hans Knudsen, *Deutsche Theatergeschichte* (Stuttgart: Kroner, 1970), 338–39.
50. Bauland, *Hooded Eagle*, 41–42.
51. Thimig, *Wie Max Reinhardt lebte*, 360.
52. Ibid, 353
53. Gottfried Reinhardt, *Der Liebhaber*, 176.
54. "Wherever Reinhardt wanted to play, wherever he wanted to build a theatre, he always wanted to follow the plan of the Theater an der Josefstadt and its actors." Ernst Haeussermann, "Max Reinhardt," *Max Reinhardt 1873–1973: A Centennial Festschrift* (Binghamton, N.Y.: Max Reinhardt Archive, 1973), 50.
55. Kindermann, *Max Reinhardts Weltwirkung*, 57.

Sabine Feisst

Schoenberg in the United States Reconsidered
A Historiographic Investigation

Like innumerable émigrés from Nazi Europe, Arnold Schoenberg, pioneer of musical modernism, spent an important part of his creative life in the United States. During this time (1933–51), he not only produced significant compositions, but also contributed greatly to musical culture in the United States. Research has been done on his U.S. sojourn, his works composed in his new homeland, and the U.S. reception of his music and ideas, although there is not as much material devoted to his work during this period as to that done prior to his immigration, which is not surprising, given how much longer he lived in Europe.[1] In some cases critics and scholars have perpetuated clichés and a variety of predominantly negative interpretations of his U.S. career. It is useful to trace and analyze depictions of Schoenberg's U.S. period in specialized literature about Schoenberg, exile studies and reference works in order to identify myths, gaps, changing trends, and the authors' agendas. Since there is not a balanced picture of Schoenberg in the United States to date, the focus here is on pertinent and influential themes about Schoenberg's personality and life, his U.S. compositions and his work as a teacher.

Schoenberg's Personality

Central to many accounts of his U.S. sojourn is the pejorative image of Schoenberg as a European in exile, an outsider in Southern California, a snob and untouchable icon with a forbidding and hermetic aura.[2] Jan Meyerowitz, an émigré composer (without ties to Schoenberg), declared that he "was not in the least Americanized."[3] Jost Hermand, a German-born German-literature specialist, emphasized the incompatibility of Schoenberg's nonconformist attitude toward art music and his strong interest in Zionism with his chosen place of residence, Los Angeles. He therefore declared him out of place in a commercially and hedonistically oriented environment not completely immune to xenophobia or anti-Semitism.[4] U.S. composer David Schiff described Schoenberg as "disoriented by his new cultural surroundings." And U.S. writer Anthony Heilbut pointed out that "Schoenberg's American career was plagued by disappointment and inattention."[5] U.S. historian Kevin Starr conveyed a particularly unbalanced and negative image of Schoenberg: "Despite his long residence in Los Angeles, from 1934 to 1951 . . . Schoenberg remained a figure so detached, so alienated, as to seem not to exist in Los Angeles at all, or at the least, not to derive much satisfaction from his life there."[6] Finally the British music critic Malcolm MacDonald summarized that "for most of his time in America he felt isolated and bypassed by the musical world, little performed and little understood in a comparative cultural backwater."[7] But if this was the case, had not Schoenberg also been an elitist and outsider in Europe? How did these and other writers arrive at such views?

The psychological complexity of Schoenberg's personality, which reveals on the one hand varying degrees of sensitivity, vulnerability, authoritarianism, and elitism and on the other hand idealism, gratitude, pragmatism, generosity, and adaptability, led to conflicting statements in letters, essays, speeches, and interviews during a particularly trying period of the composer's life. Hence Schoenberg commentators, whether aiming at a negative or a positive portrait, could always substantiate their view by using appropriate quotations from primary Schoenberg sources. To date, however, a largely one-sided and negatively flavored impression of Schoenberg's U.S. years persists. Schoenberg biographers generally omit in-depth discussions of his acculturation, his embracing of the English language, and his acceptance of U.S. life and culture and interactions with Americans, and therefore they tend to support the thesis of Schoenberg as an elitist and outsider. Biographers, however, often stress his contact with other émigrés, thereby making him appear as a so-called bei-uns-ki.[8] This approach applies to the early influential monographic studies by Hans Heinz Stuckenschmidt and Willi Reich—both students of Schoenberg, Alban Berg, or Anton Webern who stayed in Nazi Europe. Both Stuckenschmidt and Reich offer a mostly Eurocentric outlook by emphasizing the image of their "suffering hero" and by seeking to cope with their own immediate past.[9] The much-quoted collection of Schoenberg correspondence (1958) selected and compiled by European Schoenberg student Erwin Stein also reinforces—in its presentation of mostly pejorative letters from the U.S. period—the picture of a dissatisfied and disappointed Schoenberg.[10] Most "Schoenberg in America" chapters of later monographs are heavily modeled on these publications.[11]

There are, however, occasional attempts—mostly by U.S. writers—to contextualize, humanize, and popularize the "American" Schoenberg. Walter Rubsamen, a U.S. musicologist and Schoenberg's colleague at UCLA, gave a comprehensive account of his years in the United States wherein he discussed, besides his professional occupations, his interactions with numerous musicians and friends, going far beyond the popular mentioning of his friendly relationship with George Gershwin and Oscar Levant; his extraordinary hospitality and frequent parties; his leisure activities; and even his superstitions.[12] Dika Newlin, a multifaceted artist and one of Schoenberg's most unusual composition pupils, deconstructed the image of her teacher as a "disembodied historical force" and aloof authority in many articles and the book *Schoenberg Remembered,* a frank memoir of her experience as his student at UCLA.[13] She discussed, for instance, Schoenberg's secret weakness for film and television—anathema to most Schoenberg biographers, who prefer to focus on his criticisms of the Hollywood film industry.[14] Yet Rubsamen's and her efforts have been sharply criticized. And her book has even been derisively dubbed "Schoenberg Dismembered."[15] Most recently both German musicologist Matthias Henke and U.S. composer Allen Shawn humanized Schoenberg in their short biographies of him. They presented him in a new and more positive way in that they elaborated on his manifold nonmusical creative activities in America, including his designs of toys for his children and interest in bookbinding, and on his interactions with family and friends.[16] Yet Shawn's endeavor received mixed responses.[17] Beyond the above efforts, one finds scattered statements challenging the status quo of Schoenberg scholarship. U.S. exile specialist Laura Fermi remarked that "Schoenberg too benefited from his transplantation to U.S. soil. He became more human, entering into closer contact with the contemporary world."[18] MacDonald correctly pointed out that Schoenberg wrote and spoke English as much as possible and "made it almost as flexible and vivid (if somewhat idiosyncratic) a medium of self-expression as his German."[19] And the U.S. Schoenberg scholar Alexander Ringer recently wrote that because of Schoenberg's soon "thoroughly Americanized young family"—his two youngest sons were born in the United States—"American thought and behavior" gradually got a hold on him.[20] Such views should be further investigated and shape future biographies.

Health and Finances

The majority of European Schoenberg biographers, among them Stuckenschmidt, Eberhard Freitag, and Manuel Gervink, as well as authors of encyclopedia articles, elaborate on Schoenberg's health and financial problems in America suggesting a stark contrast between his seemingly prosperous European years and the depressing U.S. ones. As in the case of Béla Bartók, these writers therefore nourish the idea that the United States gave an artist of such an eminent stature an inappropriate treatment and establish what Malcolm Gillies called an "American guilt" theory.[21] The emphasis on his initial discomfort with the debilitating weather, asthma attacks, and stressful low-level teaching conditions in Boston and New York and the increased age-related health problems late in his life overshadows the fact that Schoenberg spent about twelve out of eighteen years of his U.S. career in relative good health and happiness.[22] Many writers stress that Schoenberg's heart attack in 1946 and several other ailments drove him even further into isolation and into a five-year long agony. In the *New Grove Dictionary of Music and Musicians* one can, for instance, learn that Schoenberg "led the withdrawn existence of an invalid."[23]

This point of view certainly supports the "isolation theory," but it contradicts Schoenberg's busy work schedule during that period, including private lessons and classes in composition at his home, lectures at the University of Chicago and UCLA, and courses at the Music Academy of the West in Carpinteria, California. His creative achievement since 1946, comprising his String Trio (1946), *A Survivor from Warsaw* (1947), *Fantasy for Violin with Piano Accompaniment* (1949), several vocal works, numerous writings, and the textbook *Structural Functions of Harmony* (1947), refute the notion of Schoenberg as an invalid.

Schoenberg's "financial misery" is another much discussed and distorted subject in the majority of European accounts of Schoenberg's U.S. years. Most biographers blame financial issues and thus America and U.S. institutions for Schoenberg's limited compositional output and unfinished works. Meyerowitz claimed that the "financial misery did much harm to his creative work."[24] And Wilhelm Sinkovicz assured that "during his emigration years, Schoenberg was never able to devote himself in peace to tasks which he would have liked to solve."[25] Other commentators dwelt upon Schoenberg's financial insecurity induced by his mandatory retirement from UCLA in 1944 at age seventy, which yielded a pension averaging 40 dollars (or about 465 dollars in 2007) per month for an eight year-tenure.[26] It is rarely mentioned that in Schoenberg's case UCLA extended the retirement age by five years. Stuckenschmidt describes this situation as well as the rejection of Schoenberg's application for a Guggenheim fellowship in 1945 (for which the applicants' age limit was forty years) as embarrassing.[27] Other authors dramatically claimed that Schoenberg was "suddenly forced into deep poverty" and that "Arnold Schoenberg was starving."[28] Despite the years of economic depression and World War II, Schoenberg experienced financial security with an income drawn from university teaching, lectures, private lessons, commissions, royalties and conducting engagements. In his first academic year at Malkin Conservatory, 1933–34, he earned 4,800 dollars (72,000 dollars in 2007). At USC he received 4,000 dollars(61,000 dollars in 2007) for his teaching activities between 1935 and 1936. From 1936 on he could rely on a yearly income of between 4,800 and 5,400 dollars from UCLA and lived in a Spanish Colonial style house in Brentwood Park that he had bought for 18,000 dollars and that was maintained by domestics.[29] Moreover he generously supported family members and friends with affidavits and regularly sent money to his oldest son, who was unwilling to leave Austria. And though after 1944 Schoenberg had to cut back financially, teach private students, sell manuscripts of some of his scores to the Library of Congress, and accept lucrative commissions, he never came close to starving. How could he have afforded to send CARE packages to Europe in 1946 if he had been destitute? Furthermore in this period occurred Schoenberg's greatest financial success in the United States: Antony Tudor's choreographed version of *Verklärte Nacht*, the *Pillar of Fire*, which has been performed countless times since 1942.[30] ASCAP granted him an allowance of 1,500 dollars per annum in addition to royalties, friends raised money for him, and the National Institute of Arts and Letters awarded him with 1,000 dollars in 1947.[31]

Judaism and Politics

In contrast to aspects such as Schoenberg's personality, health, and finances, his intense involvement in Judaism and the Jewish national cause (especially from 1933 to 1939 and during his last years) initially received little or no attention in early Schoenberg literature. This is an important biographical feature, since Schoenberg invested much time and energy in Jewish matters resulting in numerous writings and creative and political activities, including public speeches for Jewish organizations. Knowledge about Schoenberg's intense preoccupations with noncompositional subjects might also help to eradicate speculations as to why Schoenberg did not compose or complete more works during his U.S. years. Biographers including Meyerowitz, Reich, and Freitag limited themselves to brief remarks on this issue in discussions of Schoenberg's religious and religiously oriented works including his *Kol nidre* setting (1938) and *A Survivor from Warsaw* (1947).[32] And Stuckenschmidt, in his five hundred–page Schoenberg monograph, dedicated little more than a page specifically to Schoenberg's engagement with Judaism.[33] Similarly MacDonald touched only briefly on this subject.[34] Yet the path-breaking articles and books on Schoenberg and Judaism by the musicologists Ringer and Mäckelmann undoubtedly influenced some of the more recent Schoenberg publications and encouraged further specialized studies on this subject.[35] Ringer and Mäckelmann cast light on Schoenberg's complex attitude toward the conventions of his Jewish faith, which he never practiced in a conventional way—his wife and children remained Catholic; his unusual views about assimilation and anti-Semitism; his fight for unanimity among Jews; his attempts to found a Jewish Unity Party, and his idiosyncratic approach to Zionism, involving the establishment of an independent Jewish State through uncompromising and militant means. Lately biographers such as Gervink, Ringer, and Shawn have begun to incorporate discussions of Schoenberg's public speeches—for instance "The Jewish Situation," 1933— and his most substantial essay on Jewish politics, his "Four-Point Program for Jewry" (1933–38).[36] They mostly refrain, however, from a critical assessment of the antidemocratic and authoritarian positions, which mark many of Schoenberg's efforts.[37]

Besides Schoenberg's preoccupation with Jewish matters, his peculiar attitude toward politics in general and political writings would deserve more elaboration and clarification beyond a brief contextualization of his politically motivated settings of Byron's *Ode to Napoleon* (1942) and *A Survivor from Warsaw*. This was not achieved in early literature on Schoenberg.[38] Recent German biographies and exile studies from the early 1990s on, however, have dedicated more attention to his mostly privately kept ideas about politics. They provided more insight into his strong and continuous rejection of communism and fascism, his reservations about democracy, his concern with the rights of minorities, and his preference for monarchy.[39] Mäckelmann, Dümling, Gervink, and Ringer, for instance, explain Schoenberg's caution in most political matters, other than his political activism in the case of Jewish matters, and long-term restraint from open criticism of Hitler as a measure to protect his family and friends in Nazi Europe.[40]

Schoenberg's Late Work

In 1954 musician, philosopher, and Schoenberg champion Theodor W. Adorno expressed his belief that the problems Schoenberg posed were no longer objective, "but a product of public opinion, which keeps ready so many clichés for his work."[41] This observation has been especially true for Schoenberg's U.S. works. By the time he came to the United States, he was already infamously known as a radical and nonconformist composer of structurally complex and aesthetically challenging works. He was considered the "Avatar of twelve-tone music."[42] The works Schoenberg promoted and composed in the United States, however, often contradict this image. Soon many commentators remarked on the different nature of his "U.S." works, pitting the steadily progressive "European" against the eclectic and retrogressive "American" Schoenberg, despite Schoenberg's claim that he was unaware of any changes caused by his immigration.[43]

Heterogeneity

Many early Schoenberg biographers, most notably Stuckenschmidt and Reich, included very favorable descriptions of his U.S. compositions. Yet their commitment did not prevent numerous other commentators from viewing his U.S. oeuvre as more eclectic and heterogeneous than his European output. In their eyes Schoenberg seemed to sacrifice his former stringent "l'art pour l'art" principles by using both traditionally tonal and novel twelve-tone elements and by conceiving utilitarian, sacred, and politically engaged music. Adorno explained his late works as "fragmentary" and "catastrophes" whereby the compositional procedure meant everything and the musical material had no significance.[44] He criticized Schoenberg's mixing of old and new compositional techniques in *Ode to Napoleon* and his Piano Concerto (1942) as "forced" and "impure."[45] Pierre Boulez, the French composer and adherent of the post–World War II serialist movement, went even further,[46] bluntly declaring this approach as vain and flawed: "But what are we to think of Schoenberg's U.S. period, during which the greatest disarray and most deplorable demagnetization appeared? How could we, unless with a supplementary—and superfluous—measure, judge such lack of comprehension and cohesion, that reevaluation of polarizing functions, even of tonal functions? Rigorous writing was abandoned in those works. In them we see appearing again the octave intervals, the false cadences, the exact canons at the octave. Such an attitude attests to maximum incoherence—a paroxysm in the absurdity of Schoenberg's incompatibilities."[47]

These verdicts seem to have influenced Schoenberg scholarship since research on the majority of Schoenberg's U.S. works was for a long time limited. More recently, however, new and positive interpretations of the disparate tendencies in Schoenberg's late works have been offered. His efforts are now also understood as "processes of disjuncture and disruption, establishing frames of narrative, language and musical style only to shatter them by the intrusion of radically dissimilar elements that refuse assimilation."[48] Other commentators drew attention to Schoenberg's anticipation of "the broad availability of historical styles and self-conscious manipulation of earlier music in the output of composers we do not normally associate with Schoenberg, such as Crumb, Foss, Berio, and Rochberg."[49] They also emphasized that most of Schoenberg's European works revealed conflicting tendencies as well—rigorous modernism and elements referring to the past.[50]

Tonality—Accessibility

But the most puzzling and controversial aspect of Schoenberg's U.S. works was his more frequent and emphatic consideration of triadic harmony in works such as his Suite in G for String Orchestra (1934) and Theme and Variations for Wind Band (1942). They reveal an unmistakably retrospective quality. The premiere of Schoenberg's first U.S. work, his Suite in G, triggered, for instance, the following response by *New York Times* critic Olin Downes: "Only one thing more fantastical than the thought of Arnold Schönberg in Hollywood is possible, and that thing has happened. Since arriving there about a year ago, Schönberg has composed in a melodic manner and in recognizable keys. That is what Hollywood has done to Schönberg. We may now expect atonal fugues by Shirley Temple."[51]

After many attempts to avoid speculations about a possible capitulation of twelve-tone composition, Schoenberg wrote an article entitled "On revient toujours" in the *New York Times* in which he defended his continuous "longing to return to the older style" and his occasional decision to "yield to that urge."[52] While Schoenberg classified his tonal Suite in G and Theme and Variations for Windband only as "Nebenwerke" (secondary or minor works) and utilitarian or pedagogical music, Adorno spoke of a "long list of 'secondary works'" ("parerga") including such compositions as the Second Chamber Symphony (1939) and *Kol nidre* (1941).[53]

Adorno, Hanns Eisler, and others did not overlook that these works were more accessible and conciliatory toward audiences.[54] The rebellious Schoenberg student and temporary exile Eisler even declared after his immigration to East Germany in 1948 that Schoenberg "fell prey to the delusions that accompany capitalist culture."[55] And while in 1950 Schoenberg firmly maintained he had "made no concessions to the market," young composers in Darmstadt including Boulez followed Adorno's and Eisler's footsteps and accused Schoenberg of adapting to the new cultural situation with retrogressive and accessible compositions.[56] According to avant-garde-oriented or left-wing perspectives, Schoenberg's as well as Bartók's, Erich Korngold's and Kurt Weill's tonal or audience-friendly works appear as examples of "deradicalization" and thus of "slight importance."[57] This view can still be found in some Schoenberg monographs and exile narratives of the 1990s where authors attach more importance to the "adversarial energy of émigrés" and state that the "artistically significant works, which came forth . . . owe nothing to their adaptation to the new circumstances, but everything to their opposition."[58]

In recent years, however, some less negative interpretations have emerged. Schoenberg commentators now tend to interpret his increased number of tonal and other retrospectively marked works less as a compromise of the composer's integrity, but more positively as reflections of his émigré experience. Perhaps the historian Jarrell Jackman's observation that for exiles their "past is almost everything and the present is like a bottomless night" served them as an inspiration.[59] In this sense Schoenberg's tonal works can be viewed as "anchors to a more solid past to which he [Schoenberg] remained actively connected in a way that Webern and even Berg and succeeding generations did not."[60] Schoenberg's tonal music as well as his arrangements of his own and classical works of the past are also considered as sincere attempts to reach out to U.S. publishers, conductors, performers, and audiences from a desire or necessity to communicate with the new environment.[61] They are seen as "responses to the unfamiliar culture," as directed by outer circumstances such as commissions and encouragements from publishers or performers and as works "influenced by the pragmatic atmosphere of the United States."[62] The musicologist Alan Lessem interestingly viewed Schoenberg's tonal pieces as "public" and his dodecaphonic compositions as "private" works.[63] Others believe that the exile freed Schoenberg from the pressure to stay the modernist course and enabled him to handle compositional materials more flexibly, allowing an interaction between law and freedom.[64]

Yet in contrast to such views, some writers have kept stressing Schoenberg's resistance to adapt to U.S. culture. In support of an isolation theory, these commentators deny instances of acculturation and conformist tendencies in Schoenberg's artistic output after 1933. Schoenberg is either praised for challenging U.S. culture or criticized for exhibiting European cultural superiority.[65] Freitag stated that "in the USA Schoenberg remained non-conformist, an outsider, not least because he did not subordinate himself to the mechanisms of the market."[66] Similarly, music writer Dorothy Crawford asserted that the "American idea of market force—which necessarily lowers the aspirations of the individual in order to satisfy the greatest number of consumers—remained alien to him."[67] Hermand insisted that Schoenberg never changed his elitist attitude toward art as mass entertainment, that he composed German music, and that his late works, including his tonal works, remained complex and incomprehensible to a general audience.[68] Other authors elaborated on the new more sophisticated and freer kind of tonality used in Schoenberg's U.S. works and on the supposedly great contrast between his retrospective works such as the Suite in G and neoclassical compositions by Stravinsky.[69]

Engaged Music

Unlike most of Schoenberg's European works, his *Ode to Napoleon* and *A Survivor from Warsaw* document more evidently than his other tonally marked dodecaphonic and nondodecaphonic late works an unusual change in his artistic approach and acculturation and have caused controversies among Schoenberg commentators. Here Schoenberg not only used the English language, but also embraced the concept of engaged art, an idea that was very topical among his compatriots, U.S. composers Marc Blitzstein, Aaron Copland, Elie Siegmeister, and others in the 1940s. In his vivid musical indictments of Hitler, Nazism, and the Holocaust, Schoenberg—who once objected to Berg's *Wozzeck* of 1922 on the grounds that "music should rather deal with angels than with officer servants" and rejected Eisler's engaged music in the 1920s—seems to have contradicted his ideals of autonomous music.[70] Purists such as Adorno therefore questioned whether these works belonged to the aesthetic realm.[71] On the other hand, some scholars maintained that Schoenberg's engaged music did not sacrifice but rather enlarged the concept of autonomous art.[72] Although most Schoenberg biographers described his politically inspired works in positive terms and compared them to masterpieces of the past, including Beethoven's opera *Fidelio,* other commentators took exception to the Napoleon-Hitler parallel invoked by Schoenberg's setting of Lord Byron's *Ode to Napoleon* and the "super-topicality" of *A Survivor from Warsaw.*[73] The latter work in particular has received a wide variety of interpretations. It has been considered as a "testament to Schoenberg's own spiritual struggle," a "personal parable of his experiences as a Jew," a manifestation of "political eschatology" and a modern "Ode to Joy."[74] It has also been viewed as a reflection of Schoenberg's alienation, anger, and withdrawal from German music as well as a work whose "impetus came more from immediate external circumstances than from an intrinsic imperative to create such a piece."[75] The work was inspired by the dancer Corinne Chochem and commissioned by the Koussevitzky Music Foundation. Further *A Survivor from Warsaw* has been rejected as an "abominable banality" and Hollywood kitsch.[76]

Number of Completed Works

A further misconception and cliché pertaining to Schoenberg's U.S. works arises from speculations about the reason for their limited number. During his seventeen-year sojourn in the United States, he completed fifteen original compositions, several canons (some based on existing melodies), and six arrangements of his own and other composers' works. Numerous pieces including music for piano, organ, string quartet, a large-scale programmatic symphony based on Jewish themes, and last but not least his oratorio *Jacob's Ladder* (begun in 1917) and opera *Moses and Aron* (begun in 1930) were left unfinished. Many commentators therefore suggest that Schoenberg's mental state, heavy teaching load, and financial struggle in the United States prevented him from composing more works and from finishing others. Biographers, for instance, see the Guggenheim Foundation, which denied Schoenberg a grant in 1945, as being more or less responsible for foiling the completion of *Jacob's Ladder* and *Moses and Aron*.[77] Often the United States per se is blamed for his meager creative output:[78] "The United States was not the place where Schoenberg's ideas could fall on fertile ground," stated Sinkovicz.[79] And Lessem viewed the supposed "unresponsiveness of publishers, performers, and audiences" in the United States as an inhibiting factor for his artistic productivity.[80]

In this respect most Schoenberg commentators fail to consider his many non-musical interests and activities—political, religious, and social engagements, extensive writing (theory books, poems, essays, correspondence), painting, handcraft, sports, card and chess playing, dedication to his young family, relatives, and countless friends—which at times became his priority and undoubtedly took away time from composing.[81] These activities could explain at least in part why Schoenberg was not a generally prolific composer. And although Schoenberg's biographers tend to take his own words at face value, to the detriment of a more balanced portrait, they seem to have overlooked his comment on this issue: "Maybe I would have written more when remaining in Europe, but I think: nothing comes out, what was not in. And two times two equals four in every climate."[82]

Schoenberg: The Teacher and His Students

Another negative and in part misleading impression, emerging from most accounts of Schoenberg's U.S. teaching career, is that Schoenberg was dissatisfied with the teaching conditions—teaching load, educational system, and students. In most biographies this impression is created by quoting some critical remarks Schoenberg made about teaching in the United States, by a primary focus on his first and stressful teaching job at the Malkin Conservatory in Boston and New York, and by a sparse coverage of his eight-year tenure at USC and UCLA, where the teaching conditions were more favorable.[83] Detailed information on his private composition lessons and seminars and elaborate discussions on the nature of his teaching activities are generally omitted.[84] Such a perspective certainly underscores the image of Schoenberg as a European elitist and undermines his unwavering pragmatism, idealism, and adaptability. Yet it is indisputable that Schoenberg, a passionate and devoted teacher throughout his life, quickly adjusted to the needs and expectations of the U.S. educational system by providing a high-minded and conservative teaching approach, preferred in academia.[85] Further it should be assumed that

Schoenberg—while less happy about teaching music minors—would have enjoyed working with such gifted and prepared students as Wayne Barlow, John Cage, Patricia Carpenter, Lou Harrison, Richard Hoffmann, Earl Kim, Leon Kirchner, Oscar Levant, Alfred Newman, Dika Newlin, David Raksin, Leroy Robertson, Leonard Rosenman, William Russell, Leonard Stein, and Gerald Strang. All of these students went on to make distinguished careers as composers, performers, scholars, and teachers.

While much has been made of his European students in Schoenberg monographs, little has been said about his U.S. pupils.[86] In fact the majority of biographies generally accuse his U.S. students of lacking qualification, perseverance, and a thorough knowledge of the musical canon.[87] Composers from the Hollywood film industry, who studied with Schoenberg, come off even worse as they are charged with superficial curiosity and with only wanting to learn a few tricks in little time.[88] This distorted view was furthered by Oscar Levant's more entertaining than accurate satirical memoir, *A Smattering of Ignorance* (1940).[89] Most of the above mentioned student names are absent from the majority of biographical accounts. Cage and Levant and Schoenberg's teaching assistants, Newlin, Stein, Strang, and Hoffmann, are generally mentioned only in passing.[90] Their voices have been neglected too, although much could be learned from an in-depth study of their accounts and notes. Thus the impression arises that Schoenberg's U.S. students could not withstand comparison to his European disciples—a view underpinned by the following statement of 1951: "Strangely enough, only a very few out of the hundreds of musicians who studied with Schoenberg at UCLA have become composers of some reputation: Gerald Strang, Leon Kirchner, Simon Carfagno, Earl Kim, Dika Newlin, and Don Estep."[91] In 1967 Meyerowitz bluntly concluded that "among the hundreds of U.S. students Schoenberg taught there is not one composer worth mentioning."[92]

In the past few years some Schoenberg commentators have begun to cast a different, more positive light on Schoenberg's teaching activities in the United States.[93] Others embarked on more detailed studies of Schoenberg's late teaching methods and his development of textbooks tailored to the need of U.S. students.[94] Yet studies focusing on Schoenberg's interactions with his students are still rare.[95] Such studies could in part illuminate reasons for his immense popularity with younger generations of musicians and the great influence Schoenberg had on U.S. academia after his death.

Influence and Reception in the United States

The common perception that "Schoenberg's ideas could not fall on fertile ground," that there was no "productive preoccupation" with his work, and that his music was "practically not performed" in the United States is a myth that invites scrutiny.[96] Undoubtedly this misconception grew out of Schoenberg's own worries about his legacy and the dissemination of his music, which contradict the assumption that he was not interested in the music market. Schoenberg's concern about being neglected was prompted in part by the feeling of what his fellow émigré Ernst Krenek called the "echolessness of the vast American expanses"—a notion implying that artists for lack of feedback were often unaware of the full scope of the reception of their work in this large country.[97]

While Schoenberg commentators stress that he was first of all and undeniably a highly popular and influential teacher and elevated academic standards, they do not mention that his innumerable students spread his gospel and perpetuated his legacy in manifold ways. European biographers report about Schoenberg's revival in Europe after World War II, yet they tend to overlook that his presence in the United States also nurtured interest in modernism among the young composers and performers who did not study with him, including Milton Babbitt, Elliott Carter, Robert Craft, George Perle, and George Rochberg.[98] In the 1950s and 1960s Schoenberg's compositional ideas not only became important and much respected subjects of study in academia, but atonality and dodecaphony also came to be the preferred compositional techniques for many U.S. composers. Schoenberg gained visibility in the U.S. press through his own contributions, articles, and letters to the editors, and he regularly provoked invigorating debates about modernism by others. After his death discussions of his music and ideas have continued to appear profusely in journalistic and scholarly venues.

Furthermore the much-deplored small number of performances, amounting to hundreds of events, that Schoenberg received between 1933 and 1951 in the United States has to be considered in relative terms and must be seen against the background of a country coping with the Great Depression, countless other struggling indigenous and exile-seeking composers in the 1930s, and the economic burden caused by World War II in the 1940s. Thus it is not surprising that during these years populist leanings dominated concert programming and that, if Schoenberg's music was performed, his most accessible works were given preference. The number of Schoenberg performances also needs to be compared with the much smaller number of performances of modernist works by such fellow émigrés as Bartók, Krenek, and Edgard Varèse or indigenous composers including John Becker, Ruth Crawford, Charles Ives, Wallingford Riegger, Carl Ruggles, and Roger Sessions.

Conclusion

In surveying most literature on Schoenberg in the United States, three pejorative perspectives seem to prevail. In one view the emphasis is on Schoenberg the elitist, lone genius, and composer of complex music who stubbornly refused to adapt to his chosen new environment of Southern California. In another view Schoenberg's manifold attempts to acclimate to life in the United States and to its music scene by compromising his progressive European compositional approach is severely criticized and even derided (two Schoenbergs?).[99] In a further perspective certain problems, including financial issues that were aggravated by increased health problems, the type of teaching activity Schoenberg had "to put up with," and a reluctant reception of his music, are indirectly blamed on the United States and its underdeveloped or commercially oriented culture (see Gillies on "American guilt theory").[100]

Reasons for such one-sided viewpoints lie in the fact that Schoenberg's personality and work reveal conflicting tendencies, that his music and aesthetics are still controversial and polarizing, and that Schoenberg commentators approach their subject with widely differing agendas. Biographers are often heavily influenced, if not blinded, by his sometimes pessimistic perspectives. Schoenberg's own preference of biographies stressing discussions of his works, his strong opinions, and his European students' worshipful attitude toward him led to hagiography-like portraits suggesting the image of Schoenberg as a strong and incorruptible musical prophet.[101] Thus most Schoenberg biographies, especially in their treatment of his U.S. period, distinguish themselves by a strong focus on his works to the detriment of a comprehensive biographical contextualization. As these texts are primarily written by Europeans, principally German and Austrian Schoenberg adherents, and are still widely used, a Eurocentric outlook tends to mark the U.S. view of Schoenberg.[102] As a result concerns with Schoenberg's threatened yet unshakeable artistic identity and curtailed conditions of his life are prominent, and a successful European career is thereby pitched against a disappointing U.S. period. Other predominantly European left-wing Schoenberg commentators observed and criticized instances of acculturation and reproved Schoenberg's changes in artistic attitude and direction in the United States, which they interpreted as character weakness. New and more holistic perspectives have been explored occasionally and with increased frequency in recent years by a younger generation of biographers that includes Henke and Shawn. Yet balanced and elaborate discussions of Schoenberg's U.S. years are still rare. More broadly based biographical approaches informed by ideas of cultural theory, by new exile studies, and by more research on Schoenberg's manifold interactions with Americans have yet to be applied to Schoenberg's life and work in the United States. Such research is urgently needed to overcome the still widespread view of his later years as "la douloureuse période américaine."[103]

Notes

1. Among the most informative, though sometimes inaccurate, articles are Walter Rubsamen, "Schoenberg in America," *Musical Quarterly* 37, no. 4 (1951): 469–89; Alan Philip Lessem, "The Émigré Experience: Schoenberg in America," in *Constructive Dissonance: Arnold Schoenberg and the Transformations of Twentieth-Century Culture*, ed. Juliane Brand and Christopher Hailey, 58–68 (Berkley: University of California Press, 1997); and Dorothy Lamb Crawford, "Arnold Schoenberg in Los Angeles," *Musical Quarterly*, 86 (Spring 2002): 6–48.

2. Elizabeth Keathley and Richard Taruskin have lately criticized this one-sided view, which has been furthered by innumerable positivistically oriented studies of Schoenberg's music. See Elizabeth L. Keathley "Dick, Dika, Dickest: Dika Newlin's 'Thick Description' of Schönberg in America," Arnold Schoenberg in America. Bericht zum Symposium—Report of the Symposium, 2–4 May 2001. Herausgegeben von Christian Meyer. Arnold Schönberg Center 2002, *Journal of the Arnold Schönberg Center* (April 2002); and Richard Taruskin, "The Poietic Fallacy: Review of *Arnold Schoenberg's Journey*, by Allen Shawn," *Musical Times* (Spring 2004): 13.

3. "Er hat sich aber, wie es bei einer so großartigen Persönlichkeit gar nicht anders möglich war, nicht im geringsten amerikanisiert" (He had not, as was obviously impossible for such a tremendous personality, americanized himself in the least). Jan Meyerowitz, *Arnold Schönberg* (Berlin: Colloquium Verlag, 1967), 30. See also Michael Mäckelmann, *Arnold Schönberg und das Judentum. Der Komponist und sein religiöses, nationales und politisches Selbstverständnis nach 1921*(Hamburg: Verlag der Musikalienhandlung K. D. Wagner, 1984), 257.

4. See Jost Hermand, "A Survivor from Germany: Schönberg im Exil," in *Exil. Literatur und Künste nach 1933*, ed. Alexander Stephan (Bonn: Bouvier Verlag, 1990), 108; and "Ein Überlebender aus Deutschland. Zur Radikalität von Arnold Schönbergs zionistischer Wende," in *Judentum und deutsche Kultur. Beispiele einer schmerzhaften Symbiose* (Cologne: Böhlau, 1996), 177. Hermand also claimed that Schoenberg "sprach, empfand und dachte weiterhin 'deutsch,' ja komponierte sogar 'deutsch'" (spoke, felt, and furthermore thought "German," even composed "German"). Hermand, "A Survivor," 108.

5. See David Schiff, "Schoenberg's Cool Eye for the Erotic," *New York Times*, August 8, 1999, 30; and Anthony Heilbut, *Exiled in Paradise: German Refugee Artists and Intellectuals in America, from the 1930s to the Present* (New York: Viking Press, 1983), 135–36.

6. Kevin Starr, *The Dream Endures: California Enters the 1940s* (New York: Oxford University Press, 1997), 382–83 and 363.

7. Malcolm MacDonald, *Schoenberg* (London: J. M. Dent, 1976), 49–50. All in all MacDonald, however, strives more than other authors for a balanced Schoenberg portrait. See also Eberhard Freitag, *Schönberg* (Reinbek bei Hamburg: Rowohlt, 1973), 136–37.

8. German-speaking exiles who exclusively moved in émigré circles in Los Angeles and used to say complainingly "bei uns daheim war alles besser" (Back home [in Europe] everything was better) were dubbed "bei-uns-kis."

9. See Hans Heinz Stuckenschmidt, *Arnold Schoenberg: His Life, World and Work* (New York: Schirmer, 1977), 476–78 and 483, originally published as *Schönberg. Leben, Umwelt, Werk* (Zurich: Atlantis Verlag, 1974). Reich's two short chapters dedicated to Schoenberg's American years consist for the most part of quotations. Willi Reich, *Schoenberg: A Critical Biography*, trans. Leo Black (Edinburgh: Longman, 1971), 189–235, originally published as *Arnold Schönberg oder Der konservative Revolutionär* (Vienna: Fritz Molden, 1968).

10. See *Arnold Schoenberg Letters*, ed. Erwin Stein and trans. Eithne Wilkins and Ernst Kaiser (London: Faber, 1964), 197–301, originally published as *Arnold Schönberg Briefe* (Mainz: B. Schott's Söhne, 1958). Thousands of letters Schoenberg wrote during his U.S. years have remained unpublished and have not been taken into consideration by recent Schoenberg biographers.

11. See for instance Wilhelm Sinkovicz, *Mehr als zwölf Töne: Arnold Schönberg* (Vienna: Paul Zsolnay Verlag, 1998); and Manuel Gervink, *Arnold Schönberg und seine Zeit* (Laaber: Laaber Verlag, 2000). Sinkovicz titled the chapter on Schoenberg's U.S. years "Isolation—der Komponist im amerikanischen Exil," and he preferred to call the United States Schoenberg's "Gastland" (host land), Sinkovicz, *Mehr als zwölf Töne*, 249–313.

12. Rubsamen, "Schoenberg in America," 469–89. Besides Gershwin, Schoenberg's musician friends included Richard Buhlig, Henry Cowell, Oscar Levant, Alfred Newman, Roger Sessions, and Adolph Weiss and émigré musicians such as Joseph Achron, Hanns Eisler, Rudolf Kolisch, Darius Milhaud, Nicolas Slonimsky and Edgard Varèse. Schoenberg also socialized with figures from other fields, writers, critics, architects, filmmakers, actors, psychologists, and physicists. Many of them were regular guests at his home and some became his regular tennis or Ping-Pong partners. For a discussion of Schoenberg's friendship with Henry Cowell and artists from Hollywood, see Sabine Feisst, "Henry Cowell und Arnold Schönberg: Eine unbekannte Freundschaft," *Archiv für Musikwissenschaft* 55, no. 1 (1998): 57–71; and "Schoenberg and the Cinematic Art," *Musical Quarterly* 38, no. 1 (1999): 93–113.

13. See, for instance, Dika Newlin, "Schönberg in America, 1933–1948: Retrospect and Prospect I," *Music Survey* 1, no. 5 (1949): 128–31; and "Schönberg in America, 1933–1948. Retrospect and Prospect II," *Music Survey* 1, no. 6 (1949): 185–89, and *Schoenberg Remembered. Diaries and Recollections, 1938–1976* (New York: Pendragon, 1980). Newlin (1923–2006) was a musicologist, composer, pianist, and teacher who turned to punk rock performances and acting in the last two decades of her life.

Newlin recounts that Schoenberg toward the end of his life discovered television and like many other Americans watched with a TV tray in his lap, enjoying shows such as *Hopalong Cassidy*. Newlin, *Schoenberg Remembered*, 337–38. Pauline Alderman also reports about Schoenberg's thorough enjoyment of spy and Western films in the 1930s in her article "I Remember Arnold Schoenberg," *Facets—University of Southern California* (1976): 49–58. See also Feisst, "Schoenberg and the Cinematic Art."

15. Newlin conveyed that Rubsamen's essay "drew the wrath of some Schoenberg friends for its stress on the composer's superstition." See *Schoenberg Remembered*, 90. German musicologist Michael Mäckelmann criticized Newlin's "Schoenberg in America" articles as follows: "Verklärte Schilderungen seiner amerikanischen 'Laufbahn,' zumal wenn sie diese als 'erfolgreich' bezeichnen, verfehlen mit Sicherheit die Realität der künstlerischen wie auch der persönlichen und materiellen Nöte, denen Schönberg bis zum Lebensende in Amerika ausgesetzt war"(Transfigured descriptions of his American "career," particularly as they present it as "successful," definitely miss the reality of his artistic, personal, and material troubles, to which Schoenberg was

exposed until the end of his life). See Mäckelmann, *Arnold Schönberg und das Judentum*, 256.

16. Matthias Henke, *Arnold Schönberg* (Hamburg: Deutscher Taschenbuch Verlag, 2001), and Allen Shawn, *Arnold Schoenberg's Journey* (New York: Farrar, Straus and Giroux, 2002), 248–49 and 264.

17. Richard Taruskin, "The Poietic Fallacy," 7–34.

18. Laura Fermi, *Illustrious Immigrants: The Intellectual Migration from Europe, 1930–41* (Chicago: University of Chicago Press, 1968), 223.

19. MacDonald, *Schoenberg*, 44. This can be seen in Schoenberg's innumerable English letters and other writings and recordings of speeches. A negative take on Schoenberg's linguistic efforts is, not surprisingly, offered by Starr: "While Schoenberg was willing to surrender his German cursive handwriting in favor of standard Latin script and even to make a headlong assault on the English language, which he blended with German to achieve a new tongue, he refused to accommodate either himself or his music to émigré, much less to American tastes," 282.

20. Alexander Ringer, *Arnold Schönberg. Das Leben im Werk* (Stuttgart: Verlag J. B. Metzler, 2002), 287.

21. Malcolm Gillies, "Bartók in America," *The Cambridge Companion to Bartók*, ed. Amanda Bayley (Cambridge: Cambridge University Press, 2001), 194.

22. Schoenberg already suffered from asthma and other health problems in Europe.

23. See Reich, *Schoenberg*, 227; Sinkovicz, *Mehr als zwölf Töne*, 304; and Oliver Neighbour and H. Wiley Hitchcock, "Arnold Schoenberg," *The New Grove Dictionary of American Music*, ed. H. Wiley Hitchcock and Stanley Sadie (London: MacMillan Press Limited, 1986), 158–59.

24. "Die finanzielle Not hat seiner schöpferischen Arbeit viel Schaden zugefügt" (The financial crisis did much damage to his creative work), Meyerowitz, *Arnold Schönberg*, 5.

25. "Schönberg war während seiner Emigrationsjahre nie imstande, sich in Ruhe jenen Aufgaben zuzuwenden, die er gern gelöst hätte." Sinkovicz, *Mehr als zwölf Töne*, 286.

26. Ibid., 285. The pension was initially $28.50 and rose to $40.38 per month by 1945.

27. Stuckenschmidt, *Arnold Schoenberg*, 469. Edgard Varèse's several applications for a Guggenheim were also rejected.

28. "Arnold Schönberg ist am Verhungern" in Alma Mahler-Werfel, *Mein Leben* (Frankfurt am Main: Fischer, 1960), 278; see Alma Mahler quoted in Freitag, *Schönberg*, 151, and Hermand, "A Survivor,"112.

29. Michael Kater believes that with an annual salary between $4,800 and $5,400, Schoenberg was exploited by UCLA authorities. See Michael Kater, *Composers of the Nazi Era. Eight Portraits* (New York: Oxford University Press, 2000), 187. Kater, however, fails to mention that Schoenberg's salary was well above the average full-time American wage of $1,146 (1936) and $2,292 (1944) equaling $14,691 and 23,307 today. See *The Value of a Dollar, 1860–1999*, ed. Scott Derks (Lakeville, Conn.: Grey

House Publishing 1999), 207–30, and *National Income and Product Accounts of the United States, 1929–2000*, electronic resource (Washington, D.C.: U.S. Department of Commerce, Economics and Statistics Administration Bureau of Economic Analysis, 2001).

30. This success is mentioned by Rubsamen, Reich, and Ringer. See Rubsamen, *Schoenberg Remembered*, 480; Reich, *Schoenberg*, 214; and Ringer, *Arnold Schönberg*, 59. Yet Stuckenschmidt touches only briefly on two performances of *Pillar of Fire*, one of which was conducted by Schoenberg himself on February 8, 1945. Stuckenschmidt, *Arnold Schoenberg*, 453 and 470.

31. Schoenberg had been a member of ASCAP (American Society of Composers, Authors, and Publishers) since 1939. Rubsamen stated in 1951, "As it turned out, the royalties from ASCAP, subsequently increased in most generous fashion, were a boon to the composer during the last years of his life." Rubsamen, *Schoenberg Remembered*, 471.

32. Sinkovicz, who completely omitted discussions of Schoenberg's occupation with Judaism in his monograph, also belongs in this list of names.

33. Stuckenschmidt, *Arnold Schoenberg*, 368–67.

34. MacDonald, *Schoenberg*, 56.

35. See Mäckelmann's monograph, quoted above, and Alexander Ringer, *Arnold Schönberg: The Composer as Jew* (New York: Oxford University Press, 1990). See also Hermand's two essays, quoted above, and Charlotte Cross and Russell Berman, eds., *Political and Religious Ideas in the Works of Arnold Schoenberg* (New York: Garland Publishing, 2000). Steven J. Cahn, *Dépasser L'universalisme: une écoute particulariste d'Un Survivant de Varsovie, op. 46 et du Kol Nidre, op. 39 de Schoenberg (traduit de l'anglais par Jean-Claude Teboul)*, in *Arnold Schoenberg. Ostinato rigore. Revue internationale d'études musicales* (Paris: Éditions Jean-Michel Place, 2001), 221–34; and David M. Schiller, *Bloch, Schoenberg, Bernstein: Assimilating Jewish Music* (New York: Oxford University Press, 2003)

36. Gervink, *Arnold Schönberg und seine Zeit*, 290–91 and 302–6; Ringer, *Arnold Schönberg*, 252ff., 271–73 and 288. Ringer provides political contextualization throughout his very personally written Schoenberg biography. The importance of Schoenberg's engagement with Judaism was recently questioned because he neither practiced his Jewish faith at home nor at the temple. Camille Crittenden, "Texts and Contexts of *A Survivor from Warsaw*, op. 46," in Cross and Berman, eds., *Political and Religious Ideas*, 246.

37. See for instance Bluma Goldstein, "Schoenberg's *Moses and Aron*: A Vanishing Biblical Nation," *Cross and Berman, eds., Political and Religious Ideas*, 187–89.

38. See, for instance, Stuckenschmidt's, Reich's, and Freitag's monographs. Schoenberg's political views, his residency in the United States and not least his musical individualism hindered his reception in the former D.D.R. for many years. Yet, from the mid-1970s on, musicologists such as Mathias Hansen and Frank Schneider approached the topic of Schoenberg in America by focusing on his antifascist engagement. Frank Schneider, "Versuch einer musikgeschichtlichen Positionsbestimmung," *Beiträge zur Musikwissenschaft* 16 (1974): 75–95 and 277–96; Frank Schneider, "Schönberg und die 'politische Musik,'" *Beiträge der Musikwissenschaft* 20 (1978): 23–27; Mathias Hansen,

"*Ode to Napoleon*—Zum antifaschistischen Engagement Arnold Schönbergs," *Arbeitsheft 24. Forum: Musik in der DDR. Arnold Schönberg 1874–1951. Zum 25. Todestag des Komponisten,* ed. Mathias Hansen and Christa Müller (Berlin, 1976), 79–88. See also Hanns-Werner Heister, "Zum politischen Engagement des Unpolitischen," *Herausforderung Schönberg. Was die Musik des Jahrhunderts veränderte,* ed. Ulrich Dibelius (Munich: Hanser Verlag, 1974), 27–46, and Hanns-Werner Heister, "Musikalische Reaktion und politisches Engagement. Über drei Werke Arnold Schönbergs," *Beiträge zur Musikwissenschaft* 16 (1974): 261–76. Wes Blomster, "The Reception of Arnold Schoenberg in the German Democratic Republic," *Perspectives of New Music,* 21, nos. 1/2 (1982): 114–32.

39. Albrecht Dümling, "Zwischen Außenseiterstatus und Integration. Musiker-Exil an der amerikanischen Westküste," *Musik im Exil. Folgen des Nazismus für die internationale Musikkultur,* ed. Hanns-Werner Heister, Claudia Maurer-Zenck, and Peter Petersen (Frankfurt: Fischer Verlag, 1993), 315; Gervink, *Arnold Schönberg und seine Zeit,* 309, Ringer, *Arnold Schönberg,* 286–93.

40. See Gervink, *Arnold Schönberg und seine Zeit,* 309–10, and Ringer, *Arnold Schönberg,* 286.

41. Theodor W. Adorno, "Einführung in die Zweite Kammersymphonie von Schönberg (1954)," *Theodor W. Adorno: Gesammelte Schriften,* vol. 18, ed. Rolf Tiedemann (Darmstadt: Wissenschaftliche Buchgesellschaft, 1998), 629.

42. Heilbut, *Exiled in Paradise,* 74.

43. Albert Goldberg, "The Sounding Board: The Transplanted Composer," *Los Angeles Times,* May 14, 1950.

44. Theodor W. Adorno, "Arnold Schoenberg, 1874–1951," *Prisms,* trans. Samuel and Shierry Weber (London: Neville Spearman, 1967), 171, originally published as *Prismen. Kulturkritik und Gesellschaft* (Frankfurt: Suhrkamp, 1955); and Adorno, *Philosophy of Modern Music,* trans. Anne. G. Mitchel and Wesley V. Bloomster (New York: Seabury Press, 1973), 119–20, originally published in German as *Philosophie der neuen Musik* (Tübingen: Mohr, 1949).

45. Adorno, "Arnold Schoenberg, 1874–1951," 168. Boulez also wrote in 1961: "Son activité américaine est bizarrement partagée entre certaines oeuvres purement sérielles et des úuvres de 'conciliation,' où il s'efforça d'opérer une synthèse entre des données tonales et des exigences de la série . . . c'est pourquoi les dernières úuvres de Schoenberg apparaissent entachées d'une certaine vanité: les composantes n'en sont guère homogènes" (His activity in America is strangely divided between certain works which are purely serial and conciliatory works, in which he strove for a synthesis between tonal elements and the requirements of the row . . . for that reason Schoenberg's late works seem to be stained with a certain vanity: the components are hardly homogeneous). Pierre Boulez, "Arnold Schoenberg," *Encyclopédie de la Musique,* ed. François Michel (Paris: Fasquelle, 1961).

47. Pierre Boulez, "Schoenberg Is Dead," *Notes of an Apprenticeship,* trans. Herbert Weinstock (New York: Alfred Knopf, 1968), 268–76, originally published in French as *Pierre Boulez. Relevés d'apprenti,* ed. Jean-Jacques Nattiez (Paris: Editions du Seuil, 1966) and in a short version in English in *Score* 6 (1952): 18–22.

48. Arnold Whittall, "Schoenberg since 1951: Overlapping Opposites," *Musical Times*, (Autumn 2001): 18, and David Isadore Lieberman, "Schoenberg Rewrites His Will: *A Survivor from Warsaw*, op. 46," Cross and Berman, eds., *Political and Religious Ideas*, 212

49. Joseph Auner, "Schoenberg's Handel Concerto and the Ruins of Tradition," *Journal of the American Musicological Society* 49, no. 2 (1996): 312.

50. Many works from his dodecaphonic Suite, op. 25 (1921) through his String Trio (1946) combine twelve-tone ideas and elements and techniques of the past. Dahlhaus already wrote in 1983 that "all the impulses that emerged in the last decade were already present (albeit under different historical conditions) in Schoenberg's late works." Carl Dahlhaus, "Schoenberg's Late Works," *Schoenberg and the New Music*, trans. Derrick Puffet and Alfred Clayton (Cambridge: Cambridge University Press, 1987), 168; see also Auner, "Schoenberg's Handel Concerto," 312, and Whittall, "Schoenberg since 1951," 12–14.

51. Olin Downes, "New Suite by Arnold Schoenberg," *New York Times*, October 13, 1935. See also Lawrence Gilman, "New Music by Schoenberg," *New York Herald Tribune*, October 19, 1935.

52. Leonard Stein, ed., *Style and Idea: Selected Writings of Arnold Schoenberg*, trans. Leo Black (Berkeley: University of California Press, 1984), 109.

53. Adorno, *Philosophy*, 120. This led other authors to conclude that tonally marked works such as the Second Chamber Symphony, the *Variations on a Recitative* for organ, and the *Ode to Napoleon* are inferior within Schoenberg's U.S. compositions: "Au cours des années 1939, 1940 et 1941, Schoenberg n'écrit pas d'úuvre importante" (In the course of the years of 1939, 1940, and 1941, Schoenberg did not write any important works). Pierre Barbaud, *Schoenberg* (Paris: Editions Main D'Œuvre, 1997), 151.

54. "It is hardly a matter of coincidence that all of these secondary works of his later years have one thing in common: a more conciliatory attitude towards the public. There is a deep relationship between Schoenberg's inexorability and his particular manner of conciliation." Adorno, *Philosophy*, 121; Adorno also tried to explain Schoenberg's desire to compose tonally again: "It is common knowledge that Schoenberg in his earlier years was forced to earn his living through the orchestration of operettas. The investigation of these forgotten scores might well be worth the effort, not only because it can safely be assumed that therein he was not able completely to suppress himself as a composer but, above all, because they might possibly give evidence of that counter-tendency which emerges more and more clearly in the 'secondary works' of his later years, precisely at that point in his career when he gained total command over his material." Adorno, *Philosophy*, 121; In a further step, Adorno claims that Schoenberg's conciliatory music was written for a false society and acknowledges thus its right to consume such music: "His inexorable music represents social truth against society. His conciliatory music recognizes the right to music which, in spite of everything, is still valid even in a false society—in the very same way that a false society reproduces itself and thus by virtue of its very survival objectively establishes elements of its own truth." Adorno, *Philosophy*, 121.

55. Eisler, quoted in Heilbut, *Exiled in Paradise*, 157. Unlike Schoenberg, Eisler successfully made concessions to the American market as a film composer in Hollywood from 1942 to 1948. Soon thereafter, back in the D.D.R., Eisler unsuccessfully attempted to rehabilitate Schoenberg's music, which had been branded as "decadent formalism."

56. See Goldberg, "The Sounding Board"; see also Ernst Krenek, "America's Influence on its Émigré Composers," *Perspectives of New Music* 8, no. 2 (1970): 757–61, originally published as "Amerikas Einfluss auf eingewanderte Komponisten," *Musica* 13 (1959); and see Boulez, "Schoenberg Is Dead," 273.

57. Martin Jay, "The German Migration: Is There a Figure in the Carpet?" *Exiles and Emigrés: The Flight of European Artists from Hitler*, ed. Stephanie Barron, Sabine Eckmann, and Matthew Affron (Los Angeles: Harry Abrams, 1997), 328, 326–37. See also "The Suite with its Unexpected Return to the Principle of Tonality Is a Work of Slight Importance." Gerald Abraham, "Arnold Schoenberg," *Groves Dictionary of Music and Musicians*, ed. Henry C. Colles, 4th edition, supplementary vol. (London: MacMillan, 1940).

58. "Die künstlerisch bedeutensten Werke, die aus ihr [der viel beklagten kulturellen Isolation der Emigranten] hervorgingen, verdanken sich nicht der Anpassung an die neuen Verhältnisse, sondern der Opposition" (The artistically most important works, which came out of the much lamented cultural isolation of the emigres, owe nothing to their adaptation to the new circumstance, but everything to their opposition). Albrecht Dümling, "Zwischen Außenseiterstatus und Integration. Musiker-Exil an der US-amerikanischen Westküste," *Musik im Exil. Folgen des Nazimus für die internationale Musikkultur* (Frankfurt: Fischer Taschenbuch Verlag, 1993), 331; see also Martin Jay, "The German Migration," 332.

59. Jarrell Jackman, "Exiles in Paradise: German Emigrés in Southern California, 1933–1950," *Southern California Quarterly* 61, no. 2 (1979): 183.

60. Shawn, *Arnold Schoenberg's Journey*, 255. Crawford, on the other hand, considers Schoenberg's extensive teaching of the music of the past as a possible incentive for a stylistic change. Crawford, "Arnold Schoenberg in Los Angeles," 33.

61. Ernst Krenek, "America's Influence on Its Émigré Composers," 113.

62. Claudia Maurer Zenck, for instance, declares Schoenberg's two serial solo concertos as instances of acculturation in that they are opportunities through which Schoenberg could "present himself in a more popular way." Claudia Maurer Zenck, "Challenges and Opportunities of Acculturation. Schoenberg, Krenek, and Stravinsky in Exile," *Driven into Paradise: The Musical Migration from Nazi Germany to the United States*, ed. Reinhold Brinkmann and Christoph Wolff (Berkeley: University of California Press, 1999), 182; and see Krenek, "America's Influence," 112. Sinkovicz explained Schoenberg's motivation to complete his tonal Second Chamber Symphony (1906–39) as follows: "Jedenfalls war Schönberg bald klar, daß nur mit solchen 'Rückfällen' in die Tonalität in Amerika Fuß zu fassen war" (In any case Schoenberg was soon aware of the fact that one could gain a foothold in America only with such relapses into tonality). Sinkovicz, *Mehr als zwölf Töne*, 263.

63. Lessem, "The Émigré Experience, 59.

64. Christian Martin Schmidt, "Arnold Schönberg—Doyen der Wiener Schule in Amerika?" *Innenleben. Ansichten aus dem Exil. Ein Berliner Symposium,* ed. Hermann Haarmann (Berlin, 1995), 126; and see Marc Kerling, "Kontinuität und Bruch. Leitlinien im Spätwerk—Verarbeitungsstrategien der Exilsituation," *Journal of the Arnold Schoenberg Center,* 4 (2002): 42–43.

65. Crawford, "Arnold Schoenberg in Los Angeles," 34, and Hermand, "A Survivor," 108–10 and "Ein Überlebender," 177; see also the general discussion on opposing views of the émigrés' "deradicalization" and accommodation to U.S. culture in Jay, "The German Migration," 332–33.

66. Freitag, *Schönberg,* 136.

67. Crawford, "Arnold Schoenberg in Los Angeles," 34.

68. Schoenberg "sprach, empfand, und dachte weiterhin 'deutsch,' ja komponierte sogar 'deutsch.'" Hermand, "A Survivor," 108. "Denn auch seine nichtdodekaphonischen Werke der dreißiger und vierziger Jahre . . . sind alles andere als leicht verständlich, das heißt ebenso wenig 'eingängig' wie seine zwölftönigen Kompositionen" (Even his nondodecaphonic works of the 1930s and 1940s . . . are anything but easily understood. In other words they are as difficult to approach as his twelve-tone works). Ibid., 110.

69. See René Leibowitz, *Schoenberg and His School,* trans. Dika Newlin (New York: Philosophical Library, 1949), 389–90, originally published as *Schoenberg et son école* (Paris: Editions Janin, 1947), 118 and 126; and Stuckenschmidt, *Arnold Schoenberg.*

70. "Musik solle sich lieber mit Engeln als mit Offiziersdienern beschäftigen." Hanns-Werner Heister, "Zum politischen Engagement des Unpolitischen," *Herausforderung Schönberg—Was die Musik des Jahrhunderts veränderte,* ed. Ulrich Dibelius (Munich: Carl Hanser Verlag, 1974), 37.

71. "In this piece [*A Survivor from Warsaw*], Schoenberg, acting on his own, suspends the aesthetic sphere through the recollection of experiences which are inaccessable to art." Adorno, "Arnold Schönberg," *Prisms,* 171–72.

72. See Hermann Danuser, "Composers in Exile: The Question of Musical Identity," in Brinkman and Wolf, eds., *Driven into Paradise,* 162, and Friedrich Zehentreiter, "'Guilty Glory.' Zum Verhältnis von ästhetischer Autonomie und biographischer Krise am Beispiel der *Ode to Napoleon Buonaparte* op. 41 (1942) von Arnold Schönberg," *Exilmusik. Komponisten während der NS-Zeit,* ed. Friedrich Geiger und Thomas Schäfer (Hamburg: von Bockel Verlag, 1999), 141–62.

73. See Stuckenschmidt, *Arnold Schoenberg,* 486; see also Heister, "Zum politischen Engagement des Unpolitischen," 37, and Dirk Buhrmann, "Arnold Schönbergs *Ode to Napoleon Buonaparte* op. 41," *Journal of the Arnold Schönberg Center* 4 (2002): 68. See Meyerowitz, *Arnold Schönberg,* 82.

74. Michael Strasser, "*A Survivor from Warsaw* as Personal Parable," *Music and Letters* 76, no. 1 (1995): 52; Reinhold Brinkmann, *Arnold Schönberg und der Engel der Geschichte* (Vienna: Picus Verlag, 2001), 53–54 and 60; see also Christian Martin

Schmidt, "Schönbergs Kantate *Ein Überlebender aus Warschau,*" *Archiv für Musikwissenschaft* 33, no. 4 (1976): 277.

75. Lieberman, "Schoenberg Rewrites His Will," 212, and Crittenden, "Texts and Contexts," 247.

76. Taruskin, "The Poietic Fallacy," 34. In an earlier article Taruskin also expressed his disapproval of *A Survivor from Warsaw*'s "B-movie clichés, the Erich von Stroheim Nazi barking 'Achtung,' the kitsch-triumphalism of the climactic, suddenly tonal [*sic*] singing of the Jewish credo." Richard Taruskin, "A Sturdy Musical Bridge of the 21st Century," *New York Times*, 24 August 1997.

77. Meyerowitz, *Arnold Schönberg*, 29, Stuckenschmidt, *Arnold Schönberg*, 469, MacDonald, *Schoenberg*, 48, Sinkovicz, *Mehr als zwölf Töne*, 286, and Shawn, *Arnold Schoenberg's Journey*, 272. Few biographers point out that the age limit for applicants for a Guggenheim fellowship was forty years. See Henke, *Arnold Schönberg*, 149. Adorno's supposition that Schoenberg did not finish the large-scale oratorio and opera because "the urge to bring a work to a conclusion was totally alien to him" is outlandish. Adorno, *Philosophy*, 120–21.

78. Krenek,"America's Influence," 117.

79. "Die USA waren nicht der Platz, an dem Schönbergs Ideen auf fruchtbaren Boden fallen konnten." Sinkovicz, *Mehr als zwölf Töne*, 254–55.

80. Lessem, "The Émigré Experience," 59.

81. However, both Henke and Shawn included chapters on Schoenberg's multifarious nonmusical activities in their recent monographs. See "Lieber Vollmensch als Halbgott. Anmerkungen zur Person," Henke, *Arnold Schönberg*, 7–21; "Games" and "On Being Short," Shawn, *Arnold Schoenberg's Journey*, 247–52.

82. See Goldberg, "The Sounding Board."

83. The two most-quoted critical remarks are drawn from Schoenberg's letters to German conductor Hermann Scherchen and his fellow émigré composer Ernst Krenek. In 1936 he wrote to Scherchen: "I have been teaching at one and next year shall be teaching at the other of the two universities here. But unfortunately the material I get has had such an inadequate grounding that my work is as much a waste of time as if Einstein were having to teach mathematics at a secondary school." In 1940 Schoenberg confided to Krenek: "I share your opinion of American students of music. It's a great pity that the grounding is bad." Yet he continued, saying "I was not enthusiastic about German teaching either. . . . But American young people's intelligence is certainly remarkable." See *Arnold Schoenberg Letters*, 198 and 210. These utterances, however, should not be generalized and applied to Schoenberg's entire teaching career in the United States as they refer to his teaching of music minors and courses such as music appreciation.

84. Stuckenschmidt, *Arnold Schoenberg*, 373–80, and Freitag, *Schönberg*, 137.

85. See Lessem, "The Émigré Experience," 65. The heritage of Schoenberg's teaching in the United States can be found not only in several textbooks on harmony, counterpoint, and composition—*Models for Beginners in Composition* (1942; rev. ed.,

Pacific Palisades: Belmont Music Publishers, 1972); *Structural Functions of Harmony* (New York: Norton, 1954); *Preliminary Exercises in Counterpoint* (London: Faber, 1963); and *Fundamentals of Musical Composition*, ed. Leonard Stein and Gerald Strang (London: Faber, 1967). These are tailored to the needs of U.S. students, but also are mentioned in numerous articles on music education and proposals for music schools.

86. Gervink provides a chapter on Schoenberg as teacher in Europe in his Schoenberg monograph, yet herefrained from discussing Schoenberg's U.S. teaching career. See Gervink, *Arnold Schönberg und seine Zeit*, 216–24.

87. Meyerowitz, *Arnold Schönberg*, 29–30; Freitag, *Schönberg*, 143; Sinkovicz, *Mehr als zwölf Töne*, 264–65; Gervink, *Arnold Schönberg und seine Zeit*, 294.

88. Hans Heinz Stuckenschmidt, *Arnold Schoenberg*, trans. Edith Roberts and Humphrey Searle (New York: Grove Press, 1959), 112, originally published as *Arnold Schönberg*, Zurich: Atlantis, 1951); Reich, *Schoenberg*, 200–201; MacDonald, *Schoenberg*, 46; Lessem, "The Émigré Experience, 62–63; Kater, *Composers of the Nazi Era*, 191.

89. "There is rarely a period in Hollywood when all the orchestrators and most of the movie composers are not studying with one or another of the prominent musicians who have gone there to live recently. At one time the vogue was for Schoenberg, who came with a great reputation, of course, as a teacher. However, most of the boys wanted to take a six weeks' course and learn a handful of Schoenberg tricks." Oscar Levant, *A Smattering of Ignorance* (New York: Doubleday, 1940), 125–26. My article "Arnold Schoenberg and the Cinematic Art" seeks to correct the misconceptions about Schoenberg's interactions with composers working in the Hollywood film industry.

90. Freitag, *Schönberg*, 149; Stuckenschmidt, *Schönberg. Leben, Umwelt, Werk*, 408, 450, 455–57.

91. Rubsamen, *Schoenberg Remembered*, 473. From Rubsamen's list Simon Carfagno and Don Estep sank into obscurity. Rubsamen drew his conclusion from a statement by Schoenberg pertaining to his European and U.S. students: "The harshness of my requirements is also the reason why, of the hundreds of my pupils, only a few have become composers: Anton Webern, Alban Berg, Hanns Eisler, Karl Rankl, Winfried Zillig, Roberto Gerhard, Nikos Skalkottas, Norbert von Hannenheim, Gerald Strang, Adolph Weiss. At least I have only heard of these." See "The Blessing of the Dressing (1948)," Arnold Schoenberg, *Style and Idea*, ed. Dika Newlin (New York: Philosophical Library, 1950), 118. From Schoenberg's list von Hannenheim is now forgotten, and Rankl and Zillig are remembered as conductors. Few of his European students—Alban Berg, Anton Webern, Hanns Eisler, Roberto Gerhard and Nikos Skalkottas—became well-known composers.

92. Meyerowitz, *Arnold Schoenberg*, 30. By the 1960s John Cage and Lou Harrison had gained international recognition as composers, and Leon Kirchner and Earl Kim had become professors of composition at Harvard and Princeton.

93. Henke, *Arnold Schönberg*, 131, 135, and 143; Ringer, *Arnold Schönberg*, 287; Crawford, "Arnold Schoenberg in Los Angeles," 15–28.

94. See Murray Dineen, "Gerald Strang's Manuscript Notes to Arnold Schoenberg's Classes (1935–1937): Construction and the Two Learnings," *Journal of the Arnold Schönberg Center* 4 (2002): 104–18; Colleen Conlon, "Classical Form as Teaching Tool: Schoenberg's Pedagogy in Composition," *Journal of the Arnold Schönberg Center* 4 (2002): 271–77, and Robert Pascall, "Theory and Practice: Schoenberg's American Pedagogical Writings and the First Movement of the Fourth String Quartet, op. 37," *Journal of the Arnold Schönberg Center* 4 (2002): 229–44. See also Sointu Scharenberg, *Überwindung von Prinzipien. Betrachtungen zu Arnold Schönbergs unkonventioneller Lehrtätigkeit* (Saarbrücken: Pfau Verlag, 2002).

95. Michael Hicks, "John Cage's Studies with Schoenberg," *American Music* 8, no. 2 (1990): 125–40; David Bernstein, "John Cage, Arnold Schoenberg and the Musical Idea," *John Cage: Music, Philosophy, and Intention, 1933–50*, ed. David W. Patterson (New York: Routledge, 2002), 15–45. Schoenberg's students Patricia Carpenter, Warren Langlie, Lois Lautner, Robert Nelson, Dika Newlin, David Raksin, William Russell, Leonard Stein, and Gerald Strang provided rich source materials.

96. "Die Stätte der erhofften Triumphe aber wurde es nicht, im Gegenteil: Die USA waren nicht der Platz, an dem Schönbergs Ideen auf fruchtbaren Boden fallen konnten. . . . Die amerikanische Musikgeschichte lief nach Gesetzen ab, die denen seiner Musik diametral entgegengesetzt waren. Dessen sollte er sich bald schmerzhaft bewusst werden. . . . Die erwünschte produktive Auseinandersetzung fand nicht statt" (It never was the site of his of his hoped-for triumphs. . . . Rather, just the opposite happened. Schoenberg's ideas were not going to fall onto fertile ground in the United States. . . . American music history proceeded according to laws, which were diametrically opposed to his principles. Soon he became painfully aware of this fact. . . . The desired productive engagement did not take place.) Sinkovicz, *Mehr als zwölf Töne*, 254–55 and 279. "Sa musique n'est pour ainsi dire jamais jouée." Leibowitz, *Schoenberg*, 141.

97. Krenek, "America's Influence," 117.

98. Jameux, *L'école*, 643.

99. Such bisectional biographical views dividing a composer's career into a superior European and inferior U.S. period have also been applied to Bartók, Weill, and others. See Gillies, "Bartók in America," 190–201; Stephen Hinton, "Kurt Weill: Life, Work, and Posterity," *Amerikanismus, Americanism, Weill—Die Suche nach kultureller Identität in der Moderne*, ed. Hermann Danuser and Hermann Gottschewski (Schliengen: Edition Argus, 2003), 209–20.

100. See especially literature on Schoenberg of European provenance, for instance, Gabriele Eder, "Arnold Schönberg und die New Yorker Musikkritik," *Journal of the Arnold Schönberg Center* 4 (2002): 292–308. See also Gillies's critical discussion of Hungarian literature on Bartók where the United States is accused of treating this eminent composer inappropriately, 193–95.

101. See Egon Wellesz, *Arnold Schönberg* (Leipzig: E. P. Tal, 1921), published in English trans. by William Kerridge (London: J. M. Dent, 1925), and René Leibowitz, *Schoenberg et son école* and *Schoenberg* (Paris: Editions du Seuil, 1969).

102. Stuckenschmidt's 1974 Schoenberg monograph is still the most comprehensive biography on Schoenberg to date. While much important Schoenberg research is done by U.S. scholars, there are very few Schoenberg biographies by Americans or non-Europeans.

103. André Riotte, preface to Pierre Barbaud's 1997 book, *Schoenberg*, 9.

Yael Epstein

When the Nobel Prize Was Not Enough
Jewish Chemists from the Nazi Regime as Refugees in the United States

On April 7, 1933, the Nazis enacted the Civil Service Law, which required the dismissal of anyone who was not "Aryan" from public positions in Nazi Germany. As a consequence, many Jewish academics were expelled from their positions and thereafter immigrated to the United States. Laura Fermi called them the "Illustrious Immigrants," while Alvin Johnson, then president of the New School for Social Research, founder of the so-called University in Exile, and a leading advocate of rescue for émigré scholars, called them "Hitler's gift to American culture." Another prominent academic said, "Hitler shakes the tree and I gather the apples."[1] Among those academics, heretofore largely neglected, were prominent chemists including several Nobel Prize laureates. One account argues that at the beginning of 1933 there were about 1000–1200 Jewish chemists and engineers in Germany, to whom about 200 "non-Aryan" chemists and engineers should be added.[2] Another estimate is that the total number of chemists and biochemists who were expelled from universities and Kaiser Wilhelm Institutes was 140 (out of a total of 535 chemists who were employed in universities in Germany and Austria and the Kaiser Wilhelm Institutes). At least 122 (87 percent of the 140) had to give up their positions for "racial" reasons; they were either "non-Aryans" or married to a Jew.[3] Most estimates show chemists to be the largest disciplinary group among the scientists who fled Hitler.

The number of refugee chemists exceeds the number of refugee physicists, as only about a hundred refugee physicists came to the United States.[4] This is a relatively small figure in comparison with more than a thousand chemists, yet most of the attention in the literature has converged on the physicists, a result of the fascination with the story of their involvement in creating the atomic bomb in the United States.[5] To illustrate, Laura Fermi's well-known book *Illustrious Immigrants*, which is considered one of the most significant books on the intellectual migration from the Nazi regime, excludes the refugee chemists from the other refugee intellectuals.[6] When Fermi writes about the natural sciences, she dedicates a lengthy chapter to the European-born atomic scientists; her husband, Enrico Fermi and their circle of friends were physicists. She then dedicates a brief chapter "More Natural Scientists" to mathematicians, astronomers, and scientists in the fields of medicine and molecular biology. In the short section on molecular biology, she gives a little consideration to biochemists and ignores the field of chemistry. Similarly *The Intellectual Migration,* edited by Donald Fleming and Bernard Bailyn, contains two chapters on the physicists, "A New Site for the Seminar: The Refugees and American Physics in the Thirties," and "Émigré Physicists and the Biological Revolution."[7] This does not focus on the refugee chemists. Nor does Anthony Heilbut's *Exiled in Paradise,* which includes a chapter entitled "The Scientists and the Bomb."[8]

There is an assumption in the literature that the internationalism of science meant that the dismissed European scientists and researchers were better equipped to find work or were in greater demand abroad than their fellow refugees from Nazism who were in the arts and the humanities and that, after the initial migration, positions in the United States were readily secured.[9] Because of the success story of the refugee Jewish physicists, many believed that refugee scientists generally had no problems of adjustment and fared better than other intellectual refugees. Research demonstrates otherwise: the refugee Jewish chemists had problems of adjustment in their professional careers and sometimes had more difficulties than other intellectuals. The group of refugee chemists is especially important to Jewish historiography in the field of refugee intellectual migration from the Nazi regime, since its study introduces a more realistic and appropriate picture of the situation prominent refugee scientists experienced in the U.S. setting. This research is particularly important as a contrast to and comparison with that on the Jewish physicists, whose overwhelming success gives a false picture if extrapolated to the situation of other Jewish scientists in other disciplines.

Another significant gap that this study addresses is the question of whether the refugee Jewish chemists experienced anti-Semitism in the United States either in the universities or in the chemical industry. This issue is especially important since anti-Semitism as a phenomenon has not been thoroughly studied in relation to the refugee migration from the Nazi regime in the United States, which is mostly portrayed as the promised land or as an asylum, especially for intellectuals, to which the immigrants had to escape in order to run away from the hell in Europe. As much as this representation is at least partially accurate, the complexity of the migration experience beyond that requires exploration, which leads to a different historical narrative than what has prevailed so far. By shifting focus away from flawed historical assumptions such as the "internationalism of science," much can be learned about the experience of the refugee chemists as sociological and historical phenomena in immigration studies.

In examining the adjustment process of the refugee chemists in the United States two chief questions arise: did they have special difficulties finding positions; and if so, how did they overcome the difficulties? To answer these questions and study the adjustment and reception of the newcomers, the experiences of thirty-five European Jewish refugee chemists from the Nazi regime have been studied, Jewish refugees being persons who were considered Jewish according to the Nazi laws: persons with at least one Jewish grandparent, but in many cases with at least one Jewish parent. In an attempt to obtain a cross-section as representative of the group as a whole as possible, the selection included chemists who were well known and established before immigrating and others who were not known or famous, but were more ordinary and worked as research chemists in the European chemical industry or academy in Germany and Austria. It is important to note that all the chemists included in the sample had already been educated as chemists before coming to the United States, having earned at least a bachelor's degree in chemistry or completed professional training. In most cases they had already earned graduate degrees, such as doctorates in chemistry. The refugees from the Nazi regime started leaving for the United States in the 1930s because of the Nazi persecution and continued to come after World War II under the Displaced Persons Act, signed in June 1948, allowing 205,000 refugees.[10] This sample limits itself to those refugees whose date of arrival falls within the span 1933–45. Representative case examples and stories both of successful adjustment and of failure to adjust as part of the general narrative of the refugee chemists' experience serve to illustrate general patterns of adjustment.

Table 1 The refugee chemists and date of their arrival in the U.S.

Name of the refugee chemist	Year of arrival in the U.S.	Name of the refugee chemist	Year of arrival in the U.S.
Max Bergmann	1933	Herbert Freundlich	1938
Ernst Berl	1933	Walter M. Fuchs	1934
Hans Beutler	1936	Gertrud Kornfeld	1937
Jacob J. Bikerman	1945	Rosa L. Kubin	1938
Konrad Bloch	1935	Fritz Lipmann	1939
Erwin Chargaff	1934	Otto Loewi	1940
Zacharias Dische	1941	Fritz W. London	1938
Immanuel Estermann	1933	Herman F. Mark	1940
Kasimir Fajans	1936	Otto Meyerhof	1940
Conrat Fraenkel	1936	David Nachmansohn	1939
James Franck	1936	Carl Neuberg	1940

Table 1 (*continued*)

Name of the refugee chemist	Year of arrival in the U.S.	Name of the refugee chemist	Year of arrival in the U.S.
Hans Neurath	1935	Otto Stern	1933
Eugene Rabinowitch	1938	Kurt G. Stern	1935
Otto Redlich	1938	Leo H. Sternbach	1941
Otto Rosenthal	1935	Heinrich Waelsch	1938
Rudolf Schoenheimer	1933	Arnold Weissberger	1936
Robert Simha	1938	Kurt Wohl	1942
Carl Sollner	1937		

A few general details about the sample of refugee chemists should be considered here first. The average age of the refugee chemists who came to the United States was forty-one. This highlights the fact that many of the chemists were already established when they immigrated to the United States. The highest percentage of the refugee chemists (37 percent) were in the forty to forty-nine age range, while 31 percent were between thirty and thirty-nine years old. The refugee chemists were therefore much older than the general population of Jewish refugees who came to the United States. According to Arieh Tartakower, in the years 1939–1940, 21.5 percent of arriving Jewish refugees were thirty-one to forty years old, and 18.9 percent were from age forty-one to fifty. Similarly, in the years 1940–1941, 20.9 percent of Jewish refugees (not specifically chemists) were thirty-one to forty years old, and 19.6 percent were from age forty-one to fifty.[11]

The refugee chemists came steadily to the United States throughout the 1930s, with the highest percentage (20 percent) immigrating in 1938. After 1941 there was a decrease in the rate of arrival of refugee chemists because of the war and the difficulty of getting out of Nazi-occupied Europe. That many refugee chemists came in the late 1930s suggests either that they were slow to run from Nazism or that many were in transition, mainly leaving Germany to live and work in other European nations before leaving Europe permanently. According to U.S. Immigration Service figures for immigrants between 1933 and 1941, the number of immigrant aliens admitted to the United States peaked in 1939.[12] In the sample under consideration, 80 percent (28 out of 35) of the refugee chemists lived in a transition state elsewhere in Europe for different periods of time before coming to America. Some 45 percent of the refugee chemists immigrated for the first time to transition states in 1932–34, at the beginning of the Nazi regime. The most popular destination, attracting 42 percent of the chemists studied in the sample, was the United Kingdom. Another 17 percent of the refugee chemists found temporary refuge in France. A majority, 60 percent, of the refugee chemists went to one country only, while a minority, 20 percent, spent time in at least two countries. The range of time spent in a transition country varied from a few weeks to nine years. To illustrate, Otto

Loewi, professor of pharmacology in Austria, who received the Nobel Prize for Physiology and Medicine in 1936 for the discovery of the chemical transmission of nerve impulses, immigrated to England in 1938 and stayed there until 1940, when he came to the United States. Fritz Lipmann a prominent biochemist, who would receive the Nobel Prize in 1953 for the discovery of coenzyme A and its importance for intermediary metabolism, stayed in Denmark for seven years, 1932–39, then immigrated to the United States.

Doron Niederland has stressed that the high percentage of immigrants among chemists was due to the great demand for this profession in the host countries.[13] On the other hand, in a study on the impact of German medical scientists on British medicine at Oxford University, Weindling has argued that certain biomedical scientists and chemists came to the United Kingdom as domestic servants or gardeners and pursued careers in fringe industrial laboratories. Moreover a coordinating committee in Oxford University gave preference to scientists with prospects for remigration, given the lack of permanent positions in England. On top of that, after the beginning of the war, some refugee scholars feared internment as enemy aliens in England because they were considered "alien academics."[14] It appears that the refugee chemists were not so much in demand in the transition countries, but as temporary refugees they were able to find temporary positions there, with the common belief that the Hitler regime would not last long.

In regard to country of origin for immigration, twenty-seven out of thirty-five of the refugee chemists in the selected sample were emigrants from Germany, the country that before Hitler's rise was the world leader in science, including both the academy and the chemical industry. Of the others six were from Austria while one refugee chemist emigrated from Czechoslovakia and another emigrated from Switzerland.

All but one of the chemists in the sample already had doctorates when they arrived in the United States. The single exception was Konrad Bloch, then still a graduate student. Before their immigration twenty-nine of the refugee chemists worked mainly in universities in Germany and Austria and also in the Kaiser Wilhelm Institutes in Germany, where they held positions as lecturers, professors, heads of departments, and directors. Six of the chemists in the sample had positions as researchers in the chemical industry.

Once in the United States, some twenty-two had more than one position, and in many cases more than two positions, indicating that many refugee chemists either were prepared to move from one position to another or, on the other hand, perhaps did not receive tenure in their initial place of work and had problems of instability, mostly in academic institutes. To illustrate, Jacob J. Bikerman had five positions in the United States, four in the chemical industry and one in the academy. Although eight refugee chemists in the sample worked in the U.S. chemical industry at least once in their lives, most refugee chemists were mainly oriented to academic work and followed careers in U.S. universities and different academic institutions. Twenty-eight of the refugee chemists at least once in their life resettled on the East Coast, mainly in the states of New York, Pennsylvania, and Massachusetts and in New York City, Philadelphia, Pittsburgh, and Boston. Additionally nine resettled at least once in their life in the Midwest, mainly in big cities and university towns: Chicago, Ann Arbor, Cleveland and Minneapolis.

An important question to consider as part of gauging the adjustment process of the newcomers is whether the refugee Jewish chemists suffered anti-Semitism in the U.S. scientific environment. The case of James Franck, a scientist who emigrated from Germany at age fifty-one with a Nobel Prize in physics and became a physical chemist in the United States, provides an interesting example. In 1935 he accepted a professorship at Johns Hopkins University in Baltimore and moved his family there. At Hopkins, Franck was initially happy with his position and turned down an opportunity to work at the University of Illinois–Urbana. But in 1938 he accepted a call to the University of Chicago, where he would have greater opportunities and support, such as sufficient equipment, which he lacked at Hopkins, and the chance to work with others.

When he accepted this offer, he was astonished and humiliated when President Isaiah Bowman of Johns Hopkins University reproached him, telling him that he had acted in an un-American fashion in making the move, and these feelings became unbearable when Provost Berry tried to print a statement in the press accusing Franck of heeding the call from Chicago because it offered better financial arrangements.[15] Although the statement eventually was not published, Franck was furious about the incident and demanded an apology, which never came. Moreover Alan D. Beyerchen wrote that "James Franck decided to leave Hopkins, at least in part because of the anti-Semitic attitude of some officials there."[16] These officials included Isaiah Bowman, according to Franck, who emphasized in an interview that the president made life very difficult for Jewish faculty.[17] Interestingly Isaiah Bowman, in addition to serving as the president of Johns Hopkins University from 1935 to 1948, was an adviser to President Roosevelt on U.S. refugee policy, charged particularly with finding resettlement possibilities for Jewish refugees. In this position Bowman found every excuse to deny possible schemes and was indifferent to finding a real solution to the problem. To illustrate, when he assessed the possibility of Jewish refugee resettlement in Australia in 1939 he wrote, "Regarding Australia now, the economic organization is already completed and the danger lies in Jewish control of that organization if too many are allowed into the country and particularly the cities."[18]

James Franck together with Gustav Hertz won the Nobel Prize in 1925 for the discovery of excitation potentials, the amount of energy that an electron must absorb before it can move further away from the nucleus of the atom. His discovery confirmed the quantum hypothesis and Bohr-Sommerfeld atomic theory. In the United States his subsequent main scientific contributions were in the field of photosynthesis. Franck's important contribution to the field was that he first applied the criteria of physics and physical chemistry to devising experiments and to the interpretation of their results in photosynthesis.[19] At the meeting of the American Academy of Arts and Sciences on March 9, 1955, James Franck was awarded the 1955 Rumford Medal and Premium, an award established in 1796 to be given to "the author of the most important discovery or useful improvement on heat or on light." The award recognized that James Franck was one of the world's leading authorities in photosynthesis, to which he had made fundamental contributions, both theoretical and experimental.[20]

Rosa Kubin, a chemist who arrived from Austria in 1938, found a position in the University of Oregon Medical School, and also experienced anti-Semitism—as she recorded in an interview in 1971: "I'll never forget—I was in Bar Harbor, in a restaurant, and one of my worst experiences, I must say, was when I was in this country maybe for three or four months, . . . and I was already associated with this research work at the University of Oregon Medical School, when I was approached by one of the professors and he told me, 'Someone said that you are Jewish, is it true?' And I said, 'Yes, it's true.' He said, 'It's not that I have anything against Jews, but I said nobody who would be a Jew would become a member of the faculty at the University of Oregon.' And then he added to it, because he had met my husband, and my husband really didn't look like a Jew, and he said, 'But your husband is gentile.' You know, grasping for a straw that there is something. And I said, 'No, my husband is Jewish from head to toe, and probably more so.' So, this [anti-Semitism] was something which was quite general. Quite general."[21]

Rosa Kubin was one of the few women in the group of refugee chemists. She had received a doctorate in biochemistry from the University of Vienna in 1931 and had filled several positions in Europe before immigrating, mostly doing research in the European chemical industry. After her first position at the University of Oregon Medical School as a research assistant, she came to Waltham, a suburb of Boston where her husband had found a job as a physician. She worked in Waltham Hospital's laboratory for one year. Afterward she found a temporary position as assistant professor of chemistry in Middlesex University. She worked there until 1947, when Middlesex closed, and the property became part of Brandeis University. The new president of Brandeis, Abram L. Sachar, who was himself Jewish, decided to fire her because of her German accent. After this she worked temporarily in different colleges in the Boston area, and in the meantime she opened her own laboratory for veterinarians. Eventually, in order to receive a regular job with an eventual pension, she realized she had to work in high schools. Rosa worked in different high schools from 1956 to 1973 as a chemistry teacher.[22]

Although anti-Semitism was broadly prevalent in the U.S. academy, it was not ubiquitous. Herman Mark, who in 1947 established the first graduate school for the study of polymers in the United States, the Polymer Research Institute in the Polytechnic Institute of Brooklyn, did not experience anti-Semitism and never felt that he was discriminated against because he was Jewish, according to his son Hans Mark.[23] Mark was happy to get an academic offer at the Polytechnic Institute of Brooklyn in 1940, a position that enabled him to come to the United States. But at the same time, he did not have much of a choice. When asked in an interview if he had other offers, Herman Mark replied:

> In 1939 I visited several conferences here in the United States, ACS meetings and such, and gave lectures. Of course, it eventually became known that I would be interested in leaving Hawkesbury. One opportunity was from Dr. Emil Ott who was the research director of Hercules Powder, also a cellulose company. He was on the board of Rutgers University. . . . Ott talked with the president of Rutgers and said, "Look here, there is a fellow who wants first to come to the United States and second to go back into the academic world. Why don't you have a look at him?" I went to New Brunswick and gave a lecture there; it was a very nice place. I don't know today whether it would have been better to go to Rutgers, but I didn't. There was another opportunity at the University of Chicago on one of the various visits. I also visited Chicago, giving three lectures there. There was a very well-known organic chemist who knew of my work from Professor Schlenk. He said, "Well, if you really want to come to the United States, maybe we can do something here at the University of Chicago." But these two things were just more or less tentative.[24]

Herman Mark's main scientific achievement in the United States was to push the science of polymers from the periphery to the mainstream of U.S. science. Despite conservatism in the U.S. scientific community in both the academy and in industry, he succeeded in importing a new field and establishing it as one of the dominant new directions in the U.S. academy and industry. Besides the fact that he set up the Polymer Research Institute, he also organized conferences on polymers, established the first U.S. journal for polymer research, and initiated and sponsored the founding of similar institutions that would constitute a network of polymer research centers cooperating closely with each other all over the world. As a result of his activities, U.S. universities started to introduce the teaching of polymer chemistry in 1956, just sixteen years after Mark's arrival, and to endorse polymer research on a fully organized scale. For his lifetime of contributions to the development of polymer science, Herman Mark received the National Medal of Science in 1980 from President Jimmy Carter.

Mark's experience notwithstanding, we can find additional evidence of anti-Semitism at that time in the U.S. chemical industry. Arthur Beiser, for instance, less well-known than Franck, came to the United States with a Ph.D. in organic chemistry. He had worked from 1929 until 1933 as an assistant at the First Chemical Institute at the Berlin University and then was thrown out, finding alternative work in the German chemical industry in a Jewish owned firm. After fleeing to Cuba in January 1939, where he stayed ten months, he came with his wife to the United States in December 1939. Beiser tried to find a job in the U.S. chemical industry and contacted several companies, but all answers were negative. Beiser explains the reason: "All negative. I had a recommendation to a research director, to the Agfa in Bingham. I had a frank talk with him. He said the trouble with you is in one way you are a German and in the other way you are a Jew."[25] For a year, until 1941, he was unemployed, while his wife worked in a household taking care of small children.

An interesting phenomenon occurred with the prestigious and famous chemists, some of whom were Nobel laureates. Often the attitude toward them was hostile, disrespectful, and unwelcoming. This group of scientists includes James Franck and Otto Meyerhof, who were both already Nobel laureates when they arrived, Carl Neuberg, Otto Stern, and others. One must remember that although these were scientists who were originally given preference by the U.S. immigration laws and by private foundations and refugee committees that gave them favored treatment in rescue efforts, the reality in U.S. universities was different. As Max Bergmann describes in a letter in 1943: "As a rule, every scientist from abroad, even if he is famous the world over and he is a Nobel Laureate, has to start here on a small scale, that is, with a small salary and one or two collaborators, and it depends upon his achievements in his new position whether he makes progress."[26]

To illustrate, Otto Stern, a prestigious physicist and physical chemist, encountered a hostile environment at Carnegie Tech in Pittsburgh (today's Carnegie-Mellon University), where there was no support from the faculty. Stern had been distinguished professor of physical chemistry at the University of Hamburg and the director of its Institute for Physical Chemistry from 1923 until 1933. He is especially known for his development of the molecular beam method, for which he received the Nobel Prize in Physics in 1943. The molecular beam method is a scientific technique to research the properties of any stream or ray of molecules moving in the same general direction, usually in a vacuum.

It is interesting to note that in 1933 the president of Carnegie Tech made a trip to Germany to try to find some good scientists who might be induced to come to Carnegie. This was how Stern and his coworker Immanuel Estermann were brought to Carnegie. The president made this whole arrangement on his own without consulting his subordinates. The president became ill and after the first year Stern received no research support from the dean and from the department, especially in terms of funds, and instead encountered harsh local politics. The head of the department was very unsympathetic, there was no research going on in the physics department, and there were no Ph.D. programs running at Carnegie, just a master's degree. Thus Stern and Estermann worked by themselves, except for one machinist. The president resigned after a few years of illness. An additional factor that contributed to Stern's difficulties in adjusting at Carnegie was the fact that he had acted as "a prima donna" and had not behaved diplomatically toward the dean and other faculty.[27] This atmosphere at Carnegie was also a major factor in preventing Stern from continuing his scientific achievements. The momentum of the atom beam research that Stern had conducted in Hamburg laboratory was never regained. Stern did not have the energy any more or the emotional stamina to struggle in Pittsburgh.[28]

Another example of the difficulties of established and older chemists can be found in the case of Carl Neuberg. Neuberg, a prominent biochemist, is considered one of the fathers of biochemistry because of his scientific achievements and the fact that he actually coined the term *biochemistry*. He was professor of chemistry at the University of Berlin and was the director of the Kaiser Wilhelm Institute for Biochemistry until 1937, when the Nazis drove him out of both posts. In 1939 he left Germany. At the age of 64 he arrived at New York University, in 1941. In a letter to Karl Thomas he describes his situation there: "The people were horrified that I wanted to work, they wanted me to take walks."[29] For a year he was paid one hundred dollars per month out of grant funds, but when the funding ran out, he had to make a living as a consultant for industry and looked constantly for grants that would support his salary and research. First, Neuberg was consultant at Merck, later at Interchemical. That ceased in the fall of 1949, and he had a grant for a year until 1950. The laboratory at NYU was an unventilated room with no natural light, sufficient for only one person. As Neuberg describes it: "The cleaning woman in Dahlem would have rejected being in this room even if it had been only for an hour."[30] He kept it anyway for lack of a better one until the beginning of 1949, when he had to retire, having already passed the age limit by six and a half years. It is worth noting that other NYU professors beyond retirement age were not pressured to leave. Later in 1949, Neuberg found a position in the Polymer Research Institute at the Polytechnic Institute of Brooklyn, where he conducted his studies on polymeric nucleic acids and earned a salary as a visiting professor twice as high as his former NYU salary.[31] Even here, though, he had difficulty raising the funds for his research.[32]

Neuberg's struggles as an émigré chemist and the inadequate research conditions described above resulted in his being unable to conduct productive research, as he had done in the past. Nevertheless Neuberg will be remembered mainly for the scientific achievements in his career prior to his immigration to the United States. The rise of modern dynamic biochemistry after the turn of the century is closely associated with his name. The range of his contributions to a great variety of problems is stupendous; he stimulated many pertinent developments by his dynamism, enthusiasm, encyclopedic knowledge, and ingenuity. He was widely referred to as one of the "big three" in biochemistry at the Kaiser Wilhelm Institutes in Berlin-Dahlem (the two others were Warburg and Meyerhof). His contributions to the process of alcoholic fermentation from 1911 onward will be remembered as one of his most magnificent achievements. His discovery of the enzyme carboxylase was one of the important milestones in the elucidation of alcoholic fermentation, one of the problems that had preoccupied scientists in the nineteenth century. Neuberg's discovery showed that the zymase of Buchner was actually not a single enzyme, as Buchner had assumed, but a complex system of several enzymes. The demonstration of this important step led Neuberg to propose his ingenious schemes of fermentation.

This was a turning point in the history of enzyme chemistry, since for the first time alcoholic fermentation was envisaged as a process formed by a series of successive enzymic steps. The schemes had a deep impact on the thinking of enzyme chemists. They created the pattern of inquiry into the mechanism of metabolic pathways, thereby making a brilliant contribution that played a key role in the further study of the chemistry of cell reactions. There are in addition many other important contributions by which Neuberg initiated and stimulated various developments in biochemistry. Moreover he was a passionate and inspiring teacher and as the director of a large institute he attracted a large number of pupils from all over the world, including the United States, and created one of the largest schools of biochemistry of that period. Many scientists who were trained in his institute became leaders in their native countries.[33]

Neuberg helped establish the journal *Biochemische Zeitschrift* in 1906 and edited 278 volumes over the next thirty years. The nomenclature in the field of biochemistry bears similar traces of Neuberg's ingenuity, including the terms *phosphorylation, dismutation, desmolysis,* and *coenzyme*. Thus Carl Neuberg holds a foremost place in the early period of dynamic biochemistry.

When one analyzes the process of searching for jobs in the United States by the refugee chemists, there is a common pattern. Regardless of age and status—whether they were Nobel laureates, established and/or older, or recently qualified or younger chemists, they all used their own informal networks of connections consisting of linkages with other European Jewish refugee chemists to amplify the more formal procedures. They did so because in many cases the organizations and private committees that were created to help refugee scholars from the Nazi regime did not actually support them adequately. To illustrate, one of the main organizations, the Emergency Committee in Aid of Displaced Scholars, mainly helped and supported refugee scholars in the humanities and social sciences, thus partly neglecting the natural sciences. For example, 192 fellowships were given to scholars in the humanities and social sciences combined, in contrast to 85 fellowships that were given to scholars in natural sciences and medical sciences combined. Amazingly chemists received only 7—one of the smallest number of fellowships—while physicists were awarded 16 fellowships.[34] Thus it is no wonder that, in order to succeed, the refugee chemists utilized their own mechanisms for finding positions.

The sociological theory that most appropriately explains the basis for the professional adjustment of the refugee chemists in the United States is the "network approach." According to this theory—widely used in the literature on immigration studies—a social network consists of one or more finite sets of actors and the relation or relations defined among them.[35] A network is thus a set of individual or collective actors—ranging from individuals, families, firms and nation-states—and the relations that link them. Network patterns of ties comprise social, economic, and political interactions, as well as collective groups—kinship groups or communities—and private or public associations. The network approach makes the study of how resources, goods, and ideas flow through particular configurations of social and symbolic ties possible.[36]

Generally the network of migrants can function as a promoter of migration, sponsoring or accompanying the mover, and as an ongoing support at the destination.[37] Connections with earlier migrants provide potential migrants with many resources that they use to diminish the risks and costs of migration: information about procedures—technical as well as legal, financial support, job prospects, administrative assistance, physical presence, and emotional solidarity. Beside facilitation, the impact of social networks on migration flows is also one of channeling, since immigrants naturally serve as bridgeheads for fellow immigrants in both the geographic as well as the professional areas in which they settle. Previous studies have shown the extent to which networks allow migrants to gain access to jobs in the recipient country. The forms and characteristics of these networks may depend on their composition—friends, relatives, kin, acquaintances, professional colleagues, and so forth—but the result is similar: most positions are acquired via connections.[38]

Charles Tilly in his discussion of networks puts it simply that networks migrate. Eventually these movers transplant major segments of *existing networks* from the old country to the new country with some modification of the networks' structures.[39] When the immigrant relocates from one country to another, he has to reconstruct his interpersonal connections. He or she rebuilds in a new community a network of personal affiliations. Frequently the immigrant accomplishes this task using certain institutional set-ups. Many develop organizations of various sorts—religious, educational, political, recreational, national, and professional—varying from formally structured organizations such as welfare and mutual aid societies through more informal networks to arrangements with no formal organization at all.[40] These associations serve to strengthen the consciousness of a group's culture of origin and reproduce aspects of the traditional institutional order in a new form.[41]

Evidence of refugee chemists' networks can be demonstrated in the cases of two industrial chemists in the United States, Arthur Beiser and Leo Sternbach, the man who invented the medicine Valium. Beiser did not find a job for a year until in 1941 when he heard through his friend, a German Jew, that there was a vacancy in a cosmetics firm; he then got the job. The company was small with thirty or forty workers, and Beiser noted, "This was an American company, but Jewish. The owner was Jewish."[42] Sternbach's case is even more dependent on networks: first, when he was still working at the Eidgenossiche Technische Hochschule in Zurich with Professor L. Ruzicka, winner of the Nobel Prize for Chemistry in 1939, he was encouraged by Dr. Moses W. Goldberg, another Jewish foreigner in Switzerland, who said, "Look, the times are difficult. It will be very hard for Switzerland to house so many foreigners and it will be better for you if you are in industry." Sternbach continued, "At that time, Furter was already with Hoffman–La Roche. He had called up Goldberg and told him that they needed some chemists there. Ruzicka proposed me."[43] According to a 2001 study commissioned by the Swiss government to examine the nation's wartime past, the chemical company Hoffmann–La Roche alone among the four major Swiss chemical companies resisted pressure by the Nazis to "Aryanize" the workforce of its German units before the war. By retaining its Jewish and foreign staff Hoffmann–La Roche protected a number of employees at risk of deportation to Germany or occupied Poland as forced laborers. Hoffmann–La Roche was more sensitive to the dangers facing employees because its chairman at the time was married to a Jewish woman. Soon after Sternbach joined the company, it transferred him and other Jewish chemists to its new research facility in Nutley, New Jersey, where he worked until his retirement in 1973. "Roche saved my life," he has stated.[44]

Sternbach's first big discovery in New Jersey was a new way to make biotin, a B complex vitamin. To test the mixture, Sternbach walked into a confined space in the lab and stirred the chemicals by hand in an enamel kettle. He had to be careful: one of the chemicals involved, phosgene, becomes a poisonous gas at room temperature. His Valium breakthrough came after he followed a hunch about compounds he had tested years earlier in Poland as dyes. He wondered if they might have some effect on humans; he knew that certain anesthetics, such as novocaine, had similar molecular structures. He tested that hypothesis, but, after hitting a dead end in 1955, he moved on per instructions from his boss. Sternbach pursued his research anyway. "I always did what I wanted to do," he said. Two years later, in 1957, when clearing space in their cluttered lab, Sternbach's colleague Earl Reeder found two bottles containing the contents of old experiments with the compounds. Sternbach tinkered with the molecular structure, adding a chain of chemicals to a molecule. He sent off the new version for pharmacological testing at Hoffmann–La Roche. The compounds seemed to tranquilize mice, cats, and even monkeys, but with the unusual effect that the animals remained alert. Intrigued,

Dr. Sternbach tried the experimental drugs on himself, a practice unheard of today. Hoffman–La Roche indicated that it did not condone the practice but was aware some scientists tested drugs on themselves. One industry executive, recalling the practice, refers to such researchers as "two-legged rats." Sternbach's experiments led to the creation of benzodiazepines, a new class of drugs—with Librium hitting the market in 1960 and Valium in 1963. Widely dispensed for calming anxiety and nerves, Valium also became a cultural icon: it was the "Mother's Little Helper" of the 1966 Rolling Stones song. Hoffman–La Roche declined to provide full sales data but did report that in 1973, its peak year, Valium produced 230 million dollars in U.S. sales, or about 1 billion dollars in current figures when adjusted for inflation.[45]

Konrad Bloch, a prominent biochemist who received the Nobel Prize in 1964, arrived in the United States in a fascinating way. In 1934 the brutal Nazification of Germany prevented Bloch from continuing his studies at the Munich Technische Hochschule, where he had been a graduate student. One professor, Hans Fischer, came to his rescue by recommending an appointment at the Schweizerisches Hoehensforschungs Institute in Davos, Switzerland. In Davos, Bloch studied the lipids of the tubercle bacillus. In 1936, however, he was refused permission to continue to reside in Switzerland. Desperate, he applied to Professor R. J. Anderson at Yale, with whom he had had some correspondence concerning his research. Anderson got him a letter from the dean of the Medical School of Yale University that informed Bloch that he had been appointed assistant in biological chemistry. Anderson sent a second letter that informed Bloch that the position was unsalaried and there was no money for his research. Bloch showed only the first letter, the dean's, to the U.S. consul in Frankfurt and received a life-saving visa to immigrate to the United States.[46] Had he shown the second letter, the visa would have been denied to him.

Fischer sent Bloch to Max Bergmann, another German Jewish refugee biochemist, who had received a position at the Rockefeller Institute of Medicine. Bergmann in turn advised Bloch to meet with Hans Clarke at Columbia University, and he wrote a letter of recommendation about Bloch to Clarke, whom he knew personally, in order that he would be accepted to Clarke's biochemistry department, even though Bloch was not a student of Bergmann's.[47] Additionally he arranged a fellowship for Bloch for his studies as a Ph.D. student by approaching his friend Leo Wallerstein, a wealthy German Jew who had immigrated to the United States before the Nazis' rise to power.[48] Wallerstein was the head of the Wallerstein Laboratories on Staten Island, New York, consultants to the brewing industry; his foundation assisted refugee scholars, whether they were at the beginning of their careers or already established.[49] It is significant that in this period donors to the U.S. universities were sometimes reluctant to donate money for scholarships and fellowships to foreign students and some demanded that their donations be given to U.S. students.[50] Bloch did his postdoctoral studies at Columbia

University in the laboratory of Rudolf Schoenheimer, a prominent biochemist who was also a German Jewish refugee from the Nazi regime. Although Bloch went to Schoenheimer's laboratory because he was one of the best in the field at that time, the fact that they had similar personal backgrounds probably helped their communication, personal relationship, and understanding. Bloch's first interview for an assistant professorship was in Salt Lake City in the biochemistry department at the University of Utah. During the discussion following his seminar, he curtly responded to a comment from the audience, not realizing that the very youthful questioner was someone very high up in the administration. Bloch never learned whether his interview went well, but he suspected it did not. Breaking his return journey in Chicago, he visited Earl Evans, the recently appointed chairman of the biochemistry department of the University of Chicago, who was actively recruiting. As graduate students at Columbia, Evans and Bloch had worked at adjacent benches and had become good friends, sharing tastes in literature and music. Without any preliminaries Evans asked Bloch whether he was interested in joining his department as an assistant professor. Bloch accepted the offer: "To join Evans's department was especially attractive because an isotope laboratory with a mass spectrometer that functioned more than half of the time had already been set up by Herbert Anker, my first graduate student at Columbia."[51]

Bloch represents a story of full adjustment. He came to the United States, where he accomplished most of his scientific achievements, when he was twenty-three years old. After receiving his Ph.D. degree under the direction of Clarke, Bloch was invited by Schoenheimer to join his group and to begin the study of the biosynthesis of cholesterol, a problem that had long been of interest to Schoenheimer. The great importance of cholesterol in the development of arterial disease was already clear by the 1930s, but little was known about the synthesis in the body of this complex molecule. After Schoenheimer's death Bloch independently continued this line of work in the Department of Biochemistry at the University of Chicago. In a pathbreaking series of investigations begun in Chicago and continued after his move to Harvard in 1954, Bloch was able to identify important landmarks in the series of more than thirty reactions by which the complex structure of cholesterol is built up from simple precursors. For his work on the biosynthesis of cholesterol and his related studies on the biosynthesis of fatty acids, Bloch received a Nobel Prize in 1965, shared with Feodor Lynen.[52]

In regard to the informal system of networks and placements, it is surprising to learn that even Jewish refugee chemists who had already won the Nobel Prize years before their immigration to the United States also had to use these connections in order to receive positions at U.S. universities. Their Nobel Prize did not make a difference in facilitating an easy path to work. For example, James Franck, who won the Nobel Prize in 1925, got his first position in the United States at Johns Hopkins University. At Johns Hopkins was R. W. Wood, an old friend who knew Franck from his position as head of the physical chemistry section in the Kaiser Wilhelm Institute in Berlin in the years 1917–21. When he subsequently moved to the University of Chicago, his move was facilitated by T. R. Hogness, who had been a visitor to Göttingen, where Franck had been professor of physics and director of the second Physics Institute. Moreover, at the University of Chicago, Franck's research was financially underwritten by the Jewish philanthropist Samuel Fels.[53]

Another example of a Noble Prize laureate who needed the help of his personal connections is Otto Meyerhof—a prominent German Jewish biochemist who had won the prize in 1923. The story of his difficult road to the United States started around 1936, when Meyerhof realized that his position as a professor and director of the Department of Physiology at the Kaiser Wilhelm Institute for Medical Research in Heidelberg was untenable and that he would have to leave sooner or later. Thus he and his wife, Hedwig, visited the United States, hoping to find a position there. The only offer he got was most unsatisfactory: at a small laboratory in a commercial enterprise with a salary of five thousand dollars per annum. David Nachmansohn, another German Jewish refugee biochemist, knew Meyerhof from his days in Meyerhof's laboratory in the Kaiser Wilhelm Institute of Biology in Berlin-Dahlem; Meyerhof had been the director there from 1924 to 1930.[54] Nachmansohn, who worked at that time at the Faculté des Sciences in Paris, had spent several weeks in the United States about the same time as the Meyerhofs and had met them quite frequently. Meyerhof was depressed about his prospects. After discussing the situation with Meyerhof, Nachmansohn, knowing the great respect and admiration the French had for Meyerhof, asked him whether he would be interested in Nachmansohn's investigating the possibility of a suitable place in Paris. Meyerhof's response was enthusiastic. He had always been a great admirer of French civilization, its art and poetry, its science, its great cultural achievements. A special code was agreed on for correspondence in view of possible censorship. Although the Nazis wanted to dismiss all Jews, they were beginning to prevent them from going abroad.

On Nachmansohn's return to Paris, he immediately approached René Wurmser, Henri Laugier, and Jean Perrin. All three promised their enthusiastic and strong support. The French acknowledged Meyerhof's brilliance as a scientist, but they were also attracted by his extraordinary background in the humanities. His personality had made a great impression on them during a visit to Paris in 1934, when he gave two lectures there. During the dinner parties and receptions on that occasion, French colleagues gave strong expression to their admiration. Wurmser was at that time the head of a subdivision of the Institut de Biologie Physico-Chimique. As a brilliant biochemist and physical chemist he was familiar with Meyerhof's work and delighted with the prospect of having him in his division. He arranged very satisfactory working facilities for Meyerhof and a position as *directeur de recherches,* equivalent to a research professorship. All the negotiations were carried out by

Nachmansohn with the aid of the previously mentioned code. The problem was now to get him and his family out of Germany.

With the help of some friends, Meyerhof got permission in September 1938 to go to Switzerland for a few weeks with his wife and his youngest son, Walter, for reasons of health. His daughter, Bettina, had already left for Paris and went in November to the United States, where she had been accepted by Swarthmore College near Philadelphia. His eldest son, Geoffrey, was already living in England. The Meyerhofs never returned to Heidelberg. Of course, since they were leaving the country on the pretext of taking a few weeks of vacation, they were unable to take anything with them except the bare necessities.[55]

The reception in Paris was extremely warm. Meyerhof soon formed many friendships with his French colleagues. The Rue Pierre Curie, with several institutes and many well-known scientists, was a great intellectual center, and Meyerhof greatly enjoyed the atmosphere. For Nachmansohn the admired teacher in this period became a personal friend, and the two became even closer over the years; the relationship lasted until Meyerhof's death. The happy time in Paris, which the Meyerhofs loved and to which they became genuinely attached, was unfortunately destined to be short. Just one year later the war broke out. For a few months it was not taken seriously, but in May 1940 the Nazis invaded France, and when they threatened Paris, the Meyerhofs fled to southern France with their son Walter. Although the Meyerhofs were most cordially received everywhere and greatly helped by their colleagues, it was obvious that they had to escape as soon as possible. Nachmansohn had in the meantime accepted an invitation from Yale University, where he had arrived a few days before the outbreak of the war. He contacted a few friends. It was A. V. Hill, Meyerhof's longtime scientific colleague, who shared the Nobel Prize with him and was a personal friend, who made his escape possible. He contacted A. N. Richards of the University of Pennsylvania, who was at that time the president of the National Academy of Sciences. Richards managed to create a professorship for Meyerhof at the University of Pennsylvania in the Department of Physiological Chemistry directed by Wright Wilson. But, before coming to the United States, the Meverhofs passed through a painful and difficult period. With the help of Varian M. Fry of the Emergency Rescue Committee, a predecessor of the International Rescue Committee, they finally escaped on foot—an exhausting effort—over the Pyrenees to Spain, led by Fry's border guide, Lisa Fittko. They reached the United States via Lisbon in October 1940.[56]

The height of Meyerhof's scientific achievements occurred when Meyerhof approached the problem of the conversions of chemical energy in the living cell. He chose muscle as his experimental material. This choice was prompted by the recognition that muscle offered an excellent opportunity to correlate chemical transformations with the production of both heat and mechanical work. When he started these investigations, the formation of lactic acid, demonstrated by Fletcher and Hopkins in 1906, was about all that was known of the chemical reactions associated with muscular contraction. The source of this compound, the way in which its formation provides energy, and the manner in which the energy is utilized were completely obscure. A. V. Hill's measurements of heat production by isolated frog muscle during activity and subsequent recovery had demonstrated not only that the heat produced was proportional to the work performed, but also that about half the total heat was actually produced during recovery. Meyerhof demonstrated that muscle glycogen is the precursor of the lactic acid formed in the absence of oxygen. He further showed that, in the presence of oxygen, some of the lactic acid formed during the anaerobic contraction was oxidized, but that not all the lactic acid underwent this fate. About one-fifth to one-fourth of it was oxidized to carbon dioxide and water, and the energy of this oxidation was used to reconvert the remaining four-fifths or three-fourths to glycogen. His observations actually proved Pasteur's assumption that less carbohydrate is consumed in the presence of oxygen than in its absence. The depression of glycolysis by respiration has since been referred to as the Pasteur-Meyerhof effect. Meyerhof's brilliant analysis of the glycogen–lactic acid cycle and its relation to respiration explained the course of the heat production and for the first time established the cyclic character of energy transformations in the living cell. For this accomplishment Meyerhof received the Nobel Prize in Physiology and Medicine in 1923, when he was only thirty-nine years old; it was awarded to both him and his colleague and friend A. V. Hill.

When Meyerhof arrived in the United States, he was provided with a small laboratory at the University of Pennsylvania. But he continued to work actively and productively, as shown by the number and importance of his publications during the U.S. period. More than fifty papers appeared, bringing the total of his publications to about four hundred.[57] During this later part of Meyerhof's life, although nothing emerged that was as sensational as his earlier work, he did much significant work. He found a new enzyme breaking down adenosine triphosphate (ATP) and succeeded in tidying up several points in the glycolytic scheme. He also took up the problem of transfer of phosphate groups by acid and alkaline phosphatases.[58] This amazing productivity is all the more remarkable if one considers that Meyerhof's health was undermined by a severe heart attack in 1944 at Woods Hole, where he spent most of his summers. Through the devoted care of his wife, he was able to surmount his difficulties and to continue his activities with undiminished energy, until a second heart attack led to his death, which came suddenly in the midst of creative work and the preparation of various projects for the future.[59]

The phenomenon of Max Bergmann is extremely fascinating. He was a one-man unofficial employment agency for the Jewish refugee chemists. Other Jewish refugee chemists—the established and the young, and from all ranks—sent him letters with their curricula vitae, asking if he could find them a job or if he knew about a position. He corresponded with persons who were in dangerous or uncomfortable situations. Karl Klanfer was sending him letters while imprisoned in an internment camp in Ottawa, Canada. Bergmann constantly looked for positions for the refugee chemists in the U.S. academy and industry and sent letters to his refugee scientist friends such as Albert Einstein, Fajans Kasimir, and many others, recommending persons for different fellowships or positions. Bergmann was active or cooperated with several organizations that aided the Jewish refugee scholars, and they sent him the documents of many refugee chemists in order to ask for his help in finding them positions or writing recommendations on their behalf. He specifically worked with the previously mentioned Emergency Committee in Aid of Displaced Foreign Scholars and the Emergency Society for German Scholars in Exile (or *Notgemeinschaft deutscher Wissenschaftler im Ausland*); he was especially active in the organization Self-help of Émigrés from Central Europe and contributed funds to this organization.[60] His wife, Martha, also worked in this organization and was a co-founder.[61]

Self-help was founded in 1936 by émigrés from Germany, but it was supported by a group of Quakers and also received support from some outstanding personalities connected with the New School for Social Research, or, as it was then called by most people, the "University in Exile." Self-help was founded by people who knew what the experience of exile was all about and therefore helper and client understood each other. They had in common not only language but also the shared past and the joint struggle to create a better tomorrow. At all times Self-help was infused with the spirit and intellectual influence of former teachers such as Gertrud Baumer, Alice Salomon, and Bertha Pappenheim. They inspired the deeply felt tradition of noblesse oblige. This explains how Self-help, which charged only fifty cents for membership, came into being with little money and on a volunteer basis. Volunteerism was the lifeblood of the early Self-help, and it was the women who carried the main burden. The women worked as caseworkers who explained the new country to the clients and tried to help them adjust. One of the many functions of the organization was serving as an employment agency.[62]

Bergmann was the only biochemist of the older generation—that is, of those who had an influential position in Germany before they were forced to leave—who managed to found a biochemical school in the United States. Bergmann, formerly director of the Kaiser Wilhelm Institute for leather research in Dresden and professor at the city's Technical University, left Germany in summer 1933 and received a position at the Rockefeller Institute of Medicine. His coworker Leonidas Zervas, who had developed the carbobenzoxy method of peptide synthesis with Bergmann in 1932, followed Bergmann to New York. At the Rockefeller Institute, Bergmann founded an influential school of protein chemistry, himself continuing research in the tradition of Emil Fischer. He not only worked on analytical methods to determine the amino-acid composition of peptides; he also conducted studies into protein-degrading enzymes and peptide synthesis. In cooperation with coworker William H. Stein, Bergmann developed the "solubility product method," the first reliable method of determining the amino-acid composition of proteins. The breakthrough in the methodology of separation and analysis was achieved after Bergmann's death in 1944, by Moore and Stein, who succeeded in using chromatography for the separation of amino acids and received the Nobel Prize in 1972.[63]

Further evidence for the transplanted professional network that the refugee chemists created in the United States can be found in their 1941 establishing of the American Society of European Chemists and Pharmacists. The society's chief purpose was to establish and foster close professional and personal relations between scientists who graduated from European universities but were residing in the United States. Another aim of the society was to maintain relations with colleagues abroad and to work for international cooperation in the field of science, with particular emphasis on chemistry and physics. The society published a bulletin containing brief reviews of lectures presented before the society and news of special interest to the members, but the main activity was arranging monthly meetings during the academic year at which outstanding scientists delivered lectures to the members and friends. Among those who were members were Carl Neuberg, Otto Loewi, Otto Meyerhof, Herman Mark, Kurt G. Stern, Alfred Reis, and many other refugee chemists. A medal had been created in honor of Professor Carl Neuberg, who was its first recipient. The Neuberg Medal was awarded each year to a distinguished member among the refugee chemists, who had not only contributed materially to the knowledge of chemistry but who had also made contributions to the development of the American Society of European Chemists and Pharmacists and the creation of good will in international scientific relations.[64]

There were several places in the United States that were receptive toward refugee Jewish chemists, in contrast to those chemical companies or academic institutions that had not made room, such as Harvard University, which was the only Ivy League institution among the thirty-one leading U.S. universities not to open teaching positions to scholars who had lost their places through Nazi persecution.[65] Especially receptive places were the Brooklyn Polytechnic Institute, Columbia University, Mount Sinai Hospital in New York, and the chemical company Hoffman–La Roche. The Brooklyn Polytechnic Institute employed Herman Mark (hired in 1940), Kurt G. Stern (hired in 1944), Carl Neuberg (hired in 1949), and Robert Simha (who worked there from 1941 to 1942). The Polytechnic Institute of Brooklyn's open-mindedness in the hiring of refugee chemists was the result of a general policy of expansion led by President Harry S. Rogers. In the ten years following 1934, nine new degree programs were added, including bachelor's programs in science and metallurgical and aeronautical engineering, master's programs in physics and aeronautical engineering, and doctoral curricula in chemistry, including polymer chemistry, chemical engineering, and aeronautical engineering. To reinforce and advance the teaching program and to attract leading scholars with high caliber students, the administration first sought to develop the research program. Thus the Polytechnic hired people such as Herman Mark, who developed the teaching of and research in polymer chemistry in the institute and established the Polymer Research Institute,[66] in which Neuberg, Stern, and Simha later received positions.

At Columbia University the vision of one man, Hans T. Clarke, similarly created a welcoming atmosphere for European Jewish refugee biochemists escaping the Nazi regime. Clarke was chairman of the Department of Biochemistry at Columbia's Medical School, the College of Physicians and Surgeons. He was half German on his mother's side and from 1911 to 1913 had been a guest researcher at Emil Fischer's laboratory in Berlin.[67] Under Clarke's leadership the department became preeminent in organic biochemistry, reflecting his own background. This emphasis was unique at that time, especially in medical schools, given the fact that until the 1930s nutrition and physiology had been the predominant fields of biochemistry in the United States.[68] Clarke explained one of the main reasons for the preeminence of the department among the U.S. universities: "Among the benefits that accrued to Columbia University from the racial policy adopted under the Third Reich, was the arrival in our laboratory of various European trained biochemists, notably Erwin Chargaff, Zacharias Dische, Karl Meyer, Rudolf Schoenheimer, Heinrich Waelsch and Erwin Brand, David Nachmansohn, PhD refugee student Konrad Bloch and many others."[69] It is important to understand, however, that while Clarke's department hired several refugee chemists, the economic conditions offered to the refugee biochemists were generally poor. Erwin Chargaff, for instance, writes in his autobiography about Clarke: "Like many well-to-do people, Clarke was frugal and had little appreciation of the importance of money for those who had none. The salaries which he negotiated for his faculty members—one of the foremost functions of a department head in a U.S. university—were largely below the average and mostly insufficient; he had no understanding of the material difficulties that beset some of his younger colleagues, and he did little to keep those who were pushed or pulled away."[70]

To illustrate, Erwin Chargaff, who in the years 1930–34 was assistant in charge of chemistry for the Department of Bacteriology and Public Health at the University of Berlin, immigrated to the United States in 1934 and found a position in Clarke's department. Chargaff had been promised the title of assistant professor of biochemistry: "which in view of my having been on the way to a *Privatdozentur* in Berlin and of my advanced age, thirty years, was the least to be expected. But when I moved in with my spatula and my notebook, Clarke hemmed and hawed and disclosed to me that they had decided to start me at a lower rank, that of research associate."[71] Chargaff is best known for showing during 1949–52 that the molar ratio of particular bases of DNA (adenine and thymine, on the one hand, and guanine and cytosine, on the other), is close to one, a result that was decisive for the subsequent elucidation of the double helix structure of DNA by James Watson and Francis Crick.[72] Interestingly Chargaff claimed in his autobiography that almost all the recognition his work received had come from Europe. However, a major exception occurred at the very end of his scientific career, when he was awarded the National Medal of Science in 1975.[73]

At Mount Sinai Hospital in New York, several refugee chemists worked for different periods of time. On January 15, 1852, nine men representing various Hebrew charitable organizations had come together to establish the Jews' Hospital in New York to offer free medical care to indigent Hebrews in the city who were not able to provide for themselves during their illnesses.[74] In 1934 Erwin Chargaff got his visa to the United States through Harry Sobotka, who was in charge of the biochemistry department at Mount Sinai. Chargaff spent few months in his laboratory. Sobotka was a student of Willstatter and Kuhn in Germany and was sympathetic to the hiring of refugee Jewish chemists. Sobotka also hired Edith Rubin in 1940, a woman refugee chemist from the Nazi regime who worked there as a laboratory assistant.[75] Additionally, from approximately 1939 to 1940, Konrad Bloch worked in a cancer research project at Mount Sinai Hospital and earned double the salary he had had in his former position in Columbia University.[76]

Many of the refugee chemists who found positions in the U.S. academy were chemists who specialized mostly in underdeveloped fields of study in the United States, such as biochemistry. Fifteen of the thirty-five refugee chemists in the researched sample were trained biochemists. Moreover, polymer science did not exist as a field in U.S. universities. Thus polymer refugee chemists had the opportunity to enter the U.S. academy with no resentment and competition from U.S. scientists. In order to explain the pattern of scientific or academic adjustment of the refugee chemists, the immigrant niche approach fits this reality best.

The dominant paradigm of immigrant employment views immigrants as tending to cluster in a limited number of occupations or industries that make up a niche. The scholarly consensus concludes that professionals "tend to enter at the bottom of their respective occupational ladders and to progress from there according to individual merit." Nonetheless, growing evidence points in a different direction, suggesting that professionals, like less-skilled immigrants, also cluster in particular niches, establishing concentrations that grow through informal mechanisms and that differentiate newcomers from their native counterparts. Engineering is a case in point. Among engineers, where the foreign-born share rose from 9.4 to 17.5 percent between 1972 and 1982, an emergent pattern of niche creating could be detected, with immigrant engineers overconcentrated in education and private industry in research and development functions.[77]

Herbert A. Strauss stresses that, in order to adjust successfully in the U.S. academy, European Jewish refugee professors had to find academic or scientific niches that were commensurate with their talents and energy.[78] Herman Mark emphasized in his autobiography that it "was a lucky coincidence that I was able to transfer from Germany to the United States a science and technology that was interesting and valuable for my new employer . . . my new and special field of experience [polymers]."[79] Moreover biochemistry also became a niche for émigrés, among them the most talented biochemists of this century; in fact it is an example of a whole discipline that was changed dramatically by the coming of the refugees.[80]

This outcome fits into the general atmosphere at the time. Formal agencies that dealt with the refugees actually had some hope that such developments might or would occur. For example, a memo entitled "Suggestions for Development of the Emergency Committee [for Displaced Scholars] Field Program 1941–42" lists several items under the heading "In General Strengthen These Incentives in Colleges," including

> Desire to help able scholars who are in need. . . .
> Desire to import unusual intellectual or social influences
>   to the campus.
> Desire to supplement or develop offerings in certain departments
>   or to start *new departments.*[81]

It is significant to emphasize that historically in the U.S. academy, apart from a few appointments in Jewish or Semitic studies, Jews aspiring to academic work tended toward subjects that were new, among them biochemistry and polymer research.[82] Thus it is no wonder that the relatively successful adjustment of Jewish chemists was in these specific fields. Moreover Jewish chemists have apparently maintained an unusual rate of success in this niche: statistics regarding religious faculty and their various fields for the year 1971 showed that 20.6 percent of the faculty in the field of biochemistry were Jewish, an interestingly high figure given that Jews in the United States make up only approximately 1.5 percent of the total population.[83]

One theory implicates employer discrimination as a factor in niche development. Discriminating employers stereotype immigrants and either favor or exclude them, because of perceived group characteristics, for certain jobs. In many cases these employer preferences may result from wanting employees of the same ethnicity as customers, thereby catering to the potential prejudices of the consumer. Also some employers may perceive that immigrants or ethnic minorities are willing to work for lower wages. Unfortunately, in many cases, undocumented workers are often hired precisely because they are vulnerable for deportation and therefore easy to exploit.[84]

This theory helps to explain why Jewish refugee chemists received positions in secondary academic status disciplines of that period such as polymer science and earned lower salaries, and why several of them got positions in lower status academic institutions. Thus, in terms of scientific careers, they were in inferior positions. For example, because Herman Mark was in a low status field and could not publish scientific papers, he created the *Journal for Polymer Science:* "We had some difficulty in having certain polymer papers published in the *Journal of the American Chemical Society*. I visited A. A. Noyes to get his advice on the creation of a polymer journal. Noyes was encouraging, although he did not want the ACS (American Chemical Society) to be involved. Then, in 1945, I persuaded M. Dekker and E. Proskauer (both European refugees) to have Interscience Publishers launch *Polymer Bulletin,* containing mostly work carried out at Poly."[85] One can assume that if someone finds it difficult to publish, then it would likewise be difficult to obtain grants for research and to establish status as a scientist.

To conclude, in contrast with the general assumption in the literature on refugee scholars that natural scientists fared well overall and better than scholars in other disciplines, refugee chemists encountered a number of initial difficulties in adjusting. They were able to use a range of different methods to overcome these difficulties: informal networks, niche clustering, and the development of new scientific pursuits and areas served them well. It is interesting to detect connections at the individual level between a particular chemist's age, the relative ease or difficulty of his or her adjustment process, and the quality and quantity of his or her scientific achievements in the United States. In many cases the older and established chemists encountered surprisingly greater difficulty getting used to the new country and greater demands than their younger peers, who slowly but surely advanced in their careers.

Those refugee chemists who came with their highest scientific achievements behind them in Germany had limited power to prove themselves in the new country. This situation was compounded by the relatively poor conditions they encountered in the United States and by their relatively advanced ages. As Chargaff eloquently summarizes: "It would be a great mistake to believe that they [the refugee scientists] were received with open arms in those days. It was not too difficult for the young ones, with little offended pride to swallow; but the more distinguished, the more famous a man was, the greater was the reluctance to welcome him. These poor luminaries had a hard time. Their manners were imperial, their accents ridiculous; their cant was entirely different from the one practiced in the country to which they had come."[86] National pride plays a role here. While one might consider all one thousand plus refugee chemists part of a single group of scientists who had a profound impact on American science, the tendency is to think of two separate groups—the younger chemists who made their scientific discoveries in the United States and the already well-known refugee chemists who came with the discoveries they had previously made in Germany. Achievements of members of the former group, such as Konrad Bloch's Nobel Prize, are recognized as achievements for the United States, while the achievements of the latter group receive recognition on behalf of German or European science. Thus, when one asks who contributed more to U.S. science, the older and established chemists or the young and unknown, one can answer that in the case of the refugee chemists, the ones who were younger and unknown at time of arrival in the United States contributed relatively more.

Without the insanity of Hitler, the refugee Jewish chemists probably would never have immigrated to the United States on their own. But, once they did, they contributed greatly to U.S. science, while their adjustment process was full of personal struggles and achievements. Most of the literature about immigrant physicists produces an optimistic picture of their integration into U.S. science, mainly emphasizing their scientific achievements. However, many chemists, even Nobel prize laureates, encountered adjustment problems, despite their illustrious scientific achievements. Many were rejected by U.S. academic institutes because they were immigrants and Jewish.

Notes

1. Mitchell G. Ash and Alfons Sollner, eds., *Forced Migration and Scientific Change: Émigré German-Speaking Scientists and Scholars after 1933* (Washington, D.C.: Cambridge University Press, 1996), 3–4.

2. Doron Niederland, "The Emigration of Jewish Academics and Professionals from Germany in the First Years of Nazi Rule," *Leo Baeck Institute Year Book* 33 (1988): 291–92.

3. Ute Deichmann. "The Expulsion of Jewish Chemists and Biochemists from Academia in Nazi Germany," *Perspectives on Science* 7, no. 1 (1999): 15.

4. McGeorge Bundy, *Danger and Survival: Choices about the Bomb in the First Fifty Years* (New York: Random House, 1988), 30.

5. P. Thomas Carroll, "Immigrants in American Chemistry," in Jarrell C. Jackman and Carla M. Borden, eds., *The Muses Flee Hitler: Cultural Transfer and Adaptation, 1930–1945* (Washington, D.C.: Smithsonian Institution Press, 1983), 190.

6. Laura Fermi, *Illustrious Immigrants: The Intellectual Migration from Europe, 1930–41* (Chicago: University of Chicago Press, 1971).

7. Donald Fleming and Bernard Bailyn, eds., *The Intellectual Migration: Europe and America, 1930–1960* (Cambridge: Belknap Press of Harvard University Press, 1969).

8. Anthony Heilbut, *Exiled in Paradise: German Refugee Artists and Intellectuals in America from the 1930s to the Present* (New York: Viking, 1983).

9. Tom Ambrose, *Hitler's Loss: What Britain and America Gained from Europe's Cultural Exiles* (London: Peter Owen Publishers, 2001), 179; Niederland,"The Emigration of Jewish Academics," 292.

10. William B. Helmreich, *Against All Odds: Holocaust Survivors and the Successful Lives They Made in America* (New York: Simon & Schuster, 1992), 21, 46.

11. Arieh Tartakower, "The Jewish Refugees: A Sociological Survey," *Jewish Social Studies* 4, no. 4 (1942): 325.

12. Donald Peterson Kent, *The Refugee Intellectual: The Americanization of the Immigrants of 1933–1941*, (New York: Columbia University Press, 1953), 12–13.

13. Niederland, "The Emigration of Jewish Academics," 292.

14. Paul Weindling,"The Impact of German Medical Scientists on British Medicine: A Case Study of Oxford, 1933–45," in Ash and Sollner, eds., *Forced Migration*, 86, 91, 95, 102.

15. James Franck to Simon Flexner, June 6, 1938, Simon Flexner Papers, James Franck file, American Philosophical Society.

16. Alan D. Beyerchen, "Emigration from Country and Discipline: The Journey of a German Physicist into American Photosynthesis Research," in Ash and Sollner, eds., *Forced Migration*, 82; P. K. Hoch, "The Reception of Central European Refugee Physicists of the 1930s: U.S.S.R., U.K., U.S.A.," *Annals of Science* 40 (1983): 241.

17. Daniel J. Kevles, *The Physicists: The History of a Scientific Community in Modern America* (New York: Alfred A. Knopf, 1978), 281.

18. Geoffrey J. Martin, *The Life and Thought of Isaiah Bowman* (Hamden, Conn.: Archon Books, 1980), 125–29. Neil Smith, *American Empire: Roosevelt's Geographer and the Prelude to Globalization* (Los Angeles: University of California Press, 2003), 296, 309–10.

19. Eugene Rabinowitch, "James Franck—1882–1964," 18, James Franck Papers, Box 24; folder 20, Special Collections Research Center, University of Chicago Library, Chicago.

20. "Rumford Premium," *Bulletin of the American Academy of Arts and Sciences*, 8 (March 1955).

21. Rosa Kubin, interview by Michael Tietz, June 1971, tapes 205 and 210, transcript, Oral History Collection of the Research Foundation for Jewish Immigration, New York, 10.

22. Rosa Kubin, "From St. Poelten to America: An Autobiography," Rosa Kubin Collection, Leo Baeck Institute Archives, New York.

23. Hans Mark, letter to the author, December 16, 2003.

24. Herman Mark, interview by James J. Bohning and Jeffrey L. Sturchio at the Polytechnic University, Brooklyn, New York, February 3, March 17, and June 20, 1986, 47–48.

25. Arthur Beiser, interview by Michael Tietz, June 13, 1972, tape 5, transcript, Oral History Collection of the Research Foundation for Jewish Immigration, New York, 5.

26. Max Bergmann to Felix Haurowitz, July 8, 1943, Max Bergmann Papers, American Philosophical Society, Philadelphia.

27. Immanuel Estermann, interview by John L. Heilbron, December 13, 1962, transcript, tape 40a, American Institute of Physics, Center for History of Physics, Maryland, 19–22.

28. Ibid., 20–21.

29. Carl Neuberg to Karl Thomas, December 21, 1949, Carl Neuberg Papers, American Philosophical Society, Philadelphia.

30. Ibid.

31. Carl Neuberg to Israel Strauss, April 5, 1949, Carl Neuberg Papers, American Philosophical Society, Philadelphia.

32. Carl Neuberg to Karl Thomas, December 21, 1949.

33. David Nachmansohn, *German-Jewish Pioneers in Science 1900–1933: Highlights in Atomic Physics, Chemistry and Biochemistry* (New York: Springer-Verlag, 1979), 311–12.

34. Stephen Duggan and Betty Drury, *The Rescue of Science and Learning: The Story of the Emergency Committee in Aid of Displaced Foreign Scholars* (New York: Macmillan, 1948), 193.

35. Stanley Wasserman and Katherine Faust, *Social Network Analysis: Methods and Applications* (New York: Cambridge University Press, 1994), 20.

36. Steven J. Gold, "Migrant Networks: A Summary and Critique of Relational Approaches to International Migration," in Mary Romero and Eric Margolis, eds., *The Blackwell Companion to Social Inequalities* (Malden, Mass.: Blackwell, 2005).

37. Leslie Page Moch, "Networks among Bretons? The Evidence for Paris, 1875–1925," *Continuity and Change* 18, no. 3 (2003): 433.

38. Jean-Baptiste Meyer, "Network Approaches versus Brain Drain: Lessons from the Diaspora," *International Migration* 39, no. 5 (2001): 93–94.

39. Charles Tilly, "Transplanted Networks," in Virginia Yans-McLaughlin, ed., *Immigration Reconsidered: History, Sociology, and Politics* (New York: Oxford University Press, 1990), 84–85.

40. Raymond Breton, "Institutional Completeness of Ethnic Communities and the Personal Relations of Immigrants," in George E. Pozzetta, ed., *Ethnic Communities: Formation and Transformation,* American Immigration and Ethnicity 3 (New York: Garland, 1991), 194.

41. Saskia Sassen-Koob, "Formal and Informal Associations: Dominicans and Colombians in New York," *International Migration Review* 13 (1979): 315.

42. Arthur Beiser, interview by Michael Tietz, June 13, 1972, 7.

43. Leo H. Sternbach, interview by Tonja Koeppel, March 12, 1986, transcript, Beckman Center for the History of Chemistry, Oral History Program, Chemical Heritage Foundation, 19.

44. Julia Flynn, "Father and Son: In Two Generations, Drug Research Sees a Big Shift—Valium's Inventor, Now 95, Relied on His Instincts; Markets, Machines Today—Ban on 'Two-Legged Rats,'" *Wall Street Journal,* February 11, 2004, A1.

45. Ibid.

46. Eugene P. Kennedy, "Hitler's Gift and the Era of Biosynthesis," *Journal of Biological Chemistry* 276, no. 46 (2001): 426–27.

47. Max Bergmann to H. T. Clarke, December 31, 1936, Max Bergmann Papers, American Philosophical Society, Philadelphia.

48. Lore Bloch, interview by Yael Epstein, December 1, 2004, Lexington Boston.

49. Konrad Bloch, "Summing Up," *Annual Review of Biochemistry* 56 (1987): 7.

50. See the folder of correspondence from the Records of the Committee to Aid German Student Refugees, Harvard University Archives, Pusey Library.

51. Bloch, "Summing Up," 12.

52. Eugene P. Kennedy, "Konrad Bloch," *Biographical Memoirs: Proceedings of the American Philosophical Society* 147, no. 1 (2003): 70–71.

53. Alan D. Beyerchen, "Emigration from Country and Discipline: The Journey of a German Physicist into American Photosynthesis Research," in Ash and Sollner, eds., *Forced Migration*, 76, 82.

54. Obituaries, D. Nachmansohn, C. A. Kaiser, Columbia University Record, November 11, 1983, Leo Baeck Institute Archives, New York.

55. A few years ago Heidelberg honored its great citizen by naming a street after him: *Otto Meyerhof Strasse*.

56. Nachmansohn, *German-Jewish Pioneers*, 283–85.

57. David Nachmansohn, Severo Ochoa, and Fritz A. Lipmann, "Otto Meyerhof," in *Biographical Memoirs*, National Academy of Sciences 34 (New York: Columbia University Press, 1960), 155–56, 160.

58. Rudolph Peters, "Otto Meyerhof," in *Obituary Notices of Fellows of the Royal Society* 9 (London: Royal Society, 1954), 184.

59. Nachmansohn, Ochoa, and Lipmann, "Otto Meyerhof," 160.

60. Max Bergmann to William Rosenwald, June 5, 1942, Max Bergmann Papers, American Philosophical Society, Philadelphia.

61. Joan C. Lessing, *Guide to the Oral History Collection of the Research Foundation for Jewish Immigration* (New York: K. G. Saur, 1982), 11.

62. Gabriele Schiff, "'Listen sensitively and act spontaneously—but skillfully': Self-help: An Eyewitness Report," in Sibylle Quack, ed., *Between Sorrow and Strength: Women Refugees of the Nazi Period* (Washington, D.C.: Cambridge University Press, 1995), 185–88.

63. Ute Deichmann, "The Expulsion of Jewish Chemists and Biochemists from Academia in Nazi Germany," *Perspectives on Science* 7, no. 1 (1999): 29.

64. Herman F. Mark to James Franck, January 12, 1948, James Franck Papers, box 1, folder 1, Special Collections Research Center, University of Chicago Library, Chicago.

65. "German Scholars Get Places Here," *New York Times*, January 28, 1934, 22.

66. George Bugliarello, *Towards the Technological University: The Story of the Polytechnic Institute of New York* (New York: Princeton University Press, 1975), 24–27.

67. Hans T. Clarke, "Impressions of an Organic Chemist in Biochemistry," *Annual Review of Biochemistry* 27 (1958): 2.

68. Konrad Bloch, "The Origins of Intermediary Metabolism at Columbia College of Physicians and Surgeons (P&S)," *FASEB Journal* 10 (1996): 802.

69. Clarke, "Impressions of an Organic Chemist in Biochemistry," 4–5.

70. Erwin Chargaff, *Heraclitean Fire: Sketches from a Life before Nature* (New York: Rockefeller University Press, 1978), 68.

71. Ibid., 71.

72. Deichmann, "The Expulsion of Jewish Chemists," 30.

73. Chargaff, *Heraclitean Fire*, 8.

74. Arthur H. Aufses Jr. and Barbara J. Niss, *This House of Noble Deeds: The Mount Sinai Hospital, 1852–2002* (New York: New York University Press, 2002), 1.

75. Edith Rubin, "Coming to the United States," Edith Rubin Collection, Leo Baeck Institute Archives, New York.

76. Bloch, "Summing Up," 8–9.

77. Roger Waldinger, "The Making of an Immigrant Niche," *International Migration Review* 28 (Spring 1994): 3–5.

78. Herbert A. Strauss, "The Immigration and Acculturation of the German Jew in the United States of America," *Leo Baeck Institute Year Book* 16 (1971): 82.

79. Herman F. Mark, *From Small Organic Molecules to Large: A Century of Progress* (Washington, D.C.: American Chemical Society, 1993), 94.

80. Deichmann, "The Expulsion of Jewish Chemists," 28.

81. Gabriele Simon Edgcomb, *From Swastika to Jim Crow: Refugee Scholars at Black Colleges* (Malabar, Fla.: Krieger, 1993), 30–31.

82. Lewis S. Feuer, "Stages in the Social History of Jewish Professors in American Colleges and Universities," *American Jewish History* 71, no. 4 (1982): 433–35.

83. Seymour Martin Lipset and Everett Carll Ladd Jr., "Jewish Academics in the United States: Their Achievements, Culture and Politics," *American Jewish Year Book* 72 (1971): 95.

84. Margaret Hudson, "Modeling the Probability of Niche Employment: Exploring Workforce Segmentation in Metropolitan Atlanta," *Urban Geography* 23, no. 6 (2002): 534–35.

85. Mark, *From Small Organic Molecules to Large*, 127.

86. Chargaff, *Heraclitean Fire*, 76.

David Pickus

At Home with Nietzsche, at War with Germany
Walter Kaufmann and the Struggles of Nietzsche Interpretation

Nietzsche, as much as any other "product" from Europe, is an import to the United States. Yet, while a physical commodity allows a direct assessment of what it does and does not contain, a complex of philosophical ideas held together only by a proper name is considerably more difficult to evaluate. Hence, raising the question of which Nietzsche was imported to the United States and why means focusing on which aspects of his prolific work were defined as central, comparing this exposition to the Nietzsche that was offered for consumption in his native Germany. Putting the matter this way opens interesting perspectives, both in the general history of ideas and, since they played a key role in bringing Nietzsche to the United States, in the study of the fate of central European intellectual émigrés in America. Thus it is problematic that a major and—historically speaking—quite influential work in émigré Nietzsche scholarship, Walter Kaufmann's 1950 *Nietzsche: Philosopher, Psychologist, Antichrist* has not received the examination it deserves.

Kaufmann (1921–80) brought an unusual and interesting background and sensibility to Nietzsche interpretation. Born in Freiburg and raised in Berlin, Kaufmann's education enabled him to combine training in the original sources of German philosophy with a broad knowledge and genuine appreciation of German literature. In addition to the classical training of the *Gymnasiast*, Kaufmann, who was Jewish, also knew some Hebrew. This was an education that most U.S. Nietzsche scholars did not have—and still do not. At the same time, the persecution Kaufmann endured at the hands of the Nazis inadvertently guaranteed that he had a different set of intellectual priorities and attitudes than the typical German philosophy professor did. Escaping to the United States in January 1939, shortly after *Kristallnacht*, Kaufmann was in among the last group of German Jewish refugees to reach the country before the war's outbreak. He abandoned an initial plan to study for the rabbinate, majoring in philosophy instead at Williams College. Though no longer a religious believer, Kaufmann retained an abiding interest in religion. He later wrote that he took every course he could on religion and would have been a religion major had there been such a thing at Williams.[1]

On the surface, this interest of Kaufmann's may appear to hold no relevance for the study of Nietzsche. However, it helps to keep in mind that a great deal of Nietzsche's writing can only be described as speculations about, and exercises in, comparative religion. Kaufmann himself eventually wrote a comparative history of religions.[2] Accordingly he shared with Nietzsche a kind of historical sensibility that is found in several, but hardly all, philosophical commentators on Nietzsche. Given that Nietzsche's aphoristic style places special demands on a commentator's underlying principles of selection, the matter of shared sensibilities is important. Kaufmann thought that his commentary enabled readers to avoid getting lost in the details and to see the challenging vibrancy of Nietzsche as a whole. The final stanza in Kaufmann's poem "Professionals" suggests a disdain for scholarship that is outwardly correct but fails to engage the genuine issues:

> Solid, circumscribed, and
> showing a thorough command
> of all the most recent papers,
> we may not be movers and shapers;
> but if one is only solid
> a teacher, a talker, a scholar
> a colleague without any choler,
> one has a right to be pallid.[3]

All Kaufmann's work, including his own footnote-heavy volume on Nietzsche, was designed to avoid being "pallid."

After Kaufmann was graduated from Williams, he was accepted into the doctoral program in philosophy at Harvard. His decision to write on Nietzsche at a time when, as he put it, Nietzsche was "in eclipse,"[4] illuminates the stubbornly individualistic streak in Kaufmann's personality. In graduate school, and throughout his academic career, Kaufmann wrote on topics and in a manner that differed markedly from the established philosophical "guild." This remained true even after he himself became part of that establishment as a tenured philosophy professor at Princeton.[5] Moreover Kaufmann did not simply play this role but seemed to relish it, maintaining that it was "fun to swim against the current." His Nietzsche volume, reissued in three revised editions in 1956, 1968, and 1974, was the most conventional academic work Kaufmann ever wrote. It contained none of the aphorisms, poems, imaginative dialogues, and photographs with which he filled most of his later books. Nevertheless, the fact that for this book Kaufmann wrote in the same style as most academic philosophers should not lull us into thinking that he understood the self or Nietzsche in the same way as other U.S. scholars writing on Nietzsche. Kaufmann cannot be characterized squarely. He consistently did not fit in.

This outsider identity manifested itself in several ways. First, Kaufmann could not even fit in among the outsiders. Although he was a German intellectual émigré, he did not share some of the more noticeable and salient allegiances of that cohort. He did not suggest that Nazism represented a new and unique evil in history. He did not present himself as coming from a "broken world" and showed no desire to return to Europe. He evinced no affinity with or attraction to Marxism. Yet, unlike Karl Popper, for example, he did not engage in extensive polemics against Marxism either. Finally, though this may not have been his true intention, Kaufmann attracted no school of thought that sprang up around his name.

Of course, it might be tempting to say that the reason Kaufmann did not fit the profile of his older cohorts is that he simply did not belong with them; that he came to the United States when he was too young, and the manner and direction of his thinking was simply not of a piece with the German exiles who were actively writing in the 1920s and 1930s. While there is some validity in thinking that Kaufmann displayed a generational difference of opinion, it is not correct to presume that because he left Germany when he was young, after he completed high school, that his mental outlook was entirely "Americanized." Kaufmann shared the academic refugees' preoccupation with destructiveness and its hidden and unacknowledged sources. Though he did not interpret Hitler and Stalin in quite the same way as older German intellectual émigrés, references to them, as well as to the Holocaust and genocide in general, punctuate his works.[6] In addition the scholars with whom he most took issue and to whom he most responded, as is more easily documented, were German writers of the first half of the twentieth century. In fact, the heart of Kaufmann's work on Nietzsche is an *Auseinandersetzung*—a critical battle—with what had been made of Nietzsche by German scholars in the first four decades of the twentieth century.

Humanity and Treason

Kaufmann dedicated one of his books to the "Millions Murdered in the name of false beliefs by men who proscribed critical reason."[7] He genuinely seemed to think that critical rationality was a—perhaps the—key variable in determining whether humanity lived under freedom or tyranny. To find a parallel to an intellectual of Kaufmann's sort, it is best to return to interwar Europe and look at another embattled writer, Julien Benda. Benda's 1928 *Trahison des Clercs* heaped scorn on thinkers who shirked their task of being "an officiant of abstract justice."[8] Benda considered this weighing and judging to be the central and sacred vocation of intellectuals. Kaufmann had something of "an officiant" in him as well. He had an earnestness and seriousness that suggested that philosophy, done properly, could steer the world for the better. However, his language and allegiances were different. Benda placed Nietzsche in the category of those who had betrayed the intellectual vocation.

Kaufmann, on the other hand, obviously not only liked and admired Nietzsche, but, just as significantly, he thought the problem with German intellectual culture was that Nietzsche was listened to *insufficiently,* rather than too much. A comment Kaufmann made in a 1952 essay, "Jaspers's Relation to Nietzsche," is quite clear on this point. Speaking of what is lost if Nietzsche is prevented by interpreters from displaying his true forcefulness, he wrote, "In the whole history of German letters no other voice has spoken out with such prophetic vigor and withering sarcasm against the very forces which culminated in National Socialism. Neither Lessing and Schiller, nor Goethe and Heine approximated Nietzsche's brilliant indignation or the sustained wit of his scorn of nationalism and state idolatry, as well as militarism and cultural barbarism, and all the other festering vices to which he opposed his ideal of the good European."[9] To be sure, not every interpreter of Nietzsche has understood him in this light. Yet therein lies the crux of the story. By 1950 Kaufmann had worked out an exposition of Nietzsche that in his view rectified the scholarly damage done to Nietzsche. In doing so, he unquestionably imported a particular version of Nietzsche to the United States. Therefore, to understand what Kaufmann was aiming at, we have to clarify more precisely what he was aiming against.

In the opening paragraph, Kaufmann announced his overarching purpose in writing *Nietzsche: Philosopher, Psychologist, Antichrist.* His book "represents an attempt at a *constructive* refutation" of what he called the "Nietzsche legend."[10] Most commentators, including the bulk of English-speaking authors on Nietzsche, have tended to assume that the "legend" refers to the malign influence that Nietzsche's sister, Elizabeth Förster-Nietzsche, had on his reputation as a whole. She was the one who, early on and influentially, bandied the view that Nietzsche was a German militarist, fan of the "blonde beast," and everything else contained in the picture of a proto-Nazi. It is quite true that Kaufmann unleashed a great deal of scholarly thunder against Förster-Nietzsche, and he was not above quoting contemporary sources that cast severe aspersions on her personal character. However, it is important to keep in mind that Kaufmann thought Förster-Nietzsche actively propagated only the more "common version" of the Nietzsche legend.[11]

Thus, while there have been any number of Nietzsche specialists who have maintained that Kaufmann was wrong to see this "brutality-advocating" Nietzsche as a legend, it should be acknowledged that Förster-Nietzsche was not Kaufmann's primary target. As he saw it, the truly misleading exponents of the Nietzsche legend were other, much more established scholars. Whatever damage Förster-Nietzsche did or did not do, something she did without quite intending was much more fateful for Nietzsche's subsequent reception. In Kaufmann's opinion Förster-Nietzsche "unwittingly laid the foundation for the myth that Nietzsche's thought is hopelessly incoherent, ambiguous, and self-contradictory."[12] *This* is the legend

160   David Pickus

that Kaufmann spent most of his time and intellectual energies "constructively refuting." To progress in understanding him, we have to look at more famous and deep figures, ones whom Kaufmann understood to propagate a Nietzsche who simply was not Nietzsche.

Going in Circles

Kaufmann's most revealing comment in clarifying the purpose of his Nietzsche volume concerns not the Nietzsche legend itself, but the way this legend was enmeshed within the broader context of German intellectual life. He wrote, "The growth of the Nietzsche legend in Germany is so inextricably involved in, and so symptomatic of the development of German thought during the last decades that no summary account may seem possible. A study of 'Nietzsche; The History of his Fame,' or 'Nietzsche in the Twentieth Century' might grow into a cultural history of twentieth-century Germany focused in a single, but particularly revealing, perspective."[13] There is no reason to believe that Kaufmann did not mean exactly what he said about Nietzsche being a mirror reflecting modern Germany's cultural history. The implications of this claim can be summed up directly: in importing his version of Nietzsche to the United States, Kaufmann was also importing his own commentary on Germany's recent cultural history.

Grasping this commentary requires a bit of exposition, not only because Kaufmann wrote in such a way that deflected sustained focus on his own intentions, but also because cultural history travels by ways unfamiliar to most U.S. readers. For instance, though Kaufmann highlighted this point, very few U.S. Nietzsche scholars have taken up, even if only to refute, Kaufmann's highlighted claim that it was the attitude of the poet Stefan George (1868–1933) and his circle that was greatly responsible for blunting Nietzsche's message and propounding the legend of a not fully coherent Nietzsche. To a certain extent this neglect of George by Nietzsche scholars makes sense, since today George is read by only a small number of literary specialists. However, as Robert E. Norton, a recent biographer of George reminds us, George was once extremely well-known. He was even labeled "the most powerful man in the world."[14] Kaufmann himself certainly did not need to be reminded of what a powerful presence George was, particularly in the years surrounding the First World War. His argument is not so much about poetry as it is about cultural politics.

George wrote two well-known poems on Nietzsche.[15] Quoting almost completely from them, Kaufmann sought to demonstrate that Nietzsche was distorted in the very moment that he was celebrated and honored. While the language and conceits of George's poems are elaborate and involved, the key point for Kaufmann was a matter that could be summarized bluntly. It was, in Kaufmann's words, that Nietzsche was depicted as "the incarnate repudiation of modern vulgarity—a prophet driven insane by the blindness and deafness of his contemporaries."[16] From this perspective Kaufmann concluded that what was most significant for George was the fact that "Nietzsche's philosophic endeavors had been essentially futile: what was needed was the creation of a small *Kreis* as a nucleus for future regeneration." Indeed it is striking that both poems impute great honor to Nietzsche, as the "thunderer" and as the "warner," but do not make any mention of the content of his thought. Most central to the poems is the dramatic image of someone isolated from, yet elevated above, what George called "the idiotically trotting crowd." In the first poem, this Nietzsche occupied a barren and icy landscape and then died ("ging aus langer nacht zur längsten nacht") without really being acknowledged or heard. Kaufmann wanted his readers to understand this point because it paved the way for apprehending his main criticism: that George had refashioned Nietzsche in his own image.

A short look at George's overall attitude toward Nietzsche lends strong support for Kaufmann's conclusions. Essentially George could praise only his refashioned Nietzsche because he *did not really like* the Nietzsche he saw. George's reasons for wishing to remake Nietzsche are idiosyncratic in that they revolve around his overarching commitment to the centrality of the master-disciple relation. He could not forgive Nietzsche for having broken with Wagner. This has nothing to do with a predilection for Wagner himself. Robert E. Norton quoted George as having said,"Do you really think I would speak on behalf of that bad actor and his Valhalla swindle? This is about something else. Wagner . . . honestly took up the fight against the nineteenth century in his youth, and Nietzsche was his companion. And Wagner was Nietzsche's master! No, no—Nietzsche betrayed Wagner."[17] This sentiment was no passing fancy with George. He began another poem in one of his major works, the *Stern des Bundes,* with the words, "Who once circled the flame / Remain satellite to the flame!"[18] ("Wer je die flamme umschritt / Bleibe der flamme trabant!") Summing up George's general stance, Norton concluded that "this very reaction to Nietzsche's ostensible disloyalty . . . underscores again the degree to which George understood other people, including Nietzsche, through the prism of his own life and experience, judging them by how they measured up to—or more often fell far short of—the image he had of himself."[19] This explains more fully why Kaufmann saw George as a model for a writer who projected his own needs into his image of Nietzsche, sacrificing significant degrees of accuracy and proportion in the process.

Of course, for a philosophically minded reader there is a perhaps understandable tendency to skim over long discussions of poems and poets. However, there is no reason to assume that Kaufmann thought of the time he devoted to George as marginal. Rather the point he made about George signified where Kaufmann would draw the line and then dissent from the Nietzsche image that had come before his. It was not in seeing Nietzsche as an isolated figure standing against a crowd. In that respect he was sympathetic to George. Nor was Kaufmann utterly averse to seeing Nietzsche as one who is "sharp as lightning and steel."[20] Instead the difference lay in the way Nietzsche was placed in an alternate critical tradition. For Kaufmann, Nietzsche was fundamentally concerned with the health of modern civilization and the traditional virtues the individual could revive to cure it. Kaufman maintained that Nietzsche had never tried to invent new virtues and that those who think he had "have to rely on their imagination"[21] to produce them. Instead the virtues that Nietzsche praises are "honesty, courage—especially moral courage—generosity, politeness, and intellectual integrity."[22] Thus the task of the commentator on Nietzsche—Kaufmann's own task—is to demonstrate how Nietzsche's development, philosophical method, and cultural critique add up to a renewed and more forceful call for an application of these old virtues.

George, on the other hand, did not think much of this mode of interpreting and applying Nietzsche. In his first poem he speaks contemptuously of the "creatures" (*getier*) who fatten on the fumes that helped to strangle Nietzsche. Once this passes—presumably when pundits on him fade into irrelevance—"then you will stand, shining before the ages / like other leaders with the bloody crown." ("Dann aber stehst du strahlend vor den zeiten / Wie andere führer mit der blutigen krone.") In short Nietzsche is for George what he openly calls him: "Redeemer thou!" ("Erlöser du!"). He comes to herald a new epoch and at the same time sweep up those initiated in something beyond themselves, something leaving behind the drabness of the normal. It was not only poets who thought this way about Nietzsche. Naturally most scholars did not express themselves in George's elevated poetic language. However, the image of Nietzsche as herald and hero was quite dominant in Germany in the first half of the twentieth century; just as the tendency to blur the contours of the critical, skeptically philosophical Nietzsche in order to heighten this very image of him was common. To find out what Kaufmann objected to in this, we must investigate his charge that the typical scholarly method whereby Nietzsche was studied only served to distort the coherence of Nietzsche's moral and psychological claims.

Sane If Perhaps Dull Views

As Kaufmann saw it, Nietzsche was the philosopher of the "Good Life," which was nothing other than, "the powerful life, the life of those who are in full control of their impulses and need not weaken them, *and the good man is for Nietzsche the passionate man who is master of his passions.*"[23] The key to this mastery is "sublimation," a concept that Kaufmann claims plays the same central role that *Aufhebung* played in Hegel's philosophy. To a large degree, this conception has not been taken up in Nietzsche scholarship, and affinities between Hegel and Nietzsche are not emphasized to any great degree in most U.S. works.[24] Thus Kaufmann stands out in his insistence that Nietzsche's entire philosophy reaches a kind of moral apex in the insight that power is not to be desired for its own sake, but that "great power reveals itself in great self-mastery."[25] To any number of subsequent commentators, such a soft conclusion has been ascribed to Kaufmann's simple unwillingness to concede that he himself was doing what he lambasted others for, that is, reading his own ideas into Nietzsche. Furthermore the value of what Kaufmann considered centrally important in Nietzsche tended to be greeted with little or no enthusiastic echo in the literature. Thus Arthur C. Danto, in his 1965 *Nietzsche as Philosopher*, summed up the whole issue in less than a sentence, saying that Nietzsche "held the basically sane if perhaps dull view that the passions and drives of men be disciplined and guided by reason."[26] Danto then moved on to talk about any number of, to him, more interesting subjects in Nietzsche.

This is a thorny matter. Nietzsche was a complex and not always consistent writer. Pointing out that one scholar had a different emphasis than did Kaufmann does not in itself prove anything. Likewise the failure of Kaufmann's key points to find much in the way of resonance also does not mean that he distorted Nietzsche. Scholarship should not rely on this sort of consensus, which is nothing more than public opinion. Rather the point to keep in mind is that Kaufmann was a particular kind of intellectual émigré, one who—metaphorically speaking—brought two things in his suitcase. They were a strong sense of how evil masked itself in intellectual opacity and how wretched it was if great power did not reveal itself in great self-mastery. These two sentiments combined in an equally aroused conviction that it is damaging when any of Nietzsche's moral insights about the responsibility of the individual are relegated to a suburgent degree of importance.

However, one must turn back to pre–World War II Germany and to see the exposition to which Kaufmann was responding. A good place to begin is with Karl Joël, professor at Basel and, according to Kaufmann, friend of Stefan George. In 1905 Joël published an early monograph, *Nietzsche und die Romantik*.[27] Although only the first section of the book deals with the relationship between Nietzsche and romanticism, the significance lies in the fact that—as Steven E. Aschheim put it— Joël's book shaped "portentously if unwittingly the great Nietzschean themes that became enmeshed in the transformed right-winged politics of the future and in the unlimited profanity that was World War I."[28] In particular Joël "prefigured many of the Nietzschean and Romantic themes that the radical right would later stress: the disregard for systems and the emphasis on dynamic movement; the attempt to fuse will and feeling; the praise of passion over reason, and, above all, the stress on 'living dangerously' and 'overcoming.'"[29] Aschheim is right to note that Nietzsche was read this way (and by more than just right-wing thinkers, too). What intellectual method was used to understand Nietzsche in this fashion, and why was such a mode of procedure not regarded as a distortion? Indeed Kaufmann's claim that Nietzsche was obscured by a myth depends on his capacity to unmask the scholarly methods used by writers such as Joël as illegitimate.

Joël's fundamental argument about Nietzsche and romanticism was that "a link must exist between those who so strongly affect the modern soul; from the same

Zeitgeist are taken up as models of disposition [Stimmungsvorbilder]."[30] To show that there is such a link, Joël devoted the first half of his essay to demonstrating the lack of affinities between Nietzsche and romantics. Then in the second and what is meant to be the more conclusive half, he sought to show that such ostensible contradictions were resolved in a higher unity. To demonstrate this point, Joël assembled a large number of quotations from both Nietzsche and the romantics. These were used without any mention of the context in which they appeared and without any discussion of whether a similar word or concept could be understood by different writers in different ways. The consequence of this unrigorous method is that Joël could claim that both Nietzsche and romanticism are one. The language he used in showing this is evocative and imprecise enough to warrant comment. Nietzsche and romanticism are one "in that orgiastic drive that out of excess of love devours; [one] that honors its god in the highest in that it lacerates him [*in dem er ihm zerrisst*]."[31] In other words Nietzsche's notion of the death of God is rendered indistinguishable from the romantic religiosity of figures such as Novalis. And what is true in this case holds for any number of specific ideas that were important to Nietzsche. They all were amalgamated to snippets of quotes from the romantics. In doing so, Joël's book suggests on a scholarly plane what George proposed poetically, namely that Nietzsche is more to be valued for energy, conviction, and what he represents, rather than the specific content of these convictions themselves.

The practice of seeing Nietzsche this way, and of linking his life and works to a romantic striving, was quite common in Germany. Even Thomas Mann, who certainly thought carefully about Nietzsche, was willing to claim that, "in respect to his spiritual origins," Nietzsche "was a late son of romanticism."[32] Against all this, Kaufmann wrote, "Parallels between Nietzsche and the German romantics can of course be found, and it is also possible to define the notoriously equivocal word 'romantic' in a sense which would permit its application to Nietzsche; but, especially where no precise definition is given, any interpretation of Nietzsche as the typical representative or the late son of a movement which he consistently opposed seems, to say the least, highly misleading."[33]

The issue goes beyond the particular question of Nietzsche and romanticism. It is possible to read Nietzsche in an entirely different way than Joël did and still employ the same distorting method that he did. This is because what is at issue is not any parallel between Nietzsche and an intellectual movement, but rather the fact that Joël felt that Nietzsche's ideas could not really be absorbed on their own. They would have to be cut with an admixture of others. Joël felt strongly about this subject, and he justified his project when he wrote of Nietzsche:

> Wie ein zürnender Gott steht er vor den Menschen; nicht ungestraft nahen sie seinem Angesichte; denn er setzt alle in Flammen, macht alle erschauern

in Entzücken oder Entsetzen; blendender Glanz strahlt aus seinem Auge, doch von seinem Kampfesschild grinst ein Medusenhaupt.[34]

(Like a furious God he stands before humanity. Not unpunished do they approach his countenance. For he sets all in flames; makes all onlookers shiver in delight or outrage. Blinding brilliance flashes from his eyes. But from his battle shield grins a Medusa head.)

Presumably Joël does not want his reader to take this description literally, but to understand that people run serious risks in reading Nietzsche. Nietzsche's work will either intoxicate or infuriate and hence cannot be taken as is. Note that Joël did not state that Nietzsche advocated specific ideas that he or others may find extreme, and he did not seek to assess and distinguish what is solid from what is not. In his view, "Nietzsche ist weit, weit in die Fremde gewandert, fern von der übrigen Menscheit" (Nietzsche has wandered far, far into the unknown; far from the rest of humanity).[35] Thus the only proper stance toward Nietzsche is, as Joël puts it, to approach him sideways and assimilate his thought to someone else's. The justification Joël gives for this attitude toward Nietzsche is quite revealing. He says that "wir wollen ihn und uns von seiner verwirrenden Einseitigkeit erlösen" (we want to save him and us from his perplexing one-sidedness).[36] In other words, when it comes to expositing his ideas, Nietzsche has to be saved from himself.

Kaufmann fought against this idea most strenuously in his Nietzsche work. Any attempt to deflect attention away from Nietzsche's overarching conception of power, and the good life that "true" holders of power possess, was for Kaufmann a betrayal of scholarly vocation. He concluded his study by reaffirming that Nietzsche "addressed himself primarily to the few—as an educator."[37] Throughout the study he argued that this education revolves around working on oneself and giving style to one's character. Indeed, even the eternal recurrence—the most metaphysical of Nietzsche's theories—is for Kaufmann a psychological insight into the nature of self-cultivation. Kaufmann proposed that "the thought came to Nietzsche that the man who perfects himself and transfigures his *physis* achieves that happiness toward which all men grope, and feels a supreme joy which obviates any concern with the 'justification' of the world." Kaufmann elaborated that "the man who experiences this joy is the powerful man—and instead of relying on heavenly powers to redeem him, to give meaning to his life, and to justify the world, he gives meaning to his own life by achieving perfection and exulting in every moment."[38]

The obvious philosophical question that arises is whether Nietzsche's philosophy does indeed culminate in the principles that Kaufmann claims they do. This question can and should be debated by Nietzsche interpreters. Yet what is of moment here is that Kaufmann's questions simply cannot be raised if Nietzsche is seen through the eyes of writers such as George and Joël. Furthermore, and this is of central importance, though George and Joël may have been eccentric in their own respects, they were not alone in seeing Nietzsche as standing for something that he himself did not clearly advocate. The final point that needs discussion is the fact that, in the first half of the twentieth century, the amalgamation of Nietzsche to uncongenial ideals was typical in German writing on him. It is this "distortion's spirit" that Kaufmann combated. To get a true sense of what he imported to the United States, we have to understand how widespread his "enemy" was.

Misdiagnosed Homesickness

The predominant view of Kaufmann's work is best summed up in a comment by Keith Ansell-Pearson. He wrote that "Kaufmann's book succeeded in rehabilitating Nietzsche after the abuse his principal ideas suffered at the hands of the Nazis, but is perhaps guilty of interpreting Nietzsche too much as a humanist."[39] Though Kaufmann sharply opposed the Nazi appropriation of Nietzsche to their own ends, it is misleading to think that Kaufmann wrote his "constructive refutation" with only the Nazis in mind. It is also a bit unhistorical to use *humanism* as a mild term of disparagement since it requires some clarification of the antihuman trends that Kaufmann wished to oppose. As it is, it seems to suggest a Nietzsche who is made to sound more uplifting and edifying than he actually was. Whatever truth there is in that notion, it should be seen in the context of a widespread and grandiose German scholarly stance toward Nietzsche. Nietzsche for these writers was not someone who made specific claims that were to be examined normally. He was rather a phenomenon whose writings were to be treated as part of an earth-shaking effort. In 1918 Ernst Bertram, another George disciple, described Nietzsche as "the last and greatest heir of all of those who are of the clan of devilish spite—but a spite that is enigmatically mixed and almost identical with divine homesickness [*götlliche(m) Heimweh*]. . . . He is heir and destiny-brother not only of all whose generation not only strives in Goethean fashion [goethisch] from darkness to light, but which, in turn, a deep distress drives out of the light, the all-too-illuminated, into darkness into uncertainty."[40] This view of Nietzsche—that his statements take us away from clarity in the very moment that they move us toward it—was not only held by initiates of the George school, it was also held by Martin Heidegger, albeit in a different manner.

In 1943 Martin Heidegger wrote an essay, "Nietzsche's Word: God Is Dead," subsequently published in a 1950 anthology, *Holzwege*.[41] Kaufmann knew this work, and referred to it in the bibliography of the first edition of his monograph. Heidegger's sixty-page piece is an extended commentary on the well-known aphorism "The Madman" in the third book of *The Gay Science*. This is the aphorism in which a madman tells an uncomprehending crowd that the reason he seeks but cannot find God is that He is dead. He has been killed by this same sort of crowd, even though they know it not. Like everything else that Heidegger wrote, the argument advanced to explain this particular passage is part of a far-flung philosophical project, one that cannot be summarized with any ease.[42] The important thing is to note the ways that Heidegger's treatment of Nietzsche expressed the drawbacks that Kaufmann already found prevalent in German Nietzsche interpretation. Although twisting and turning, Heidegger's basic argument is identifiable. It is that Nietzsche has done something quite valuable in helping us reach the point where we can understand that nihilism should not be comprehended as something revealed by an analysis of "the spiritual situation of the age."[43] Rather, in ways so prevalent we do not experience it, nihilism is a "historical movement which is already of long duration and whose essential ground lies in metaphysics itself."[44] Nietzsche is thus valuable because he "thinks of nihilism as the 'inner logic' of western history."[45] Heidegger then goes on to consider whether Nietzsche grasps the full implications of his own insight, eventually deciding that "Nietzsche never recognized the *essence* of nihilism, like every other metaphysics before him."[46] Heidegger's conclusions should be held to some sort of scrutiny. However, it is a bit unfair to Heidegger to cast aspersions on the validity of his case without going into the actual details of his argument. Nevertheless it is reasonable to ask what sort of Nietzsche reading Heidegger's case entails and what kinds it excludes. What stands out is that Heidegger's concerns cannot be made to fit with the Nietzsche whom Kaufmann presents, and vice versa.

In particular Kaufmann wanted the parable about the death of God to be read within the context of the surrounding aphorisms. These revolve around the phenomenon of secularism, and the impossibility of maintaining a "cozy" anthropocentric view of the cosmos once the unquestioned belief in the traditional creator God had either been dropped or allowed to atrophy. At the end of aphorism 123 Nietzsche noted that "it is something new in history that knowledge wants to be more than a mere means,"[47] meaning that an unleashed *Wissensdrang* will not stop short of any time-honored moral value solely because it would make humanity uncomfortable to lose it. This set the stage for the madman's claim in aphorism 125 that the crowd simply does not understand that their own assumptions "kill" God. Thus, when it came time to provide his own answer as to whether Nietzsche helped overcome nihilism or contributed to it, Kaufmann answered that "perhaps the most precise answer to this question is to be found in a line from Zarathustra: 'what is falling, that one should also push.' Nietzsche is not speaking of 'mercy' killings of the crippled and insane, but of all values that have become hollow, all creeds out of which the faith is gone, and all that is professed only by hypocrites."[48] Furthermore, to ensure that no one takes this point in too abstract or too general a fashion, Kaufmann reminded readers of Nietzsche's identification of "the philosopher as doctor—surgeon,"[49] adding that "the health of our civilization appeared to him to be severely threatened: it looked impressively good, but seemed to Nietzsche to be thoroughly undermined—a diagnosis which, though trite today was perhaps no mean feat in the eighteen eighties."[50]

Here is where the contrast with Heidegger becomes fully apparent. As is well known, Heidegger also fiercely opposed the inauthenticity and chatter of his age. However, the denunciation of hypocrisies that so earned Kaufmann's praise is precisely what Heidegger found suspect in Nietzsche. Like George, albeit much more openly, Heidegger did not really approve of the critical project he saw in Nietzsche. At the start of his piece he asserted that Nietzsche understand his philosophy as a countermovement against Platonism. Heidegger then explained that such a philosophy was necessarily at odds with itself: "As a mere countermovement, however, it—like everything anti—necessarily remains arrested in the essence of what it tackles. Nietzsche's countermovement against metaphysics is, as the mere turning about of this, the exitless ensnarement in metaphysics; so [much] indeed, that it unties itself from its own essence, and as metaphysics never is able to think its own essence."[51]

The details involved here require more explication, but the passage's basic gist is that something about Nietzsche's philosophical stance prevented him from understanding something he needed to understand. As usual with Heidegger, the exact meaning of this missing essence remains a bit out of reach. Nevertheless two pregnant comments made at the very end of the essay give a strong hint of Heidegger's general drift. He claims that it is unequivocal according to the first sentence—and even more unequivocal "for those capable of hearing" according to the last sentences—that the madman is the one who "seeks God in that he cries after God."[52] Heidegger asked whether this is not a cry *de profundis*. He implied the answer is yes, and he concluded by stating that "thinking first begins when we have come to know that the reason glorified for centuries is the most hard-necked adversary (*Widersacherin*) of thinking."[53]

Given that Heidegger took a stand against reason, it is clear that the only value he could see in Nietzsche's word was that it helped illuminate the nature of this adversary. This is a Nietzsche very much in the mold described by Bertram, one who takes us from darkness to light and then back again into a profounder darkness. For Heidegger this was the realm of a certain kind of religiosity and prerational thinking. Here is where we see the similarity in Heidegger's treatment of Nietzsche with other pre–World War II German writers. It is not Heidegger's idiosyncratic view of the place of metaphysics in Nietzsche's thought. Rather it is the submerged disdain for the specifics of Nietzsche's strictures—particularly the rational, secular, and individualistic aspect of Nietzsche that is most squarely within the Enlightenment tradition—combined with an overall endorsement of something less precise that Nietzsche represents, something that makes Nietzsche a line of demarcation between fundamental opposing camps.

For Kaufmann to refute this appropriation of Nietzsche, he needed to do exactly what he did in his monograph: streamline Nietzsche's voluminous writings into a single, overarching argument, one stressing self-cultivation and critical rationality. Kaufmann could not stand the suggestion that Nietzsche led one away from the rigorous task of self-clarity. In later editions of his Nietzsche volume, Kaufmann was taking explicit aim at Heidegger's claim that reason is the "adversary of thinking." Quoting this point from Heidegger, he immediately added as a counterblast aphorism two from *The Gay Science*, which begins, "what is good-heartedness, refinement and genius to me, which the human being who has these virtues tolerates slack feelings in faith and judgments."[54] Of course, given the protean nature of Nietzsche's extensive writings, it will always be possible to find passages there that go against the grain of Kaufmann's exposition. Yet it is striking how little of the Nietzsche scholarship that came before him stressed rigor in faith and judgments.

For philosophical issues raised by Kaufmann to be investigated in more depth, a fuller understanding is needed of the cultural context in which Nietzsche became a phenomenon stripped of his critical, enlightened overtones. Given that in 1924 even Thomas Mann could call Nietzsche a *"Führer in die Zukunft"* without making it very clear how Nietzsche was a leader or what sort of future he was leading Germany toward, one can sympathize with Kaufmann's earnestness and urgency.[55] Whatever one thinks of the interpretation Kaufmann produced, his core concern was that Nietzsche's message not be misused by a malfunctioning republic of letters. And if it was too late for Germany, it might not be too late for the United States. It was this horizon that Kaufmann brought with him as an intellectual refugee.

Conclusion: Is That All There Is?

The literature on Nietzsche is enormous. Even if one were to give some credence to the claim that George and Joël, Bertram, Heidegger, and Mann all reveal a disturbing tendency to blunt the sharpness of Nietzsche's insights, there is no reason to conclude—on that basis alone—that Kaufmann provided the necessary antidote to misleading pictures of Nietzsche. Clearly such a vast topic as "who reads Nietzsche better?" cannot be settled in one blow. What can be assessed is the question raised at the start: do we grasp the Nietzsche whom Kaufmann imported to the United States? We cannot do this unless we acknowledge that Kaufmann identified something truly worthy of concern: another kind of betrayal of intellectuals. It was not simply Nazi hacks that played fast and loose with Nietzsche. There was indeed a pervasive disfigurement of Nietzsche within German letters, one that mirrored a wider absence of critical spirit in the society at large. Kaufmann's view from the United States passed judgment on a world he left behind. In a section of his *The Faith of a Heretic*, "The Quest for Honesty," Kaufmann wrote that "the practice of seizing on a label, instead of considering a man's ideas is common, if often unconscious."[56] What he tried to do in the work that first established him in academia was to show that so much of what was previously presented as engaging with Nietzsche's ideas was actually seizing upon a label, and a label inimical to Nietzsche at that.

Was Kaufmann heard in any of this and do his concerns matter any more? If Nietzsche were no longer an object of abiding interest, the answer would probably be no. However, given Nietzsche's continued importance in intellectual life in the United States, Kaufmann's stance toward Nietzsche reveals not only the concerns of his specific environment, but serves as a touchstone for seeing what is and is not considered "living" in Nietzsche. From this perspective a provocative conclusion emerges, one that hopefully will spark further discussion and debate. In 1968, in the preface to the third edition of his monograph, Kaufmann wrote, "the subtitle of my book still seems right to me. Nietzsche was a philosopher above all, but not only that; he was also a psychologist; and he defined his own significance very largely in terms of his opposition to Christianity."[57] This statement is more challenging than the matter-of-fact way of putting it makes it seem. As Kaufmann defined it, Nietzsche's psychology revolved around dissecting our motivations, and the degree of power they do or do not express. Likewise, opposition to Christianity was understood by Kaufmann to mean Nietzsche's advocacy of a more honest way of living and realizing value. What stands out in comparing him to the writers on Nietzsche that he criticizes is how much they disliked the Nietzsche that Kaufmann admired. Their Nietzsche was not one that compelled any introspection, nor was it one that called for a more *honest* alternative to Christianity. Fashions change, and it is unlikely that U.S. commentators will speak about Nietzsche the exact same way that German authors did in 1909, 1919, or 1939. Still styles can change and underlying affinities remain the same. For this reason it is worth asking if the trends Kaufmann combated continue in different forms. If so, the fruits of his particular exile have yet to be gathered.

George's Poem on Nietzsche and a Modified Version of Kaufmann's Translation

Translating this poem offers enormous opportunities to make errors, and criticism and correction is welcome. The poem appears here because it is not that easily accessible in English. Given the difficulty of translation, it is interesting to see how versions differ. Beyond that, the poem is quite interesting in its own right. It has a kind of evocative power, even if one disagrees strongly with the Nietzsche image it presents. Kaufmann also translated the complete poem, for inclusion in his *Twenty German Poets* (1962), but his version includes puzzling nonliteral choices. For instance, he wrote "destroyed" when George used the verb for "killed." Still, most of the passages and the basic structure of the translation given here are his, with some modification of his "heavy lifting."

The goal was to capture exactly what George said while still conveying the fact that George made each line stand on its own, though most of them have to be read in conjunction with each other. Any unclear parts of the translation reflect the current effort to reproduce this. The poem's setting and meaning are interpreted here to be the reflections of someone contemplating the house where the insane Nietzsche spent his last years. This leads to a series of reflections on Nietzsche himself. One of them deserves comment. It is that Nietzsche was not pleased with the outcome of his work. This is strikingly at odds with many of Nietzsche's own statements. In addition it is interesting to speculate on how George wanted the intentions of "one who came too late" to be understood.

Nietzsche
Schwergelbe wolken ziehen überm hügel
Und kühle stürme—halb des herbstes boten
Halb frühen frühlings . . . Also diese mauer
Umschloss den Donnerer—ihn der einzig war
Von tausenden aus rauch und staub um ihn?
Hier sandte er auf flaches mittelland
Und tote stadt die letzten stumpfen blitze
Und ging aus langer nacht zur längsten nacht.
Blöd trabt die menge drunten scheucht sie nicht!
Was wäre stich der qualle schnitt dem kraut!
Noch eine weile walte fromme stille
Und das getier das ihn mit lob befleckt
Und sich im moderdunste weiter mästet
Der ihn erwürgen half sei erst verendet!
Dann aber stehst du strahlend vor den zeiten
Wie andre führer mit der blutigen krone.
Erlöser du! selbst der unseligste—
Beladen mit der wucht von welchen losen
Hast du der sehnsucht land nie lächeln sehn?
Erschufst du götter nur um sie zu stürzen
Nie einer rast und eines baues froh?
Du hast das nächste in dir selbst getötet
Um neu begehrend dann ihm nachzuzittern
Und aufzuschrein im schmerz der einsamkeit.
Der kam zu spät der flehend zu dir sagte:
Dort ist kein weg mehr über eisige felsen
Und horste grauser vögel—nun ist not:
Sich bannen in den kreis den liebe schliesst . . .
Und wenn die strenge und gequälte stimme
Dann wie ein loblied tönt in blaue nacht

Und helle flut—so klagt: sie hätte singen
Nicht reden sollen diese neue seele!

(Heavy yellow clouds float over the hill
And chill storms—half envoys of the spring
Half early spring . . . so this wall
Enclosed the thunderer—him that was unique
Out of thousands from smoke and dust around him?
Here he sent on flat middle land
And dead city the last dull lightings
And went from long night to the longest night.
Idiotically trots the crowd down—there do not spook them
What would be a stab to the jelly-fish—cut to the weed
Yet a while reign pious silence
And the vermin that bespotted him with praise
And still fatten themselves in musty fumes
That helped to strangle him are first done with!
Then, however, you stand shining before the ages
Like other leaders with the bloody crown.
Redeemer thou! Yourself the most unblessed
Burdened with the weight of what destinies
Have you never smiling seen the land of longing?
You created gods only to topple them
Never happy in a rest or a construct?
You have killed the closest in yourself
To then tremble after it newly desiring
And to scream out in the pain of loneliness.
He came too late that said imploringly to you:
There is no way left over icy cliffs
And aeries of dreadful birds—now this is needed:
To banish oneself in the circle closed by love
And when the austere and tormented voice
Then sounds like a song of praise in blue night
And bright flood—lament: it should have sung
Not spoken this new soul

Notes

    1. This information is taken from *Faith of a Heretic* (Garden City, N.Y.: Doubleday, 1961), 3–8.

    2. See Kaufmann's *Religions in Four Dimensions* (New York: Reader's Digest Press, 1976).

    3. "Professionals," in Walter Arnold Kaufmann, *Cain and Other Poems,* 2nd ed. (New York: Vintage Books, 1971), 72.

4. This is from the preface to the fourth edition (1974) of Kaufmann's *Nietzsche*, Kaufmann, *Nietzsche: Philosopher, Psychologist, Antichrist* (Princeton: Princeton University Press, 1950).

5. He remained in the Princeton philosophy department until his death in 1980. The primary bent of the department from the 1950s through the 1970s was toward analytic philosophy. Here too Kaufmann relished his role as "odd man out." See his critical treatment on analytic philosophy and logical positivism in his *Critique of Religion and Philosophy* (London: Faber & Faber, 1959; New York: Doubleday, 1961).

6. Peter Novick in *The Holocaust in American Life* (Boston: Houghton Mifflin, 1999) has put forth the thesis that consciousness of the Holocaust did not really sink in until the late 1960s. As valuable as this reminder of the changes in historical emphasis may be, it is important to keep in mind that the fact that Kaufmann did not speak about the Holocaust at length, or in graphic detail, does not mean that he regarded it as less than central. The important point is the direct link between what he said about totalitarianism and the key themes of his books.

7. This is the dedication to *From Shakespeare to Existentialism* (Boston: Beacon Press, 1959).

8. Benda's 1928 *Trahison des Clercs* translated by Richard Aldington as *The Treason of the Intellectuals* (New York: W.W. Norton, 1969), 51. For a study of Benda both as an independent thinker and a Jew, see Louis-Albert Revah's *Julien Benda: Un Misanthrope Juif dans la Fance de Maurras* (Paris: Plon, 1991).

9. This 1952 essay appeared in Paul Arthur Schilpp, ed., *The Philosophy of Karl Jaspers* (New York: Tudor Publishing, 1957), 426.

10. Kaufmann, *Nietzsche*, 3. Unless noted, all references are to the first (1950) edition.

11. Ibid., 7. A fuller account of Elizabeth Förster-Nietzsche's role in the misreading of Nietzsche is found in Carol Diethe's *Nietzsche's Sister and the Will to Power: A Biography of Elisabeth Förster-Nietzsche* (Urbana: University of Illinois Press, 2003).

12. Kaufmann, *Nietzsche*, 7.

13. Ibid., 8.

14. Robert E. Norton, *Secret Germany: Stefan George and His Circle* (Ithaca and London: Cornell University Press), 2002. The point about his world fame is made on the first page of Norton's preface.

15. The first and longer poem, along with a translation and a short commentary, appears in the appendix.

16. Kaufmann, *Nietzsche*, 9.

17. Norton, *Secret Germany*, 236.

18. This is quoted in Kaufmann's *Twenty German Poets: A Bilingual Collection* (New York: Modern Library, 1962), 169. It should be noted that George did not follow the standard German rules for capitalizing nouns. All quotations from him are as written.

19. Norton, *Secret Germany*, 589.

20. This is from the second poem, where Nietzsche is described as "scharf wie blitz und stahl" (sharp as lightning and steel).

21. Kaufmann, *Nietzsche*, 88.

22. Ibid.

23. Ibid., 246.

24. This is not to say that no connections between Hegel and Nietzsche have been drawn. From Karl Löwith onward, there have been several efforts to examine the similarity of trope and themes between the two thinkers. For a recent volume, see Will Dudley, *Hegel, Nietzsche and Philosophy: Thinking Freedom* (Cambridge, U.K.: Cambridge University Press, 2002). Kaufmann's particular stance, however, finds little echo in the literature. In the first volume of his *Discovering the Mind* (New York: McGraw Hill, 1980), Kaufmann judged Hegel valuable but insufficient because he remained too beholden to Kant. Kaufmann concluded that "what was needed was a thinker who could develop Goethe's legacy without trying to reconcile it with Kant's. That is what Nietzsche did, and after him, Freud" (268). Although it is impossible to unpack the meaning of these comments fully in this essay, it does show that Kaufmann did not think of Nietzsche as standing alone in a moral/psychological tradition of German thought. As noted, Goethe's work plays a central role in defining the agenda of this tradition, making it that much more imperative that U.S. commentators on Nietzsche at least look at the impact of Goethe on German-born scholars.

25. Kaufmann, *Nietzsche*, 220.

26. Danto, *Nietzsche as Philosopher* (New York: Macmillian Company, 1965), 149. In later editions of his Nietzsche volume, Kaufmann included several critical comments on Danto's work. Some of them were rejoinders to criticisms Danto had made of Kaufmann. However, the main thrust was to show that Danto's approach flattened out and neglected what was really of moment in Nietzsche. See the long footnote on page 359 of the fourth edition of *Nietzsche: Philosopher, Psychologist, Antichrist*.

27. *Nietzsche und die Romantik* (Jena and Leipzig: Diedrichs, 1905).

28. Aschheim, *The Nietzsche Legacy in Germany, 1890–1990* (Berkeley and Los Angeles: University of California Press, 1992), 127.

29. Aschheim, *Nietzsche Legacy*, 126. Commenting on the general zeitgeist, David Blackbourn wrote that "there is no doubt about it: many Germans with the time and money to spare were trying to get in touch with their inner selves." The fact that Nietzsche lambasted the "more manifestly idiotic of these cults, circles and movements" did not stop him from being seen as the one who advocated such a leap into passion. Kaufmann himself tended to regard such a leap as a simple descent into irrationality. Other Jewish refugees, such as Erich Fromm, produced variations on the same theme. See Blackbourn's, *History of Germany, 1780–1918*, 2nd ed. (Oxford, U.K.: Blackwell, 2003), 302–3.

30. Joël, *Romantik*, 5.

31. Kaufmann, *Nietzsche*, 188.

32. See his talk "Rede gehalten zur Feier des 80. Geburtstages Friedrich Nietzsches am 15. Oktober 1924," in Hermann Kurzke and Stephan Stachorski, eds., *Thomas Mann Essays*, vol. 2 (Frankfurt am Main: S. Fischer, 1993), 238.

33. Kaufmann, *Nietzsche*, 14.

34. Joël, *Romantik*, 6.
35. Ibid., 5.
36. Ibid., 5.
37. Kaufmann, *Nietzsche*, 368.
38. Ibid., 285.
39. From the recommended readings listed in his edited edition of *On the Genealogy of Morality*, trans. Carol Diethe (Cambridge: Cambridge University Press, 1994), xxviii.
40. This comes from the opening section *"Einleitung: Legende"* to his 1918 *Nietzsche: Versuch einer Mythologie*, reprinted in Georg Peter Landmann, ed., *Der George-Kreis* (Stuttgart: Klett-Cotta, 1980), 272.
41. Heidegger, *Holzwege*, 1950 in *Gesamtausgabe*, vol. 5 (Frankfurt am Main: Vittorio Kostermann, 1977). It is translated and edited by Julian Young and Kenneth Haynes as *Off the Beaten Track* (Cambridge and New York: Cambridge University Press, 2002).
42. A comment David Lindenfeld made in his essay "Two Antimodern Master Narratives: Jung and Heidegger" provides a good starting point for situating Heidegger's use of Nietzsche in the wider discussion. Lindenfeld argued that "the Nietzsche lectures play a similar role in Heidegger's oeuvre to that of *Capital* in Marx's. Just as Marx began by portraying capitalism in all its power and then proceeded to show how it undermined itself by its own logic, so Heidegger performed a similar operation on Nietzsche's will-to-power, which for him represented the final stage in the history of Being—that of nihilism." Lindenfeld's claim does seem accurate, but it also raises the all-important question of why Heidegger felt justified in advancing this particular version of the will-to-power. Kaufmann saw it as a retreat from reason and as an attendant unwillingness to read Nietzsche in context. This raises the challenge of explaining why his "anti-Heideggerian" views are wrong. Lindenfeld's essay is reprinted in Suzanne Marchand and David Lindenfeld, eds., *Germany at the Fin de Siècle*, (Baton Rouge: Louisiana State University Press, 2004), 305.
43. Translation, Young and Haynes, *Off the Beaten Track*, 166. See Manfred Riedel for an explanation of this view of Nietzsche being a corrective to the more National Socialist friendly Nietzsche that Heidegger had earlier espoused in *Nietzsche in Weimar* (Leipzig: Reclam, 1997), 109–15.
44. Heidegger, "Nietzsche's Word," 166.
45. Ibid., 167.
46. Ibid., 197.
47. Kaufmann's translation of *Die Fröliche Wissenschaft* is *The Gay Science* (New York: Vintage Books, 1974), 180.
48. Kaufmann, *Nietzsche*, 87.
49. Ibid.
50. Ibid.
51. Translation is my own—see the original in Heidegger, *Holzwege*, 217. It is a modified version of the translation by Young and Haynes, "Nietzsche's Word," 162.

Although this translation is excellent at conveying what Heidegger probably intended, I have tried to reproduce some of the difficulty and obscurity of the original language.

52. Heidegger, *Holzwege*, 267. Again, I have mildly altered Young and Haynes's version of "Nietzsche's Word" in *Off the Beaten Track*, 199

53. Heidegger, *Holzwege*, 267.

54. Kaufmann, *Nietzsche; Philosopher, Psychologist, Antichrist*, 4th edition (Princeton: Princeton University Press, 1974), 230.

55. Mann, "Rede," 238.

56. Kaufmann, *The Faith of a Heretic* (1961; reprint, New York: Meridian Books, 1978), 28.

57. Preface to the third edition reprinted in the fourth edition of *Nietzsche* (1974), viii.

David Kettler

Negotiations
Learning from Three Frankfurt Schools

A recent study by Gerhard Sonnert and Gerald Holton examines the "second wave" of refugees from Nazi Germany, the individuals who were under eighteen years of age when they arrived in the United States during the years between 1933 and the beginning of the Second World War.[1] They find that a disproportionate number of these émigrés achieved a measure of success in professional—and above all in academic—pursuits. Among the examples they use to illuminate their statistics are a number of well-known scientists and scholars, but inevitably the great majority of the individuals they classify as finding a place in the careers they single out have been journeymen in their various fields. This is where I can situate myself as a detail in their story, a refugee arrival in 1940 at age nine and a faculty member of assorted colleges and universities since 1955.

In a rather commonplace naive response to good social science research, I was almost chagrined to learn how little originality there has been in my life. Even an ambivalent attitude I expressed to one of my daughters at the end of an autobiographical letter I wrote to her when she was ten proves to have been a commonplace in my cohort. I wrote at the time:

> America never captured my enthusiastic allegiance, in the gut sense of many grateful immigrants. It had been too long and too tortuous a wait at too impressionable an age, I guess, with too capricious an outcome. Oh yes. Our benefactors in Bayonne also changed our names, to make them less foreign-sounding. I had been Manfred Ketzlach, called Fredi by all my family and friends. The Nazis required that Jews who did not have obviously Jewish first names had to add the middle name "Israel" or "Sarah." But Manfred Israel Ketzlach wouldn't do. I became David Kettler. That's many decades ago, and I don't know if I'll ever manage the switch all the way. A strange business.

In a chapter called "Privatized Costs, Socialized Benefits," Sonnert and Holton cite as a case they consider representative of one of four typical syndromes a mathematician who wrote, "I suspect I never quite became an American" (183). The authors offer some psychological explanations for this response, but that is not my field of competence or interest.

Instead I would like to move to a more sociological level of analysis. Simply stated, Sonnert and Holton explain much of the "second wave" cohort's success, given the remarkably favorable opportunity structure of "cultural capital" received as legacy from home, especially in relations with fathers. They stretch this explanation a little in the cases of children who came without their parents. In reflecting on my own experience as a case study, I open up the question of individuals effectively without more than a dim echo of cultural capital who nevertheless identify early with the intellectual exiles of the first wave and return constantly to their legacy. Such identification need not be an enlistment as disciple: the object of the identification may be perceived as an admired but damaged person, the transmitter of a dilemma. It may be in short an identification with exile and thus with a lifetime of negotiations that preclude the comforts supposed to be implied by discovering or deciding who one is. Although my birthplace was Leipzig, it is rather Frankfurt that has embodied this condition for me.

I start with a brief autobiographical narrative covering the years between 1930 and 1955. Its focal point is my untimely (*unzeitgemäß*) identification with the antifascist refugee generation. The Frankfurt connection arises from my most admired teachers, Franz Neumann and Herbert Marcuse, and refers first, accordingly, to the "Frankfurt School" in the most familiar sense. Following that were my theoretical and practical preoccupations between 1955 and 1970 with the "vocation of intellectuals" during my career from instructor to professor in the political science department of the Ohio State University. Although this period actually includes a year's fellowship in the Institut für Sozialforschung, the prime Frankfurt link is nevertheless the sociological work of Karl Mannheim.

In the next phase in my life, I was at Trent University in Ontario, Canada, from 1970 to 1990, a period during which I first attempted to negotiate the differences between the two Frankfurt schools, as I understood them, and then turned to the Frankfurt school of labor law, represented by Hugo Sinzheimer, to inquire more deeply into diverse practices of negotiations and the character of various kinds of settlements. Later I enjoyed exceptionally satisfying years as scholar in residence and later research professor at Bard College, where a continued pursuit of the earlier themes eventuated in seven years of concentrated work on intellectual exiles, notably the German émigrés of the 1930s. The patron saint of this segment is once again Franz Neumann, whose track has been evident in all the earlier portions as well, and the geography shifts to the axis between Berlin and New York.

The account draws on several social science disciplines, including political science, sociology, history, cultural studies, and a bit of philosophy. Yet in the end there is a lot of narration. This is quite a long story, which cannot convey anything without a certain amount of detail, so I will have to use some rather compressed formulations elsewhere and to make some leaps from time to time. It is never clear in a case study whether the patterns are not idiosyncratic, so I cannot be certain that what I am offering is more than a personal memoir. I trust that it may nevertheless be of some value to students of the 1930s waves of immigration.

A Belated Recruit to the Last Weimar Generation

It all starts in Leipzig, where I was born on July 1, 1930. My father came to Germany from Kherson on the Dnieper, near Odessa, in 1908, at age three, and my mother from Brody on the Austro-Hungarian side of the border with Russia in 1914, at age twelve. Both were from what is now Ukraine. They were *Ostjuden,* or East European Jews, in short, like 80 percent of the Jews in Leipzig, lacking more than primary education, but they were also acculturated to the world of standing room at the opera. My mother's parents were enclosed by orthodoxy, but her brothers were worldly and reasonably successful businessmen. She overcame family opposition to marry the slightly younger, impecunious son of a thoroughly secularized and Russified household. Until the "Aryan" takeover of her family's business in 1938, my father worked as a backroom clerk in my uncles' stores; but my parents sought to educate my older brother and me to middle-class German-Jewish standards. The shelves of Goethe, Schiller, and Heine accompanied us even in our move to a single room in a *Judenhaus* in 1939. I do not remember hearing Yiddish until my early years in the United States. Until it was forced shut on November 10, 1938, my brother and I attended the Höhere Jüdische Schule, conducted by a husband and wife belonging to the famous rabbinical Carlebach family. According to my cousin Heinz, midway in age between my father and me and a survivor of seven years in concentration camps, my father was leftist in his politics and read avidly about the Soviet Union. I cannot say that based on my own knowledge since he died on April 30, 1940, four weeks after our arrival in the United States, when he had just turned thirty-five and when I was just approaching my tenth birthday.

For the first four years in the United States, my mother worked in a factory, and we were dependent on distant relations for our occasional outings to middle-class events. Although my mother was part of a small group of German-speaking refugees given employment by the proprietor of the Maidenform Brassiere Company, we stopped speaking German at home almost immediately. Eventually my mother married a widowed shopkeeper—an uneducated Jewish immigrant from prerevolutionary Russia—"for the sake of the children." My adolescence was a confused struggle, but I managed to leave high school without an education but with formal qualifications good enough to gain admission to Columbia College, as well as with sufficient savings from my summer employments to pay tuition for the first semester. I was remarkable at the end of high school only in having an exceptional vocabulary, I recall, as a result of reading popular lending library books at the rate of five a week. Although I had somewhere picked up a mildly left-liberal political inclination, which offended my patriotic teachers, and had read some Freud with my two friends in order to belittle other acquaintances by our unsolicited insights into their dreams and slips of the tongue, it is safe to say that everything I encountered in college was new. I was an eager, grateful student.

Columbia College at the time did not even require students to select a major field, as long as we accumulated credits in advanced courses, so I balanced classes in philosophy, economics, political science, and history. My honors thesis, however, was on Marx's *German Ideology*. I could not say much about it since I wanted to believe it all, but I had misgivings. By then I was nevertheless one of six members of the moribund campus front organization, Young Progressives of America, where the other five, constituting the Communist Party cell, used to caucus beforehand in order to work out the party line for the meeting, where I would join their number. We demonstrated against the Korean War, as I recall, as well as against the awarding of an honorary degree to a Rightist dictator from Chile. Our primary contribution was a lecture series entitled "Negro History," which no one attended. It was my conviction at the time that my involvement with Communists was strictly a tactical maneuver, that I was using them to promote my own causes, and that this opportunistic affiliation did not oblige me to believe most of what they claimed, especially about the Soviet Union and its allies. Still, my cooperation with them also inclined me to discount or undervalue reports of abuses so harsh as to upset my tacit, fanciful compact.

As an undergraduate, I approached academic culture quite passively. I was a "good student," and my typical grade was an A-minus. After a course on the history of political thought, taught by a shy, young Canadian who followed Franz Neumann's syllabus, I knew that I would somehow pursue this study, but I had no idea how that might happen since I had no conception of academic careers. Mostly I studied diligently what I was assigned. It should be added that I had little time to be intellectually adventurous, since on weekdays I spent more than eight hours at work, helping to administer—and eventually teaching in—a proprietary adult high school. An obvious result of this routine was that I had some self-confidence but no familiarity with student culture.

My transition into graduate school at Columbia happened as if by itself. My job in the evening high school was secure; there was never any doubt of my being admitted to graduate studies; and a fellowship was found to cover my tuition. It was just as natural that I would now become a student of Franz L. Neumann, although I had never seen him until I entered his large lecture course "Democracy and Dictatorship" in my last undergraduate summer. Now I was more confident as some sort of Marxist, having been introduced to Georg Lukács in a class that also examined Karl Mannheim and Karl Popper. Put somewhat paradoxically, I had found a home in the antifascist immigration, becoming in my habitus an "untimely" member of a generation whose actual members were fifteen to thirty years older. My political self-identification, moreover, was with a "popular front" that had ceased to exist even as a hope at about the time of the Stalin-Hitler Pact. Especially at the emotional level, my emancipation from this morally contradictory *Unzeitmäßigkeit* (untimeliness) has been gradual and uneven.

In addition to my classes and seminars with Neumann, as well as courses with Robert K. Merton and Seymour Martin Lipset, great names of the U.S. sociology of the time, I heard Herbert Marcuse for a year in a course significantly called "the" theory of social change (in contrast to a course in the same department called "theories of social change"). My master's essay "Plato and the Problem of Social Change," a critique of Popper's "Open Society," originated as a paper for Neumann's seminar but derived its problem formulation from Marcuse's course. It was my second choice of a topic, selected after a noted specialist in U.S. political studies, anxious about my vulnerability to McCarthyist blacklisting, persuaded me not to undertake a study of "political crime" as an implicit category of U.S. law. Oddly the advice to pay attention to Plato rather than to politically provocative themes was repeated in 1970, when a department chair sought to help me overcome a political blacklisting at his institution. But that is a different, not very interesting story, with a happy ending in Canada.

In any event both Neumann and Marcuse read and approved the master's essay on Plato. The thesis was so far from being afflicted with "historicism" in Karl Popper's sense that Plato lacked any theory of social or political transformation. The confrontation with Popper was continued in my doctoral dissertation, which began as a grandiose critique of historical theories from Plato to Marx and ended as a narrow study of Adam Ferguson, who was to have been the subject of only a chapter. I continued to look for ways of understanding the uses of history in the construction of social theory without succumbing to the logical errors whose diagnoses I conceded to Popper. Neither Neumann nor Marcuse, notwithstanding their posthumous consignment to the Frankfurt School, directed students' attention to the philosophical writings of Horkheimer or Adorno. The political theories surveyed in the courses, even in doctoral level seminars, were indiscriminately labeled theories or ideologies, to be assessed for their respective contributions to the expansion of "human freedom," whose elements were largely taken for granted.

My doctoral work on Ferguson consequently sought a strategy for bypassing philosophical issues in the technical sense and ended up—five years later and long after Neumann's early death and Marcuse's departure for Brandeis—in a conception of eighteenth-century "moral philosophy" as a tension-ridden paradigmatic mode of orientation for modern intellectuals, a study unexpectedly indebted more to Karl Mannheim than to the critical theory of the Horkheimer-Adorno Frankfurt School. Notwithstanding the work's eccentric sociological approach and thesis, which were evidently little remarked on except by some skeptical but kind members of the doctoral committee, the book remains a standard work in the admittedly small field, and it has been recently republished.[2]

The Vocation of Intellectuals

In 1960, when the dissertation was approved, I had been a faculty member in the Department of Political Science at Ohio State University for five years. I owed the appointment to a surprising upsurge of interest in political theory initiated by the Rockefeller Foundation in the early 1950s and to the openness to this initiative of a worldly political scientist, Harvey C. Mansfield, who had recently returned to the university from wartime service in Washington and was newly appointed not only as chairman of Ohio State's ambitious program but also as editor of the profession's principal journal. He indulged the overlong maturation of my dissertation project in part because he quickly employed me as his assistant in editing the *American Political Science Review,* a position that I held for five years and that required me to prepare a summary and preliminary assessment of nearly ten manuscripts a week, a sustained and thorough education in the discipline of political science, which I had largely neglected during my postgraduate studies.

Except for some book reviews, I published nothing during these apprenticeship years, as I was preoccupied as well with learning the teaching trade, although one of the reviews, not accidentally called "Dilemmas of Radicalism," was the first of many attempts to come to grips with Neumann. It was a critique of the posthumous collection of his U.S. essays in which I repeated some criticisms I had made to his face after he asked me to referee his newly prepared article on freedom in the spring of 1953, when I was an auditor in his doctoral seminar. The key question was how his requirement of a rational policy could be met without violating his standards of participatory and liberal freedoms if the crisis of culture and society was as severe as his diagnosis suggested.[3] He never liked the question, perhaps because he considered it hid a Stalinist rationalization. In any case I spent many years attempting to render my critical question less crude . . . and perhaps more answerable.

Not quite coincidentally, 1960 was also the year I first met Max Horkheimer. Kurt H. Wolff, who had brought him on a visit to Ohio State, helped me to secure him as a guest lecturer in my class: he surprised me by speaking with Schopenhauer against Nietzsche. We talked later about my coming to Frankfurt for a year, to follow up my Ferguson study with the study of Marx, to which it had always been meant to be an introduction.

Yet by the time I finished writing my applications for a postdoctoral grant to both the Social Science Research Council and the Fulbright Commission—with success in both cases—I realized that I had first to work through the implications of my practical preference for Karl Mannheim's approaches. As a result, however, my year of research in the Institute of Social Research in 1961–62 proved to be a largely fictitious affiliation. Neither Adorno nor Horkheimer were at all disposed to encourage my studies of Mannheim, for reasons I barely grasped at the time; and I was too arrogant to recast myself as merely their student. With my newfound partner, who became my wife in the course of the year, I lived in Königstein, which was not yet a suburb, and I came to Frankfurt only to acquire a new supply of library books once in a while. My notes of my sole interview with Adorno show that he had referred me to an advanced student named Jürgen Habermas, but I was too discouraged by Adorno's manifest contempt for my subject to follow any of his leads. Horkheimer reproached me when I sought him out at the end of my stay, because I had not requested permission to attend the institute seminar. On balance my failure to do so in the absence of an invitation was probably a good thing: I would take my Frankfurt School in small, digestible doses—a metaphor that also comes to mind because my nervous system responded to my first return to Germany with no end of abdominal discomfort, one of my few topics in common with Horkheimer.

Despite the intense demands of my largely internalized confrontation with Germany during that year—I had an ulcer by Thanksgiving—I made headway in my independent studies of Mannheim. The two publications originating then had to await an additional summer of research, mostly in London. One attempted to show structural parallels between Ferguson and Mannheim as two ends of a continuum of intellectuals' orientations.[4] The other was a monograph reporting my findings, unpublished at the time even in Hungary, about Mannheim, Lukács, and the so-called Sunday Circle. Georg Lukács, whom I visited both in 1962 and 1963, had little patience himself with my historical questions, but he was kind and sent me to Zoltán Horváth, who was just completing a well-informed if quite traditional historical survey. My own thesis was that the Sunday Circle and its immediate aftermath demonstrated the insufficiency of what I called "revolutionary culturism" and highlighted the urgency of a search for a more adequate political concept, which I thought informed their divergent paths.[5] I discovered that I had little stomach for the transcendent revolutionary option—either in its practical Communist Party form or in its esoteric virtual adaptation in Frankfurt. An indirect testimonial to this conclusion in quite a different idiom was a small article on Montesquieu's *Persian Letters*, in which I argued, with express reference to Marcuse's *Eros and Civilization*, that Montesquieu had correctly showed that love cannot be a political principle and that politics had to be a more limited project.[6]

My own 1960s, then, was divided between my largely localized experiments with reformist political activism on behalf of the usual causes of those years, which made me think of myself as a radical, and a series of essay publications on the relations between such activism and democratic theory, a return to the issues raised in my Neumann review, but now deepened by my first round of studies of Mannheim, as well as the explorations of New Left, notably in its British manifestations. Further enriching my work during those years was a second year in Europe in 1966–67, the unexpected gift of a year as political science Fulbright lecturer at the University of Leiden, supplemented by a semester as instructor in the Institute of Social Studies in The Hague. The respite from activism and the opportunity to observe a Left that ranged from dissenting socialists to playful Amsterdam anarchists confirmed my habits of distinguishing between the distance required for reflections on radical political theory and the immediacy of mobilizing ideologies associated with direct practice, a main theme of my writings on my return.[7]

In the meantime I focused on Mannheim, obsessively compiling detailed notes on all of his writings and informing myself as well about the Weimar context of his best known work. Yet I was not ready to publish anything. Back in the United States, I shifted the locus of my activism to the political science profession, about which I thought I knew a good deal from my days as assistant to the editor of the *Review*. My writings and minor political campaigning were focused on reintroducing social theory themes into the discipline, rather than proclaiming a revolutionary revelation. I became chairman of something called the "Caucus for a New Political Science" active in the profession, but I disappointed the more activist recruits to this cause by my insistence on academic standards and a scholarly tone.[8] While this rather moderate tendency was clear enough to disgust my younger associates, it was little attended by my more senior professional colleagues, not least because the purely political lines of division in the discipline were reinforced by a cleavage between the strongly emplaced advocates of a scientific style and the scattered adherents of alternatives accumulated over the decades, as well as new converts to assorted philosophical radicalisms of the time. In 1970, then, I was abruptly removed from this disputed terrain, caught unaware in a transition from my full professorship at Ohio State, which had become unbearable because of the local state of the methodological wars, to a comparable position in a department with a strong political theory core, where I could expect to protect my students from prejudicial requirements. When Ohio State joined other campuses in an outburst of militant protest in the Spring, I invented a kind of peacekeeping role for faculty unwilling to see the dissent simply stifled, but I was nevertheless cast in the role of faculty agitator that was required by the conservative scenarios of those events—and, having resigned earlier in anticipation of the move that was now foreclosed, I found myself without a job and virtually unemployable. The combination of insufficient hostility to rebellious students and disciplinary dissidence sufficed to bring about a kind of polite blacklisting, especially effective for a candidate for a senior appointment.

Politics: Science or Negotiation

After a year of safe haven (at an instructor's salary) in a small, unorthodox college, I moved to a new, welcoming undergraduate university in Canada, where my alien status effectively disqualified me from active political engagements and freed me to return to my more strictly academic quandaries. After writing an article on the Ohio State events, drawing on Neumann for the first time in some years, to help me think about the legal forms of those conflicts,[9] as well as revising an English version of my Lukács and Mannheim study for a theoretical-political journal, I accepted an assignment to write an article on Herbert Marcuse for a textbook edited by two conservative scholars. It would give me a chance to balance my accounts, notwithstanding the curious venue and the near certainty that none of my peers would ever read it. In the end, as I rethought Marcuse's achievement, I found surprisingly little substantive loss when I abandoned the supposed dynamic of the dialectic in favor of a three-fold division into a "negation" of bourgeois society, a utopian projection, and a theory of political change. In defiance of Marcuse's express strictures, then, I could extract value only after detotalizing the design to reveal a vigorous and often quite brilliant version of the leftist civic humanism that was the lingua franca of the antifascist exile.[10] I stopped thinking of the Frankfurt School as a vast mountain that I had yet to climb and went for walks instead in the lower-lying woods by incorporating both Adorno and Horkheimer in the cultural studies courses I was beginning to develop and by finding nothing anomalous about distinguishing in their texts between self-dramatizing exaggerations and deep questions. Habermas was a help in all this, although I knew right away that this was not a school that would have me as a regular pupil.

The combination of regard and reservation towards Habermas's grand design initiated an assignment that led me from my earlier topics to a new cycle. In the spring before a full sabbatical for 1975–76, which I had arranged to spend at Balliol College, Oxford, and which I had expected to devote wholly to a book on Karl Mannheim, picking up where I had left off almost ten years earlier,[11] I was asked to review a treatment of the Scottish moral philosophers of the eighteenth century, which followed Habermas's lead in interpreting these texts. The most important question that arose in the course of the review was precisely about my initial assumption when I first addressed Ferguson, whether his moral philosophy, insofar as it was also a social theory, actually rested on the scheme of historical stages that was doubtless present, but whose actual work in the design, I now decided, had to be discovered rather than imputed on the strength of later theorists he was thought to anticipate.[12] I was able to gain a three-month residency at the Institute for Advanced Studies in the Humanities in Edinburgh and to work through Ferguson's archival remains, notably his class lectures. The historical stages were important to his practical reading of situations appropriate to the actor, I concluded, but not to the spectator's scientific explanation. The relationship between the intellectual and the scholar was thus one of complementarity, not displacement. In a major article published in 1976, then, and in a less formal sequel a year later, I concluded that I had been right in treating Ferguson's theory as a composite structure but that I had been wrong in relying on a standard paradigm and that I had consequently underestimated the element of constitutional bargaining and political openness in the essayistic theoretical design as well as in the substance of the political theory itself.[13]

Despite renewed immersion in the subject, a few book reviews, and a premature book contract, my Mannheim project did not really gain momentum until a year or two after my return to Canada, when two German-Canadian sociologists already well known for contributions to Mannheim studies and sociology of knowledge persuaded me to begin a collaboration with them. Most important was Volker Meja, with whom I began a collaboration that has been productive for more than thirty years. Born in Germany at the beginning of the war, with a father in the army and childhood experiences as a refugee from his grandmother's home in Silesia, Meja is an academic product of Frankfurt and the Institut für Sozialforschung, at least until his departure for postgraduate study in North America, where he was a student of Kurt H. Wolff at Brandeis University. Some might wonder at this re-enactment of the famous German-Jewish symbiosis, but it has always seemed obvious to us. We edited and in effect translated two book-length manuscripts by Mannheim, for which we also provided interpretive introductions,[14] and we then jointly wrote a brief overall account of Mannheim's intellectual project, giving due weight to my earlier treatments of his Hungarian beginnings, our new reading of the standard works in the light of the new discoveries, and a nonreductionist treatment of his time in English exile, which I had researched years earlier. Perhaps because the book was so short—and notwithstanding inattentive, somewhat patronizing reviews—there were translations in German, French, Spanish, and Japanese.[15] Our reading of Mannheim emphasized the experimental character of Mannheim's essays, even when misleadingly presented as integral chapters in his well-known *Ideologie und Utopie,* as well as the centrality of the theme of "politics as a science," construed as a need to recognize but to render controllable what was historically called the "irrational" element in human social life. Fifteen years later, when Meja and I recast the analysis to incorporate the fistful of specialized Mannheim studies we had published in the interim, we characterized the project as the constitution of an open, multidimensional bargaining regime designed to manage without resolution a classic constellation of difficulties confronting liberalism since its first articulation by John Stuart Mill.[16] While the structural analysis of liberalism derived from R. D. Cumming's marvelous and marvelously eccentric book—another return to one of my teachers—the account of bargaining regimes drew on quite a different return and overdetermination.

In the autumn of 1979, I became chairman of the Faculty Association at Trent—an office that normally went begging—but I set as a condition for accepting the chore that the established core group would help me to convert the association into a proper trade union under Ontario labor law, with the capacity of negotiating a binding collective agreement and backed by a right to strike. In this eminently pragmatic and localized form, some of my old political responses revived. The unionization campaign succeeded, and for the next eighteen months, more or less, I spent twelve hours a week at the bargaining table, renegotiating all the rules and procedures governing faculty up to the actual terms of compensation. Two things gave added weight to the things I learned from this experience in applied labor law. First, a publisher asked me to advise on the question of publishing Franz Neumann's 1934 London School of Economics dissertation on the "Domination of the Rule of Law," which I had never read. And, second, I was unexpectedly invited to spend 1981–82 as a Fellow of the Netherlands Institute of Advanced Study in the Social Sciences and Humanities. I actually advised against publishing the Neumann, unless it could be paired with a companion volume on the historical context and meaning of the work, and—of course—I decided to spend the NIAS year researching Neumann's legal theorizing, beginning with his Weimar years as labor lawyer. This brought me back to school in Frankfurt for the third time, since Neumann's labor law thinking derived from his years with Hugo Sinzheimer, including his service as instructor in the Akademie der Arbeit, which was attached to the university.

The labor law established by Sinzheimer was essentially collective bargaining law with the prime theoretical puzzle being the legal status of the collective agreement. The central political questions had to do with the relationships between the regimes constituted by relations among state, worker, and employer collective actors and the democratic political constitution, especially insofar as the latter was seen as an agency of social change toward socialism. I concluded from my studies that not even the disastrous outcome of the Weimar experiment disproved the case for a complementarity between quasi-corporatist regimes and the sphere of political action. A defeat is not necessarily a refutation, although it is eminently understandable why the defeated—such as Neumann and his associates—should have thought so, at least for a while. With a second year at NIAS, I was able to play a part in the belated Dutch reception of Sinzheimer's contribution in exile to the formation of a labor-law field in Holland and to learn from the German discussions of the time about hyper-juridification (*Verrechtlichung*) and deformalization of law, which coincided with a revival of interest in Weimar socialist legal theory.[17] Then too, there was the early work on reflexive law by Gunther Teubner, now in Frankfurt, which derived in turn from U.S. labor law approaches reminiscent of Weimar labor law. The contrast between the mode of legality for which labor law was paradigmatic and the mode of legality grounded in property law led me then to attempt a critique of "new property" approaches to the welfare state and a proposal for a theoretical approach based on the labor law experience.[18]

All the while, however, I wanted to get a clearer understanding of the differences among bargaining regimes and their various capacities for constituting relationships congruent with reasonable management of conflicts, as well as their capacities for changes in the parties to be recognized and the matters to be deemed proper for negotiation, with special emphasis, of course, on the role of reflexive law in these designs. My studies went in two directions. First, there was a case study of the role of labor lawyers in the early bargaining regime experiments of the International Ladies Garment Workers Union, mostly in New York City and around the time of the First World War, a publication that had a sequel some years later in a study of the labor regime sources of the Japanese lifetime employment institution.[19] The latter was initiated by a specialist on Japanese labor relations, who was astonished to find Hugo Sinzheimer and Weimar labor law playing a prominent role in Japanese practice, notwithstanding the postwar statutory incorporation of the U.S. design.[20] The second direction was initiated by Seymour Martin Lipset's challenge to show whether differences in the labor regime could contribute to explaining the divergences between U.S. and Canadian trade union density in the years after 1960. This resulted in a series of three publications, done with different combinations of specialist collaborators.[21] One was fittingly published in a collection of articles on reflexive labor law issued by the Hugo Sinzheimer Institute of the University of Amsterdam.[22] Common to all these studies, which drew on European neocorporatist experiences as well, was a rejection of the militant conflict models commonplace in North American labor history studies, in favor of recognizing the versatility and resiliency of bargaining models. At the same time, the work culminated in the recognition that the trade unions and labor regimes I had been examining, whatever their merits, were being irretrievably marginalized by the end of the 1980s.[23] It was time to collect what I had learned from my empirical explorations and to move once more to more reflexive questions.

Exile and Return

In 1990 I accepted a visiting appointment from the Graduate Center of the City University of New York followed by an invitation to be scholar in residence at nearby Bard College. I returned from Canada to the United States. The first order of business then was to complete the work on Mannheim that Meja and I had begun, even as I was primarily focused on labor and the law. We published a series of articles probing more deeply into Mannheim's German research project and into the complex and ultimately unsatisfying negotiations that constituted his reception in the years of his immigration to England. This phase of my many encounters with Mannheim was introduced by a mild but gratifying academic adventure, which also pointed toward a new level of reflection.

Around 1985 my attention was called to Nina Rubinstein, who had studied with Mannheim and whose completed dissertation had been pushed aside by the Nazi dismissal of her teacher and by the forced immediate exile of her Menshevik family. A group of us, in the United States and Frankfurt, notably Claudia Honegger, who soon after became professor of sociology in Bern, persuaded the Johann-Wolfgang-Goethe University to award Rubinstein the earned doctorate, after a memorable viva voce examination of Rubinstein, then age eighty-one; and the dissertation was subsequently published on its merits, together with my laudation and some other documents.[24] As someone at home in the Menshevik immigration in Berlin, Rubinstein undertook a study of exile through a comparison between the White Russian immigrants of the Soviet era and the French émigrés of 1789, although the work ultimately concentrated on the latter. My encounter with Rubinstein's study suggested a new way of settling my unfinished business with both Mannheim and Neumann, since both cases had already raised questions about the consequences of their forced immigrations and complex subsequent dealings with representatives of their fields in their lands of asylum.[25]

This shift of emphasis was delayed, however, by an unexpected new find in 1997 of a major Mannheim text, a verbatim transcript of his introduction to sociology course in his first Frankfurt semester. Although his own quite detailed lecture notes for other courses had been available in the University of Keele collection, this text comprised a dramatic presentation of his distinctive idea about the forms and purposes of sociology.[26] A conference on the new materials brought me together with Colin Loader, the author of a well-respected study of Mannheim, and we decided to publish an English translation of the text, with supporting materials, as well as a book on a theme given new urgency by these documents, Mannheim's conception of sociology as the mode of *Bildung* appropriate to the democratic era.[27] Questions of education, namely political education, had already played a part in our separate earlier interpretations, but the 1930 record showed the scope of Mannheim's claims for sociology, in view of the historical place of *Bildung* as a major issue of political as well as cultural conflict in Germany. The lectures moreover offered new insights into Mannheim's relations with writers he located in the fascist forefield, notably Carl Schmitt and Martin Heidegger, as well as those he considered orthodox Marxists. Despite the narrow focus on the years between 1930 and 1933, the study with Loader struck me as profoundly instructive not only about Mannheim but also, in view of his character as a representative intellectual, about the state of the question of democracy and culture in those years, so bitterly regretted and so harshly judged by the intellectual exiles of 1933.

Beginning in 2001, then, I turned to an intense if always exploratory study of intellectual exile, picking up the theme from Rubinstein and perhaps also from my own oblique biographical relations to it. Some of the issues had already been raised by my monographic work on Mannheim, Neumann, and Sinzheimer, of course, but now I decided to seek the cooperation of colleagues, notably younger scholars. There have been three stages in this project, centered respectively on a workshop, a large conference, and a special issue of an interdisciplinary journal. The challenge to the twenty workshop participants at the first stage was epitomized in the title "No Happy End," inspired by the deep disappointment and self-blame evident in the late writings of Mannheim and Neumann, notwithstanding their reputed status as models of émigré success. Out of the workshop arose a large conference with a less one-sided problematic, namely "contested legacies," which referred to three distinct sites of contestation: the Weimar scene, the diverse bargaining regimes among the exiles themselves and in their relations with their respective fields in the places of asylum, and in the successive waves of reception.[28] The ancestry of this kind of contextualization in my confrontations with Mannheim's approaches is evident, but my own actual contributions to the project had mostly to do with Neumann, although the momentum also led me to publish some narrowly focused studies of Nina Rubinstein, Hans Mayer, and Erich Kahler.[29] The principal result of the effort was reported in an introduction to the main collective publication arising out of the project, written with the Germanist Gerhard Lauer. Taking up the insight developed in the book on Mannheim and "political education," we contrasted the way in which the dispute between *Bildung* and *Wissenschaft* was structured during the Weimar years with the contest in U.S. higher education between proponents of "liberal arts" and "professionalism." The aim was to interrogate the exiles' various negotiations of the translation and transition, as documented in their work.[30]

The "contested legacies" project led me to three questions, which I have only begun to address. The first of these, corresponding to the third phase mentioned above, is documented in a collection entitled *Limits of Exile*, which brings together studies of numerous intellectual immigrations, ranging from Iraqi Jewish novelists in Israel and Iranian students in the United States to Spanish Civil War exiles in Mexico and Russian philosophers in Weimar Germany.[31] The unifying question had to do with the postmodern and postcolonial versions of the long-established metaphorical extension of the exile concept to comprehend states of estrangement that had no specific political source or character, a complex of issues commonly identified with the work of Edward Said. My proposal was to limit the concept of exile to its less metaphorical dimensions, lest we impoverish our abilities to examine the limits imposed by the condition—and even blur the inquiry into changes that may indeed render exile in the politically charged sense an anachronism.[32] The contributors to the collection, including my coeditor, were not all agreed, and the project remains open.

The second new question deriving from my renewed attention to Neumann as a representative social science émigré had to do with the interplay between the immigrants and the academic disciplines in which some of them found a home. Specifically I wrote two studies, drawing on archival records as well as my own recollections of my work on the *American Political Science Review* with the focus on the unexpected upsurge in the mid 1950s of "political theory" in modes inconsistent with accepted science models, at a time when quite simple positivist models of social science were so strongly in the ascendant.[33] These were then presented to audiences of U.S. political scientists, marking a return to this disciplinary setting after many decades.

In the spirit of such a reorientation, Volker Meja and I are returning one last time to Mannheim in order to focus on the less self-reflexive dimension of his project, the side he presented to disciplinary professionals inspired by Max Weber, especially through an examination of the projects Mannheim set his doctoral students during his lamentably brief but extraordinarily fruitful three years in Frankfurt, a time in which he managed nevertheless to fill the place of Oppenheimer's Frankfurt School, in its competition with the "Kölner Schule" (Cologne School) of von Wiese. This book, to be offered to the present generation of scholars who are looking at Mannheim anew, notably in Frankfurt, will bring together some past publications of ours on several of his women students, as well as my recently published papers on Kaethe Truhel, who wrote on social workers and bureaucrats in the Weimar welfare state, and on Jacob Katz, who wrote on the ideology of Jewish assimilation.[34] The last of these papers, written with Volker Meja during a joint month at Dan Diner's Jewish Studies Institute in Leipzig, resonates with a friendship earlier dramatized on a day in Poland, twenty years earlier. We first visited the village where Volker, born in 1940, had spent some war years with his grandmother until they were forced on the road by the approach of Russian armies, and then we then drove on to Auschwitz, just before dusk, where I lost beloved aunts and uncles and cousins of my age, and where I would have died myself, if it had not been for an unlikely combination of lucky accidents.

The Leipzig paper on Mannheim was called "Mannheim's Jewish Question," and it attempted to answer, with the help of his dealings with Katz, why Mannheim never once addressed the inhuman happenings later described as the Holocaust, although he never denied his Jewish parents, who both survived the years of the Budapest ghetto, in his personal life. Our thesis, uncertain and speculative, was that Mannheim's intellectual, if he were Jewish, had strong reasons, unrelated to cliches about self-hatred, to impose a silence about Jewishness, in order to reproduce a setting free of Christianness on which the constitution of the *Bildungsschicht* depended—a counterpart, perhaps, of Adam Ferguson's never-explained decision to surrender his standing and title as a clergyman when he returned to the Edinburgh of David Hume and Adam Smith.

That half-serious allusion underlines the obvious reflexive implications of the thesis of the Katz paper for my attempt to make sense of my own intellectual course. After all, questions about Jewishness and the Holocaust are absent from my own record as well. Yet the argument about intellectuals is too vague. Much more to the point, I think, is the generational identification I introduced at the outset. Antifascism was a reading of the short twentieth century that precluded anything like the centering of anti-Semitism, not to speak of the Holocaust. Until constrained to adapt by events at the bargaining table where the continued legitimacy as well as the financial viability of Horkheimer's Institute in New York was at issue, Franz Neumann opposed the turn toward anti-Semitism in their studies, claiming that he had exposed National Socialism in his *Behemoth* virtually without a serious reference to the phenomenon. My present projects accordingly include an attempt to understand the vicissitudes of antifascism in its transformations in the course of exile and return. My contribution to *Limits of Exile* deals with return from concentration camp as a mode of exile and return.[35] All the attention I can spare from the Mannheim project is going to a larger, comparative study, including especially all the phenomena that my late-born arrival in the antifascist exile generation spared me from having to face, notably the terrors of Stalinism. There can be no dramatic conclusion to this painful inquiry. I am not about to kick over the negotiating table. And, perhaps, given the realities registered on tables of another sort—actuarial tables—it will not end at all, because it will simply have to stop. The bell will ring, and school will be out.

In their treatment of cultural capital, Sonnert and Holton distinguish among embodied, objectified, and institutionalized states of that resource. The cultural objects and credentials intended by the last two types are largely irrelevant for young refugees, so the issue is about the first. Under embodied cultural capital, they "count the deportment, values, and expected behaviors that the young refugees imbibed in their early years from their families and the surrounding environment."[36] Inasmuch as the cultural aspirations in my own family could only be thinly symbolized during my childhood years and ceased in any case to be a presence after my arrival at a young age, when neither my mother nor our most frequent family contacts were at all oriented to the German-Jewish habitus of *Bildung*, I am tempted to speak of being haunted by the specter of a disembodied cultural capital, a deep preoccupation with a rumor of irretrievable loss. A more optimistic rendering might speak of the quest for a legacy, depending very much on guides, and yielding at best the sort of reward that Georg Simmel associated with the heirs who enhanced the fertility of a field simply by digging for the treasure to which they were directed by their father's will. Or perhaps the search is after all nothing but a reenactment of Dickens's famously bleak case of *Jarndyce v. Jarndyce*.

Notes

1. Gerhard Sonnert and Gerald Holton, *What Happened to the Children Who Fled Nazi Persecution* (New York: Palgrave Macmillan, 206).

2. *The Social and Political Thought of Adam Ferguson* (Columbus, Ohio: Ohio State University Press, 1965); republished with a new introduction and afterword as *Adam Ferguson: His Social and Political Thought* (New Brunswick: Transaction, 2005).

3. "Dilemmas of Radicalism," review of Franz L. Neumann, *The Democratic and the Authoritarian State*, *Dissent* (Autumn 1957): 386–92.

4. "Sociology of Knowledge and Moral Philosophy: The Place of Traditional Problems in the Formation of Mannheim's Thought," *Political Science Quarterly* 82 (September 1967): 399–426

5. *Marxismus und Kultur: Mannheim und Lukács in den ungarischen Revolutionen 1918/19* (Neuwied: Luchterhand Verlag, 1967); revised and published in English as "Culture and Revolution: Lukács in the Hungarian Revolutions of 1918/19," *Telos* 10 (Winter 1971): 35–92.

6. "Montesquieu on Love: Notes on the *Persian Letters*," *American Political Science Review* 58 (September 1964): 658–61, and as "The Cheerful Discourses of Michael Oakeshott," *World Politics* 16 (April 1964): 883–89.

7. "Political Science and Political Rationality," in David Spitz, ed., *Political Theory and Social Change* (New York: Atherton Press, 1967), 59–89; "The Politics of Social Change: The Relevance of Democratic Approaches," in William E. Connolly, ed. *The Bias of Pluralism* (New York: Atherton Press, 1969), 213–49; "Beyond Republicanism: The Socialist Critique of Political Idealism," in Marvin Surkin and Alan Wolfe, eds., *An End to Political Science. The Caucus Papers* (New York: Basic Books, 1970), 34–81.

8. "The Vocation of Radical Intellectuals," *Politics and Society* 1 (Autumn 1970): 23–49, and in Ira Katznelson et al., eds., *The Politics and Society Reader* (New York: David McKay Company, 1974), 333–59; with Godfried van Benthem van den Bergh, *Intellectuellen tussen macht en wetenschap* (Amsterdam: van Gennep, 1973).

9. With Harry R. Blaine, "Law as a Political Weapon," *Politics and Society* 1 (November 1971): 479–526

10. "Herbert Marcuse. The Critique of Bourgeois Civilization and Its Transcendence," in Anthony de Crespigny and Kenneth Minogue, eds., *Contemporary Political Philosophers* (New York: Dodd, Mead & Co., 1975, and London: Methuen & Co., Ltd., 1976), 1–48. See also "The Aesthetic Dimension of Herbert Marcuse's Social Theory," *Political Theory* 10 (May 1982): 267–75

11. "Political Theory, Ideology, Sociology: The Question of Karl Mannheim," *Cultural Hermeneutics* 3 (May 1975): 69–80.

12. "History and Theory in the Scottish Enlightenment," *Journal of Modern History* 48 (March 1976): 95–100

13. "History and Theory in Ferguson's *Essay on the History of Civil Society:* A Reconsideration," *Political Theory* 5 (November 1977): 437–60; "Ferguson's *Principles:* Constitution in Permanence," *Studies in Burke and His Time* 19 (1978): 208–22.

14. Karl Mannheim, *Strukturen des Denkens,* eds. David Kettler, Volker Meja, and Nico Stehr (1980; Frankfurt: Suhrkamp Verlag, 2003); in English as *Structures of Thinking* (London: Routledge and Kegan Paul, 1982, 2001); Karl Mannheim, *Konservatismus. Ein Beitrag zur Soziologie des Wissens,* eds. David Kettler, Volker Meja, and Nico Stehr (1984; Frankfurt: Suhrkamp Verlag, 2003); in English as *Conservatism,* London: Routledge and Kegan Paul, 1986, 2001.

15. With Volker Meja and Nico Stehr, *Karl Mannheim* (Chichester: Ellis Horwood Limited; London and New York: Tavistock Publications, 1984).

16. With Volker Meja, "Politik als Wissenschaft: über Theorie und Praxis bei Karl Mannheim," *Angewandte Sozialforschung* 11 (1983): 403–17; co-authored in English

with Volker Meja and Nico Stehr, "Is a Science of Politics Possible?," *Transactions/Society*, 24 (March/April 1987): 76–82. With Volker Meja and Nico Stehr, "Karl Mannheim and Conservatism: The Ancestry of Historical Thinking," *American Sociological Review* 49 (February 1984): 71–85. With Volker Meja, "Settling with Mannheim," *State, Culture, and Society* 1 (April 1985): 225–37; Mary Gluck, "The Romance of Modernism: Review-essay of *George Lukács and His Generation*," *Canadian Journal of Sociology* (Winter 1986–87): 443–55. With Volker Meja and Nico Stehr, "The Reconstitution of Political Life: The Contemporary Relevance of Karl Mannheim's Political Project," *Polity* 20 (Summer 1988): 623–47. With Volker Meja and Nico Stehr, "Rationalizing the Irrational: Karl Mannheim and the Besetting Sin of German Intellectuals," *American Journal of Sociology* 95 (May 1990): 1441–1473; With Volker Meja and Nico Stehr, "Karl Mannheim und die Entmutigung der Intelligenz," *Zeitschrift für Soziologie* 19 (April 1990): 117–30. With Volker Meja, "That 'typically German kind of sociology which verges towards philosophy': The Dispute about *Ideology and Utopia* in the United States," *Sociological Theory* 12 (November 1994): 279–303.With Volker Meja, *Karl Mannheim and the Crisis of Liberalism: "The Secret of These New Times"* (New Brunswick: Transaction Publishers, 1995).

17. "The Question of 'Legal Conservatism' in Canada: A Review of *Essays in the History of Canadian Law I*," *Journal of Canadian Studies* 18 (Spring 1983): 136–42; "Works Community and Workers' Organizations: A Central Problem in Weimar Labour Law," *Economy and Society* 13 (August 1984): 278–303. "Sociological Classics and the Contemporary State of the Law," *Canadian Journal of Sociology* 9 (1984): 447–58; "A Review of *Essays in the History of Canadian Law II*," *Journal of Canadian Studies* 19 (Winter 1984): 150–64; with Volker Meja, "'Sancho Pansa als Statthalter.' Max Weber und das Problem der materiellen Gerechtigkeit," in Heinz Zipprian and Gerhard Wagner, eds., *Max Webers Wissenschaftslehre. Interpretation und Kritik*, 713–54 (Frankfurt: Suhrkamp, 1993). With Volker Meja, "Legal Formalism and Disillusioned Realism in Max Weber," *Polity* 28 (Spring 1996): 307–31. "Hugo Sinzheimer: Advocacy, Law and Social Change," in A. J. Hoekema, ed. *Mededelingen 6. Hugo Sinzheimer Instituut voor onderzoek van arbeid en recht* (Amsterdam: Hugo Sinzheimer Instituut, 1993); expanded in *Bard Journal of Social Sciences* 2 (April–May 1994): 12–20.

18. "Law and Constitution in the Welfare State: Impasse or Evolution," in M. David Gelfand et al., *Law in the Welfare State: An Interdisciplinary Perspective* (N.p.: HIMON, Universität-Gesamthochschule Siegen, n.d.). "The Reconstitution of the Welfare State: A Latent Social-Democratic Legacy," *Law & Society Review* 21 (1987): 9–47.

19. "Interest, Ideology, and Culture: From the Protocols of Peace to *Schlesinger v. Quinto*," in Ian Angus, ed., *Anarcho-Modernism: Toward a New Critical Theory*, 271–90 (Vancouver: Talonbooks, 2001).

20. With Charles T. Tackney, "Light from a Dead Sun: The Japanese Lifetime Employment System and Weimar Labor Law," *Comparative Labor Law and Policy* 19, no. 101 (1997): 101–42.

21. With Christopher Huxley and James Struthers, "Is Canada's Experience 'Especially Instructive'?," in Seymour Martin Lipset, ed., *Unions in Transition: Entering the*

Second Century, 113–32 (San Francisco: Institute for Contemporary Studies, 1986); reprinted as "Trade Unions in North America since 1945: A Comparison," in Donald Avery and Roger Hall, eds., *Coming of Age: Readings in Canadian History since World War II*, 148–65 (Toronto: Harcourt Brace Jovanovich, 1996); with James Struthers and Christopher Huxley, "Unionization and Labour Regimes in Canada and the United States: Considerations for Comparative Research," *Labour / Le Travail* 25 (Spring 1990): 161–87

22. With Peter Warrian, "American and Canadian Labor Law Regimes and the Reflexive Law Approach," in Ralf Rogowski and Ton Wilthagen, eds., *Reflexive Labour Law*, 95–137 (Deventer and Cambridge: Kluwer, 1994).

23. With Volker Meja, "The End of Western Trade Unionism? Social Progress after the Age of Progressivism," in Jeffrey C. Alexander and Piotr Sztompka, eds., *Rethinking Progress*, 123–58 (London and New York: Unwin Hyman, 1990). The principal articles cited in notes 19–25 are collected in *Domestic Regimes: The Rule of Law, and Democratic Social Change*, vol. 3 of *Mobility and Norm Change* (Berlin and Cambridge, Mass.: Galda & Wilch Glienecke 2001).

24. "Wie kam es zu Nina Rubinsteins Promotion," in Nina Rubinstein, *Die französische Emigration nach 1789. Ein Beitrag zur Soziologie der politischen Emigration* (Graz: Nausner & Nausner 2000), 73–85.

25. With Volker Meja, "Schattenseiten einer erfolgreichen Emigration: Karl Mannheim im englischen Exil," in *Exilforschung. Ein internationales Jahrbuch*, vol. 5 *Fluchtpunkte des Exils*, 170–95 (Munich: edition text + kritik, 1987).

26. "Can We Master the Global Tensions or must We Suffer Shipwreck on Our Own History?," in Martin Endreß/Ilja Srubar, eds., *Karl Mannheims Beitrag zur Analyse moderner Gesellschaften*, 293–308 (Opladen: Leske + Budrich, 1999).

27. Karl Mannheim, *Sociology as Political Education*, David Kettler and Colin Loader, eds. and trans. (New Brunswick: Transaction Publishers, 2001); with Colin Loader *Karl Mannheim's Sociology as Political Education* (New Brunswick: Transaction Publishers, 2002). "Political Education for a Polity of Dissensus: Karl Mannheim and the Legacy of Max Weber." *European Journal of Political Theory* 1, no. 1 (2002): 31–51; with Colin Loader, "Temporizing with Time Wars: Karl Mannheim and Problems of Historical Time," *Time and Society* 13, nos. 2/3 (2004): 155–72; "The Secrets of Mannheim's Success," in Eberhard Demm, ed., *Soziologie, Politik und Kultur. Von Alfred Weber zur Frankfurter Schule*, 141–53 (Frankfurt: Peter Lang, 2003); translated, revised, and expanded as "Das Geheimnis des bemerkenswerten Aufstiegs Karl Mannheims," in Bálint Balla, Vera Sparschuh, Anton Sterbling, eds., *Karl Mannheim. Leben, Werk, Wirkung, und Bedeutung für die Osteuropaforschung*, 149–68 (Hamburg: Krämer, 2007).

28. David Kettler, ed., *Contested Legacies: The German-Speaking Intellectual and Cultural Emigration to the US and UK, 1933–1945* (Berlin and Cambridge Mass.: Galda & Wilch, 2002).

29. "Self-Knowledge and Sociology: Nina Rubinstein's Studies in Exile," in Edward Timms and Jon Hughes, eds., *Intellectual Migration and Cultural Transformation*, 195–206 (Vienna and New York: Springer, 2003); "The Symbolic Uses of Exile: Erich

Kahler at Ohio State University," in Alexander Stephan, ed., *Exile and Otherness*, 269-310 (Oxford and Bern: Peter Lang, 2005); "A German Subject to Recall: Hans Mayer as Internationalist, Cosmopolitan, Outsider and/or Exile," *New German Critique* 96 (June 2006): 171-81.

30. With Gerhard Lauer, "The 'Other Germany' and the Question of *Bildung*," in Kettler and Lauer, eds., *Exile, Science, and Bildung: The Contested Legacies of German Emigre Intellectuals*, 1-18 (New York and London: Palgrave, 2005); David Kettler and Thomas Wheatland, eds., *Contested Legacies: Political Theory and the Hitler Regime* special issue of the *European Journal of Political Theory* (June 2004); "'Weimar and Labor' as Legacy: Ernst Fraenkel, Otto Kahn-Freund, and Franz L. Neumann," in Helga Schreckenberger, ed., *Die Alchemie des Exils. Exil als schöpferischer Impuls*, 129-47 (Vienna: Edition Praesens, 2005).

31. David Kettler and Zvi Ben-Dor, eds., *The Limits of Exile*, special issue of the *Journal of the Interdisciplinary Crossroads* (April 2006).

32. "'Les émigrés sont les vaincus.' Spiritual Diaspora and Political Exile." *Journal of Interdisciplinary Crossroads* 1, no. 3 (2004): 269-82.

33. "Political Science and Political Theory: The Heart of the Matter," in Brian Caterino and Sanford Schram, eds., *Making Political Science Matter: the Flyvbjerg Debate and Beyond*, 234-51 (New York: NYU Press, 2006); "The Political Theory Question in Political Science, 1956-1967," *American Political Science Review* 100 (November 2006): 531-39.

34. With Volker Meja, "Their Own 'peculiar way': Karl Mannheim and the Rise of Women," *International Sociology* 8 (March 1993): 5-55; "Women and the State: Käthe Truhel and the Idea of a Social Bureaucracy," *History of the Human Sciences* 20, no. 1 (2007): 19-44; with Volker Meja, "Karl Mannheim's Jewish Question: History, Sociology, and the Epistemics of Reflexivity," *Simon Dubnow Institute Yearbook* 3 (2004): 325-47.

35. "Exile and Return: Forever Winter," *Journal of the Interdisciplinary Crossroads* 3 (April 2006): 181-200.

36. Sonnert and Holton, *What Happened to the Children*, 144.

Tibor Frank

Budapest—Berlin—New York
Stepmigration from Hungary to the United States, 1919–1945

Emigration from interwar Hungary was different from that of most other European countries.[1] Hungary suffered the consequences of World War I enormously. The Austro-Hungarian defeat ended all pretensions Hungary had to at least the semblance of a semi–Great Power status. The country went through two agonizing revolutions in 1918–1919, Romanian occupation in 1919, and a counterrevolution in 1919–20, followed by the devastating Peace Treaty of Trianon in 1920. The treaty partitioned the country and gave over two-thirds of its territory to the newly created or aggrandized neighboring countries of Romania, Czechoslovakia, and Yugoslavia. The territorial and population concessions dictated by the Treaty of Trianon turned Hungary overnight into an independent but small, landlocked, and vulnerable state with a full-blown small-country complex.

Whereas the total population of Hungary rose from 13,663,691 in 1869 to 18,264,533 in 1910, with only 54.5 percent ethnic Magyars of the total population in 1910, the census of 1920 recorded only 7.89 million people in Hungary after Trianon, with a mere 2.4 percent representing all the national minorities. By 1930 the overall population was 8.68 million, which by 1941 had reached 9.32 million. The number of Jews in 1869 was 542,257 (4 percent), while in 1910 the number rose to 911,227 (5 percent), and remained around 5 percent in the interwar era.[2]

The Postwar Years

Hungary's postwar misfortune was partly attributed to the country's Jewish population, which was scapegoated to take a huge share of the blame for the catastrophe. As in Austria and Germany, the Jews were often perceived as an alien and disruptive group in society. Though a gross travesty, this perception gained credence from the fact that the overwhelming majority of the leaders of the 1919 "Republic of Councils," a short-lived offshoot of Lenin's Bolshevik Revolution of 1917, were of Jewish descent.

The new regime that was installed under Admiral Miklós Horthy in the fall and winter of 1919–20 produced the continent's first anti-Semitic legislation of that century, a quota system that compared the number of Hungarian Jews to the overall population of Hungary and allowed only 5 percent of the total number of students to be of Jewish origin in higher education. This new "numerus clausus" system was particularly painful for Hungarian Jews as they were disproportionately represented in the "free" professions, comprising more than 50 percent of private medical doctors, lawyers, journalists, merchants, and businessmen. By contrast there were traditionally few Jews among officials employed by the state of Hungary or by the municipal authorities or among teachers and professors.[3] Though the system lapsed for a while by the end of the decade, it was a powerful spur for many brilliant young Hungarian intellectuals and professionals of Jewish descent to leave the country and complete their education or seek employment elsewhere. Many would have preferred to immigrate to the United States, but entry there was restricted by the introduction of the quota system, starting with the emergency immigration restriction law of 1921 and finalized by the even-more-restrictive national origins scheme of the Reed-Johnson Act of 1924, under which only 869 persons from Hungary could be admitted annually, a number later reduced to a mere 473.

Hungary thereby lost a host of prospective mathematicians, scientists, engineers, physicians, architects, musicians, artists, filmmakers, sociologists, and authors who would go on to make distinguished names for themselves in Europe and particularly in the United States. That was compounded by further rounds of increasingly drastic anti-Jewish legislation in 1938–41, modeled on that introduced in Nazi Germany.

Assimilation

By contrast to that in other East-Central European countries, assimilation was particularly strong in late-nineteenth- and early-twentieth-century Hungary. It was considered the most important gateway of opportunity in a country where Magyarization proved a guiding principle of building the Hungarian nation, itself traditionally a composite mixture of ethnic, religious, and language groups of various sorts. Before World War I, the country provided an almost unparalleled measure of religious tolerance. Assimilation often included language shift, name change, ennoblement, mixed marriage, and religious conversion. This was particularly the case in Budapest, a city referred to by the contemporary poet Endre Ady as "made by Jews for us."[4] The change from German or Yiddish into Hungarian, from Jewish families into Hungarian ones, from Judaism to Roman Catholicism or various forms of Protestantism all served the purpose of integration into Hungarian society, and yet these various forms of assimilation also created a sense of mental vacuum, an aura of lost identity, a religious no man's land.

Assimilation, along with its various manifestations, reflected the measure of psychological insecurity, social uneasiness, and inner unrest of generations of Jews in Budapest as well as elsewhere in the Austro-Hungarian monarchy and even beyond.[5] This issue has been discussed by a growing literature on Jewish insecurity.[6] The price of assimilation for religious converts was the loss of roots, social and psychological; its reward was promotion and social recognition. In the increasingly secularizing world of fin de siècle Budapest, it often seemed a reasonable bargain to exchange socially undesirable traditions for the psychological and commercial benefits of a seemingly secure position in Hungarian society.

For the converts of the World War I era and the immediate postwar years, these benefits were short-lived. Nevertheless assimilation into Hungarian society provided the Jewish middle class with a set of experiences that prepared them for successful immigration and naturalization in the United States. This was expedited by their having already experienced comparable change in Hungary and the Austro-Hungarian Empire. They were prepared for the typical problems of émigrés/immigrants, having already experienced multiple values, double identities, and a sense of living, as it were, in between different societies.

The single most remarkable characteristic of assimilation in Hungary around the turn of the century, and a measure of its success, was Magyarization. The abandonment of the German language for Hungarian was rapid: the number of Jewish speakers of German dropped from 43 percent in 1880 to 21.8 percent by 1910, and the percentage of Magyar speakers in Hungary reached 75.6 percent.[7] To some degree name change, already a frequent phenomenon in Hungary by the 1840s, was also part of this movement. Changes in family name often were from Hebrew to German under Joseph II, then from German to Hungarian in the nineteenth century, and again, among many émigrés and exiles, from Hungarian to U.S. English.

Toward Germany

The average "Hungarian" middle-class person was typically German or Jewish by origin, and it was German culture and civilization that connected Hungary and the Austro-Hungarian monarchy with Europe and the rest of the world. Middle-class living rooms in Austria, Hungary, Bohemia, Galicia, and Croatia typically boasted the complete works of Goethe and Schiller, the poetry of Heine and Lenau, and the plays of Grillparzer and Schnitzler.[8] Not only were German literature and German translations read throughout these areas, German permeated the language of the entire culture. When Baron József Eötvös (1813–1871), a reputable man of letters and minister of education, visited his daughter in a castle in eastern Hungary, he noted: "What contrasts! I cross Szeged and Makó, then visit my daughter to find Kaulbach on the wall, Goethe on the bookshelf and Beethoven on the piano."[9]

German being the lingua franca in the Austro-Hungarian monarchy, most potential émigrés first went to the German-speaking countries of Europe: Germany, Austria, or Switzerland. Even Czechoslovakia had excellent German universities in both Prague and Brno. Members of the Austro-Hungarian middle classes usually spoke German well, and these countries were close to Hungary, not only in geographic, but also in cultural terms. The German influence in the Austro-Hungarian Empire was particularly strong in terms of education, the musical life, and the arts and sciences. Weimar Germany and parts of German-speaking Czechoslovakia were also liberal and democratic in spirit and politics. In addition, like the former Austro-Hungarian Empire, Germany, and to some extent Czechoslovakia, represented a multicentered world: each of the "gracious capitals of Germany's lesser princes,"[10] as the historian István Deák put it, could boast of an opera, a symphony, a university, a theater, a museum, a library, and an archive, with an appreciative and inspiring public that invited and welcomed international talent. Young musicians graduating from the Hochschule für Musik in Berlin could be reasonably sure that their diploma concerts would be attended by the music directors and conductors of most of the German operas across the country, poised to offer them a job in one of the many cultural centers of the Reich.[11] Berlin and other cities of Weimar Germany shared many of the cultural values and traditions that young Hungarian scholars, scientists, musicians, visual artists, filmmakers, and authors were accustomed to, providing an attractive setting and an intellectual environment comparable to the one that perished with prewar Austria-Hungary or that had been left behind, particularly that of Budapest.[12] The vibrant yet tolerant spirit of pre-Nazi Germany, and particularly the atmosphere of an increasingly Americanized Berlin, gave them a foretaste of the United States and some of its big cities.

After the political changes of 1918–20, small groups of intellectually gifted Hungarians started to migrate toward a variety of European countries and the United States. Following what often proved to be the first step in a chain- or stepmigration, most of the Hungarian émigrés found they had to leave the German-speaking countries on the rise of Hitler as chancellor of Germany in early 1933, and they continued on their way, in most cases to the United States. This pattern was certainly not the only one, though it was by far the most typical.

Professional migration as a European phenomenon after World War I was certainly not restricted to Hungary alone. The immense social convulsions that followed the war drove astonishing numbers of people in all directions. Russian and Ukrainian refugees fled Bolshevism, Poles were relocated in reemerging Poland, and Hungarians escaped from newly established Czechoslovakia, Romania, and Yugoslavia.[13] Outward movement from Hungary in the 1920s was part of this emerging general pattern and cannot be clearly defined as *immigration* proper. Most people simply went on substantial and extended study tours of varied length, just as others did before World War I. Contrary to general belief, migrations were not limited to Jews suffering from the political and educational consequences of the White Terror in Hungary. However, Jewish migrations were a definitive pattern of the 1920s when the *numerus clausus* law kept many of them out of the universities. The result of these migrations was the vulnerability of statelessness, or at least mental statelessness, the troubled existence of living long years without citizenship in a world built on nationality.[14]

Gentile Hungarians also left their country in considerable numbers in this era for a variety of reasons. In subsequent years many of them returned to Hungary. Their list included the likes of the authors Gyula Illyés, Lajos Kassák, and Sándor Márai; the visual artists Aurél Bernáth, Sándor Bortnyik, Béni and Noémi Ferenczy, and Károly Kernstok; the singers Anne Roselle (Anna Gyenge), Rosette (Piroska) Andai, and Koloman von Pataky; the actors Vilma Bánky, Ilona Hajmássy, Béla Lugosi, and Lya de Putti; the composers Dezső Antalffy-Zsiross and Béla Bartók, and Nobel laureate Albert Szent-Györgyi. Motivated by politics, poverty, curiosity, or longing for an international career, people of dramatically opposed convictions hit the road and tried their luck in Paris, Berlin, or Hollywood.

Many of the Hungarians who left the successor states of the former Austro-Hungarian Empire were labeled as "Romanians," "Czechoslovaks," or "Yugoslavs." Because of the quota laws, however, few Hungarians headed toward the United States: migrations were directed toward European centers, in the first place to Germany.

Moving to Germany was not only a question of survival in terms of studies, jobs, and promotions: it also meant an opportunity to resume one's original professional activities or intellectual direction. It was not merely the acquisition of a new address: it led to the reconstruction of spiritual and often bodily health, the realization of the self, a restoration of the mind. Joining prewar Hungarian groups and friends in Germany, new Hungarians came by the hundreds to Berlin in the 1920s. They found what increasingly amounted to a Hungarian community, with bass Oszkár Kálmán singing in the Staatsoper and tenor Pál Fehér in the Städtische Oper, and a host of Hungarian singers including Gitta Alpár, Rózsi Bársony, Oszkár Dénes, and Tibor Halmai featuring in Paul Abraham's popular operetta *Ball im Savoy*. Even after the Nazi takeover, Maestro Fritz Busch presented Verdi's *Ballo in maschera* in the Städtische Oper with the Hungarian stars soprano Mária Németh and tenor Koloman von Pataky. The accompanist Árpád Sándor was an organic part of the musical life of the city.[15] Berlin was certainly not the only destination. The mathematician Gábor Szegő was happy to accept a full professorship at Königsberg in 1926, the chemist Ferenc Kőrösy went to study at Karlsruhe in 1923, the philosopher Karl Mannheim settled in Heidelberg, where he had studied before World War I, and became a professor of sociology in 1930 at the University of Frankfurt am Main until escaping to Britain.[16] The mathematician Otto Szász gave up a position at the University of Frankfurt am Main in 1933 to leave for the United States, where he taught mostly in Cincinnati.[17]

Hungarian filmmakers formed an integral part of the German film industry after World War I. German film established its independence from foreign influence at the same time, and film production was supported by massive government aid: the UFA (Universum-Film Aktien Gesellschaft) was founded in 1917 and remained the dominant force of the film industry until the end of World War II. The 1920s were known as the golden age of the German cinema. A large number of Hungarians served their film apprenticeship at the UFA studios in Berlin-Babelsberg. As they did not all work there continuously until Hitler emerged, they did not all leave Germany as a group after 1933. The directors Michael Curtiz (Mihály Kertész), Joseph Pasternak, and Charles Vidor; the actors Peter Lorre, Bela Lugosi, and Paul Lukas (Pál Lukács); and S. Z. Sakall and Victor Varconi (Mihály Várkonyi) left Germany for the United States, some of them well before the Nazis came to power, as they had found Hollywood's offers more attractive.[18]

At one point toward the end of the 1920s, the Hungarian government began to realize the significance to Hungarian culture of the continuous outward flow of émigré professionals. Count Kuno Klebelsberg (1875–1932), minister of religion and education between 1922 and 1931, visited some of the key German universities, trying to invite the promising Hungarian scientists back to Hungary. Mrs. Szegő, wife of the mathematician Gábor Szegő (1895–1985), described the conversation, where Count Klebelsberg was confronted with the long list of successful Jewish Hungarian mathematicians and scientists in Germany:

> When Klebi [Klebelsberg] celebrated some time ago in Göttingen, the mathematician Courant who sat next to him at the dinner table tried to impress him by listing a number of Hungarian though non-Aryan scientists (such as [Lipót] Fejér, [George] Polya, Misi [Michael Polanyi], [John von] Neumann, [Theodore von] Kármán, Gábor [Szegő]). [Max] Born seconded. Klebi said that Misi had received an invitation to return to Budapest. . . . Tammann [also at the table that night] remarked that he doubted whether Misi would accept the invitation, and give up his position in Germany. Klebi responded with the by now classical adage: *Wenn Vaterland ruft, kommt Ungar!* [When the Fatherland calls, the Hungarian comes!][19]
>
> Mrs. Szegő added with a measure of cynicism, "*Si non è vero, è ben trovato.*" [If it's not true, it's well invented].

Returning to Budapest, the minister published a prominent article on the first page of the popular daily *Pesti Napló*. In the title of his article, Count Klebelsberg used a reference to the poet Endre Ady's well-known line from 1906, which referred to modernization in Hungary. For the minister the great national problem in 1929 was to "preserve the genuine features of the nation while at the same time raising [Hungary up] to a completely European level and learning from the nations that surround us."[20] He was cautious with literature and the humanities and suggested the importance of maintaining the strong Hungarian national character but argued differently in regard to the fields of medicine, economics, and the technical and natural sciences: "Chauvinism and particularism would take a cruel revenge there," he said, "for them we must open the gates widely. . . . May a lot of people come in, a great many of them, as many as possibly can, with the new inventions of new times, new methods of production, and, first and foremost, with new energies."[21] The minister, in an effort to induce a return migration in the key professions, wrote the article as an open invitation to all Hungarian professionals currently in other countries.

Klebelsberg's article stirred the Hungarian émigré community in Germany. At one point or another, many of them had difficulties finding jobs, and the call of the Hungarian government sounded promising. Michael Polanyi showed his copy of *Pesti Napló* to his Berlin friends. Future Nobel laureate Eugene Wigner (1902–1995) and Leo Szilard (1898–1964) actually signed it as if acknowledging the message—but they decided to stay in Germany. A day after the article appeared, the minister was interviewed about the actual intentions of the government. Klebelsberg suddenly became cautious and backpedaled when confronted with questions about returning professors, suggesting that this was in fact up to the Hungarian universities. Some scientists did return, however, and the most notable among them, and later a Nobel laureate, Albert Szent-Györgyi (1893–1986), concluded a successful period of research in Groningen (Holland), Cambridge (England), and the Mayo Clinic in Rochester, Minnesota; he returned to Hungary in 1928, apparently at the instigation of Klebelsberg.[22] Others, such as the celebrated Hungarian American conductor Fritz Reiner, based in Cincinnati at that time, also toyed with the plan of returning to Hungary, where Reiner was apparently invited to become music director of the Budapest Opera. Reiner's conditions, however, were so demanding that the appointment never materialized.[23]

The misjudgment of the German situation in late 1932 and early 1933 was not unique: as late as January 1933, the operetta *Ball im Savoy*, by the Hungarian Berliner Paul Abraham (1892–1960) was played with phenomenal success in Berlin and sung by Hungarian stars Gitta Alpár (1903–1991) and Rózsi Bársony (1909–1977). Here were a composer and two singers who, within a matter of a few weeks, had no place in Hitler's officially anti-Semitic Germany.[24] The short novels of British author Christopher Isherwood, such as *Mr. Norris Changes Trains* (1935) and *Goodbye to Berlin* (1939), as well as more recent films such as *Cabaret, Mephisto,* and *Julia* have chronicled the breathtaking immediacy of change from Weimar to Nazi Germany. Though some members of the Hungarian community attempted to survive by answering the question "Arisch oder nicht-Arisch?" (Aryan or non-Aryan?) on Nazi questionnaires by answering "Ungarisch, evangelisch" (Hungarian, Lutheran),[25] Berlin was no longer safe, with the ever-present swastika on the red Nazi banner, marching SA troops, NSDAP party rallies, book burnings, and mushrooming new anti-Semitic slogans and regulations.

Jewish Hungarian members of German scientific organizations typically severed their links after the Nazi takeover. Theodore von Kármán left Germany well before

Hitler's *Machtergreifung*, and his settling at Caltech was a consequence of developments inherent in his research area, not of political or racial persecution. Nevertheless, when the Nazis came to power, he completely turned against Germany, where he spent some twenty-five years. John von Neumann left the Deutsche Mathematiker-Vereinigung in 1935 shortly after his *Mathematische Grundlagen der Quantenmechanik* [The Mathematical Foundations of Quantum Mechanics] was published in Berlin.[26] Others followed suit.

Multiple Exiles

The life and work of Leo Szilard illustrates a characteristic form of immigration—double or even multiple exiles—with their compounding destabilizing impact on career, lifestyle, and mental health. Szilard seemed to be continually in search of himself throughout his life, to travel where his mind led him, to chase the world. Szilard's life was one of continual change and intellectual unrest; it was a quest for role, influence, and identity. His excessive sensitivity and constant alertness were products of his experiences as a young student in Budapest in 1919; consequently the mature Szilard in the Berlin of 1933, and forever after, was always ready to move.

Szilard was a member of the distinguished group of Hungarian émigré scientists whose work is most closely associated with the atomic bomb.[27] A student of Max von Laue and close associate of Albert Einstein in Berlin, Szilard probably was the most imaginative and original member of this outstanding group of scientists whose pervasive characteristics were imagination and originality. Szilard's colleagues saw him as a genius. Eugene Rabinowitch remembered him as a "brilliant, paradoxical, arrogant, lonely man of ideas and sudden action"; Eugene Wigner asserted that he had met "no one with more imagination and originality, with more independence of thought and opinion."[28] He was the ultimate problem solver, one who identified, posed, and solved problems of very different types in a variety of fields.

During the clouded months of late 1919, Szilard felt increasingly insecure in Budapest as the White Terror reigned and threatened his future. In September he and his brother Béla suffered a humiliating attack at the Technical University for being Jewish, and his recently acquired baptismal certificate, which he naively presented in self-defense, seemed to further inflame the anti-Semitic hatred of their attackers. Béla remembered that Leo had been unable to obtain a visa after the establishment of the Commune but ultimately secured an official document within twenty-four hours from the Budapest police on December 11, 1919, testifying to his "political reliability," because his name "had not been entered into the books of the political police."[29] He also acquired a written statement from the mathematician Lipót Fejér (1880–1959) on December 14 proving that he had won second prize in the student competition in physics under the auspices of the Mathematical and

Physical Society. These documents allowed him to leave Budapest for Berlin within a few days at the end of 1919.

Just as the year 1919 was one of national identity crisis for Hungary, it also was one of personal identity crisis for Szilard and was the root of major fears. The long and agonizing fall of 1919 left a lasting impression on his young mind and imprinted on it an acute awareness of history's dangerous turns. His various psychological complexes, such as his impulse to live always in hotels or rented rooms instead of setting up his own residence,[30] and his constant state of alert, allowing him to move quickly whenever necessary, probably have their roots in the terrible anguish he experienced in 1919. It is telling that he kept his most important belongings, particularly his papers, in two suitcases ready to be carried away at a moment's notice—as he did in Berlin in the beginning of March 1933, right after the Reichstag fire.[31] Like so many of his Hungarian contemporaries who were then living in Germany, he experienced a terrible sense of déjà vu of the Budapest of 1919, a disagreeable sense of familiarity with a threat that warranted steady vigilance and urgent response. It is perhaps not far off the mark to speak here of an *Angstneurose*, or anxiety neurosis, in Sigmund Freud's sense, the symptoms of which Szilard experienced throughout his life.[32] The sudden outburst of anti-Semitism, the violence of a right-wing takeover, and the threatening atmosphere of vengeance were all well known to Szilard and his Hungarian contemporaries from their experiences in Budapest well over a decade before the Nazi takeover in Germany and would remain in their minds for the rest of their lives. Szilard's excessive sensitivity and constant alertness were products of his experiences as a young student in Budapest in 1919; the mature Szilard in the Berlin of 1933 and forever after was always ready to move. The somewhat younger Jewish-Hungarian mathematician Paul Erdős (1913–1996), who lived a comparable life especially after World War II, offers an interesting parallel.

The German social historian Joachim Radkau's diagnosis of the age of *Nervosität* (nervousness) in Germany from Bismarck to Hitler also fits Hungary after World War I.[33] In a roundabout way, the rise of a distinct Hungarian school of psychology with internationally recognized achievements in psychoanalysis, fate analysis, and stress points to the psychological consequences of a society in turmoil.[34] Émigrés of Jewish origin such as Szilard had additional reasons to be nervous.[35] One may venture to think that psychological impulses motivated his pioneering efforts to build the bomb against the threat of Hitler. His Jewish Hungarian background, his upbringing, and his long and permanent exile contributed to a troubled and difficult psyche. It is also true, however, that his psychological makeup equipped him with the skills to survive and the sensitivity to help anyone who needed his support, often in the face of adversity. After World War I and the Hungarian revolutions of 1918–19, Szilard's life reveals a continuous interplay of politics and science, a drama in which he seems to have been too political for a scientist and too scientific for a politician.

After fleeing Berlin rapidly on the burning of the Reichstag on February 27, 1933, Szilard, perhaps more than anyone else, was the prime mover behind the founding of the Academic Assistance Council. Soon thereafter he accidentally met Sir William (later Lord) Beveridge in Vienna and persuaded him to form a committee to aid refugee scientists and scholars.[36] "Things in England develop very well," Szilard wrote to the distinguished Austrian chemist Friedrich A. Paneth (1887–1958) from Brussels in mid-May 1933. "Sir William Beveridge, whom I met in Vienna and who has been very active since he came back in London, succeeded in getting a very prominent group to make an appeal for raising funds in England. The first contribution will probably be made through voluntary cuts of salaries of University teachers (this is very confidential)."[37]

Szilard functioned like an entire team of people. He had followed Beveridge back to London, where he wrote to Max Delbrück (1906–1981) on May 7, 1933: "What I am concerned with at the present is to co-ordinate the foreign groups which are already in existence, and to stimulate the formation of groups in countries where there are no suitable groups as yet."[38] He then traveled for a month on the Continent. In Belgium he met the rectors of all four of the Belgian universities, the physicist Jacques Errera, and the philosopher and politician Hendrik de Man of the University of Brussels, who assisted him in mobilizing Belgian colleagues to aid refugee scientists and scholars. In Switzerland he talked to Gustave Gerard Kullman of the Committee for Intellectual Cooperation of the League of Nations and Walter Kotschnig of the International Student Service.[39]

In London, Szilard met with university leaders and prominent scientists such as Beveridge, director of the London School of Economics and Political Science; Frederick G. Donnan of University College, London; Gilbert Murray of Oxford, chair of the League of Nations Committee for Intellectual Cooperation; Sir John Russell; G. H. Hardy of Cambridge; Nobel laureates Niels Bohr of Copenhagen and Archibald V. Hill of the Royal Society and University College, London; and Henry Mond, the second Lord Melchett, chair of the Jewish Agency. He also met with Jewish leaders such as Neville Laski; Claude Joseph Goldsmid Montefiore; Sir Philip Hartog, chair of the Committee of the Jewish Board of Deputies and the Anglo-Jewish Association; and Chaim Weizmann, the future president of Israel. Living as always in a hotel and working from his office at the Academic Assistance Council headquartered at the Royal Society, Szilard apparently contacted all the agencies in London that were formed to help European Jewish scientists in trouble, including the Central Jewish Consultative Committee at 1 Finsbury Square and the Jews' Temporary Shelter at 63 Mansell Street.[40] He put Friedrich Paneth in touch with the Jewish Refugees Committee's Hospitality Committee at Woburn House in June 1933; soon thereafter Paneth was appointed as a consultant for the Imperial

Chemical Industries (ICI) and later taught at Imperial College, London, and the University of Durham from 1939 to 1953.[41] Szilard also considered mobilizing Nobel laureates to aid refugee scientists and scholars, but this plan failed to receive general approval and was soon dropped.[42]

The Academic Assistance Council helped several Hungarian scholars, including the economic historian Karl Polanyi (1886–1964), get to England; his younger brother Michael Polanyi (1891–1976), securely on his way to England, also tried to help some of his gifted students remaining in Germany to obtain scholarships in Great Britain.[43] Other Hungarian scientists as well, many of whom have been hitherto unidentified, were rescued by jobs in Great Britain, often serving as a stepping stone to employment in the United States. A case in point was the nutrition expert Paul György (1893–1976), who was dismissed from his position at the University of Heidelberg in 1934 after thirteen years there: he was offered a research fellowship at the University of Cambridge during 1934–35, then was appointed to a professorship at Western Reserve University in Cleveland (1935–44) before becoming professor of clinical pediatrics and of nutrition in pediatrics at the University of Pennsylvania in Philadelphia.[44]

Networking

Bonding, networking, cohorting within and, less often, between various members of the Hungarian American community became more intense than ever during the war years, all of which was abundantly documented by their correspondence. In order to understand the nature of networking, it is essential to appreciate the social structure of immigrant groups and their ties to prospective newcomers. Because the bulk of the quota was earmarked by preferences for one sort of immigrant rather than another, and nonquota immigration was greatly dependent on letters of recommendations, affidavits, and invitations from fellow nationals who had become U.S. citizens, the social composition of the exile community was virtually self-sustained and self-perpetuating.[45] Because of this there was very little chance to incorporate new elements or groups. Peasant communities absorbed prospective farmers, professionals attracted fellow professionals, Gentiles invited Gentiles, and Jews welcomed Jews. Thus U.S. immigration policies, especially during the long period between 1924 and 1965, contributed to the stability and growth of existing social patterns in the immigrant communities. Even given access to a limited number and type of sources regarding this information, typically in the private papers of Jewish Hungarian scientists and other professionals, this observation seems valid. Statistical evidence regarding all U.S. immigrant visas issued, including enclosed personal material, still needs to be discovered. Nonetheless it may prove enlightening to survey some case studies that have become available.

Jewish Hungarians were first warned of the increasing Nazi danger by the *Anschluss* of neighboring Austria by Germany. As the small Hungarian quota was entirely filled for years ahead, immigration seemed possible only for scientists who had received an invitation to a particular university or research institute. Thus many scientists embarked on a desperate struggle to obtain invitations. "I beg you to give me your assistance in this difficult situation," pleaded the eminent Viennese-Hungarian mycologist József Szűcs to potential employers through his mentor, Theodore von Kármán, who was one of the most willing supporters of refugee scientists.[46] Also begging for Von Kármán's support was young aeronautical engineer Miklós Hoff (1906–1997) from Budapest, who did indeed receive his first U.S. job, as an instructor in Brooklyn, through Von Kármán.[47] Vilmos Szilasi (1889–1966) explained to his cousin Theodore von Kármán that the letter of affidavit should make it very clear that "you know me since our childhood and give the explicit assurance, that my immigration would not be inimical to the interest of the United States" and "that you assume the responsibility of keeping yourself informed of my conduct in the U. St. as well as immediately reporting to the Department of Justice any irregularity in my activities."[48]

An invitation by itself was not enough: appointments to a particular job had to be for at least two years. When Professor Gábor Szegő secured sufficient funds to invite his longtime associate and friend, the distinguished mathematician George Pólya (1887–1985), from Switzerland to Stanford for a year, "the American Consul in Zurich refused to admit him on non-quota basis because of the temporary character of the appointment."[49] In a desperate attempt to get his friend out of Europe, Szegő turned to Von Kármán to secure an additional invitation for Pólya from Caltech. "You understand that although Pólya is not in a concentration camp and not yet dismissed, his situation is very dangerous and he tries desperately to get out before it is too late," Szegő wrote to Von Kármán.[50] "It is not necessary to stress how urgent the case is. Every day may bring new restrictions and difficulties."[51] The Polyas left Zurich via Portugal for the United States in 1940; Pólya ultimately succeeded in obtaining a two-year teaching position at Brown University and Smith College before joining the Stanford faculty in 1942, where he remained until the end of his very long life.[52]

The noted Budapest lung and tuberculosis specialist Gyula Holló (1890–1973), a personal physician of the authors Frigyes Karinthy and Dezső Kosztolányi, as well as of musicians Béla Bartók and Joseph Szigeti, turned to his former patient John von Neumann to support him "by drawing the attention of some influential person who could help me to get a job or an invitation or give instructions through the State Department to the Consulate in Budapest so that I get a non-quota place (which is not unprecedented) or, and this seems to be the most realistic idea, prepares the way and helps me if I come as a visitor searching for a job personally."[53] Dr. Holló succeeded in getting out of Hungary, accepted a position at Goldwater Memorial Hospital, and died in New York City in 1973.[54]

As the war came nearer to Hungary, the nonquota contingent became filled for years ahead, partly by pure and applied scientists, medical doctors, and mathematicians. Yet many did not succeed in getting an invitation. A celebrated Budapest surgeon, Professor Lajos Ádám (1879–1946) was told that the Mayo Clinic in Rochester, Minnesota, would not extend an invitation although Dr. C. W. Mayo counted him "as one of my very good friends." Ádám's well-known and well-connected Hungarian American protector, the journalist and author Emil Lengyel (1895–1985), was told that "we are up against conditions here at present which make it impossible for us to guarantee bringing him here as a Professor or to guarantee any salary."[55] Ádám stayed in Budapest and, miraculously, survived the war.

In the meantime many nonscientists managed to get out. Refugees included many people from the world of film and theater, entertainers, literary people, actors, directors and musicians. In early 1940 Von Kármán had the distinct impression that "New York and Los Angeles are full of newcomers from Budapest, but almost exclusively artists, actors, and writers. Certainly more than half of the music and literature is now in the United States," he commented to a friend in Hungary.[56] Much later, in the early 1950s, Michael Polanyi himself sought to move to the University of Chicago, but, because of his leftist political entanglement in various international groups including the Galileo Circle of pre–World War I Budapest, he was refused entrance to the United States between 1951 and 1953.[57]

For people dependent on their native language and culture, immigration was merely the lesser of two evils. It may have saved their lives, but in many cases immigration nonetheless turned out tragically. A lesser known but important case among authors was that of Ignotus (Hugo Veigelsberg, 1869–1949), the famous liberal critic, essayist, and journalist in turn-of-the-century Budapest and interwar Vienna. It is worth recalling his case in some detail as it reveals virtually the entire support mechanism that immigrants could expect in the United States.

Ignotus, a prominent Budapest literary figure, was from the perspective of immigration a pathetic figure with a difficult case. More than seventy years old and with a poor command of English, he was not in a position to rebuild his literary career. Ignotus was one of those who was forced to leave Austria after the *Anschluss*, and, after a brief stay in England, he went to Lisbon in an effort to secure a U.S. immigration visa but was stranded there. His old Hungarian American friends mobilized their best connections: Emil Lengyel, Rusztem Vambery, and Sandor Rado wrote to the influential Ingrid and Bettina Warburg as well as to Lotta Loeb, all of whom worked for the Emergency Rescue Committee, and they were able to secure their cooperation.[58] Lengyel pointed out that Ignotus had been "fighting Hitlerism in its Hungarian and German varieties" and that he was "on the blacklist of the Gestapo."[59] Rado and Edith C. Field provided moral sponsorship affidavits for the State Department; Edith C. Field added an affidavit of support as well.[60]

Rusztem Vámbéry prepared a detailed biographical sketch and emphasized how the periodical *Nyugat* under Ignotus had advocated "liberal and progressive ideas" and "was for two decades the center of young intellectuals."[61] The Emergency Rescue Committee used Vambery's text to obtain a visa for him, though they also solicited the support of Nobel laureate Thomas Mann.[62] Other sponsors included Professor Oscar Jászi and Count Ferdinand Czernin.

Ignotus was admitted to the United States in early 1941, along with his wife, but the Immigration and Naturalization Service did not provide them with unlimited permission to stay. When they were asked to leave the country in August 1942, Ignotus's friend Oscar Jászi used his personal connections to U.S. Supreme Court Justice Felix Frankfurter, and it was probably Frankfurter's support which secured an extension for the Ignotus couple.[63]

Ignotus, however, had a difficult time in New York. His wife became seriously ill, and the long years in exile made him "a very worried and fearful man" who could "get things unintentionally quite confused," as associates of the International Rescue and Relief Committee taking care of him soon found out.[64] The only income to support the couple came from charitable organizations such as the American Committee for Christian Refugees and subsequently the Community Service Society. The monthly allowance of sixty dollars that the Community Service sent him was insufficient. Furthermore this organization supported refugees only on a temporary basis and refrained as a matter of policy from helping chronic cases.[65] The International Rescue and Relief Committee and the Jewish Labor Committee took joint responsibility for additional sponsorship in the amount of another fifty dollars a month that was extended to Ignotus through 1948.[66] On the recommendation of the Writers' Project, Ignotus received a prize from New York City in May 1944 that came with one thousand dollars.[67] His wife, however, was so sick that a deportation order was pending against her because she was now in a mental institution, which made their permanent settlement plans in the United States hopeless.[68] In early 1949 he departed for Hungary via Britain, leaving his wife behind in the care of the American Committee for Foreign Scholars, Writers and Artists (subsequently the American Council for Emigres in the Professions). He also left behind bitter feelings among the various agencies that had supported him. "Mr. Hugo Ignotus has left for England," commented Charles Sternberg of IRRC, adding, "I am glad he did."[69] Ignotus was eighty then and approaching his end. On his arrival in Budapest, he was taken immediately to a hospital where he was observed by an old friend as "shriveled, . . . sitting unstoppably trembling. He was half dead."[70]

The poignant case of the great composer and piano virtuoso Béla Bartók (1881–1945) is well known.[71] In one sense he was less fortunate than Ignotus: after a few years in voluntary exile during the war years, he died in New York City in

1945 before he could fulfill his desire to return to his native country. Invited to give a concert at the Library of Congress in 1939, Bartók, of Gentile origin, was eager to leave Hungary by the time the war broke out. He described his anxieties and fears as if he spoke for all intending exile: "at the outbreak of the war, I really came into a really desperate state of mind. . . . We see that small countries are invaded from one day to another quite unexpectedly by the most terrible armies and subjected to tortures of every kind. As for my own country, now, instead of one dangerous neighbour, we have got two of them; nobody knows what will happen next day. It may happen, if I leave the country for America that I can't return, can't even have news from my family—. I hope you will understand my state of spirit—."[72]

Bartók decided to leave Hungary for the United States in late 1940, when he received the honorary degree of doctor of music from Columbia University.[73] In February 1941 he was employed by Columbia as a visiting associate in music to work on the late Professor Milman Parry's Yugoslav music collection of nearly four thousand discs.[74] Bartók enjoyed this work very much, which lasted until the end of 1942, but he was never really happy in his voluntary exile and always hoped to return to his native Hungary. While he was relatively healthy, he played a political role in the Movement for Independent Hungary, trying to convince the world that the movement represented millions of Hungarians "supporting those who fight for a free and democratic world."[75]

Anti-Semitism in the United States

It is a generally accepted historical fact that the United States gave too little support to refugees from Germany and other European countries that were overrun by the Nazis. U.S. anti-Semitism has been often quoted as one of the main reasons for this lack of compassion and cooperation.[76] Some of the arguments used to explain this today had already been voiced in the mid-1930s. In an NBC radio broadcast on July 9, 1934, Cecilia Razovsky of the National Council of Jewish Women, admitted that "the United States . . . is still confronted with the gigantic task of finding employment for some ten million of its own people. . . . Sympathetic as Americans have always been to the distress of refugees, our own grave problems have caused us to forgo our traditional historical policy of asylum for the oppressed and the homeless, and our response in this crisis has necessarily been less generous than in the past."[77]

As late as 1935, the High Commission for Refugees of the League of Nations viewed optimistically a largely European "plan for the liquidation of the refugee problem."[78] Carefully prepared by Walter M. Kotschnig, the plan calculated that the refugees from Germany could be absorbed by countries all around the world. At this point Kotschnig suggested that some 25,000 people would go to European countries and an additional 850 to the United States—considering that some 5,000 immigrants were already admitted in the first eighteen months of the immigration. Today, knowing the real figures of the German catastrophe, Kotschnig's estimate sounds naive.

In what was obviously part of a propaganda war to change the prevailing common opinion in the country, the immigration expert Louis Adamic surveyed the immigrant situation in the United States between 1932 and 1938 and voiced some of the most important and most typical prorefugee arguments of the day. He noted that the fears of patriotic, yet in many instances poorly informed, citizens prevailed. Antiforeign feelings were channeled into several hundred organizations and movements. To counterbalance common sentiment, Adamic came to a number of new conclusions. Out of the total allowance of nearly 1,100,000 people for all the quota countries "only 140,000 quota immigrants actually came in, or about 11 per cent of the quota. During the period before June 30, 1938, only 42,494 quota immigrants had been admitted, which is about 28 per cent of the 153,774 permitted under the quota."[79] He included Hungary in the list of countries that did not approach their small quota in the Depression years before 1938.[80] Adamic was quick to point out that very few of the refugee-immigrants from Germany under National Socialism "took jobs to the detriment of anyone who had been in the country before their arrival." Adamic's pamphlet emphatically suggested that not all refugees were Jewish, a common fear of contemporary Americans. He also underlined that "Catholics and Protestants have also suffered new persecutions."[81] Suggesting that the admission of Hitler's victims was good for the country, Adamic quoted Bruce Bliven of the *New Republic,* whose enthusiastic report "Thank You, Hitler!" attempted to change the generally negative attitude of the U.S. public. Almost simultaneously, *This Week,* a supplement to several major Sunday papers, published a similar article entitled "Thank You, Dictators!"[82]

The refugee question reopened the post–World War I problem of the quotas, and their eventual abolishment became a hotly debated issue once again in the late 1930s. As "professional alien-haters and Jew-baiters," organizations such as the American Coalition formed serious opposition to the elimination of the quotas. Several organizations interested in spreading antiforeign sentiment were directly connected with the Nazi propaganda machinery in Berlin.[83] Adamic was correct in his balanced assessment in 1939 that "a very large number of U.S. citizens are deeply interested in getting the refugees out of the reach of the Nazis, but many are afraid, too, that a large increase in immigration to this country is apt to help augment the sentiment against the 'foreigners' which—partly as a backwash from nationalism and anti-Semitism in Europe, partly on account of our own economic plight—has been stronger of late in several parts of the United States than ever before."[84]

The Nazi takeover in Germany and subsequent events in Europe occurred at a time when the United States was still coping with the aftermath of the great economic and financial crash of the late 1920s and early 1930s. The New Deal had begun to transform the country, but there was still considerable poverty and distress, discouraging many from contributing to foreign aid and offering a large number of jobs to displaced Europeans.

Large sections of U.S. society were reluctant to admit "foreign refugees, which could mean dispossessing Americans qualified to fill the positions."[85] Some Colorado citizens suggested sending European immigrants to Alaska rather than have them in their own state.[86] In his capacity as president of the Carnegie Endowment for International Peace, Nobel laureate Nicholas Murray Butler (1862–1947), president of Columbia University, received a large number of letters from people in Nazi-occupied countries in Europe seeking his assistance in coming to the United States. His secretary could send only discouraging answers explaining that there were "approximately ten million unemployed in this country at the present time and . . . thousands of our young men and women are graduating each year from colleges and universities and are finding great difficulty in obtaining employment."[87] Some Americans refrained from contributing in support of refugees, as they were deeply convinced in their isolationist wisdom that "charity should begin at home."[88] This was a typical, widely used argument against spending on refugees. Phelan Beale of the firm Bouvier and Beale on Broadway in New York pointed out that "I can show you in this country right at your doorstep details just as pitiful, if not more so than can be portrayed in Czechoslovakia. I can also show you a greater number of people in the United States who have lost their homes and means of livelihood than the number of deplorable victims in Czechoslovakia, who have suffered a like fate. Means that are at my disposal to unfortunates, I prefer to apply to sufferers in the United States, because it is my sincere belief that we should put our own house in order before we proceed elsewhere."[89]

The same argument was used by C. Ledyard Blair of Wall Street who declared to "have the greatest sympathy not only for those in Czechoslovakia but those in China, Spain, Palestine and the jews [sic] in Germany. We also have, as you know, in this country some ten or eleven millions of American unemployed citizens, for whose support we are unnecessarily taxed."[90] Delavan M. Baldwin of New York, who had recently returned from Germany, went so far as to put the question to President Butler, chairman of the American Committee for Relief in Czechoslovakia, "should not Americans give aid to American institutions for Americans in America, in view of the on rush of emigrants now from Germany to the United States?"[91] Louis Adamic warned that "the situation which the refugees and our economic crisis jointly create is so delicate and dangerous," especially "in an atmosphere in which alien-baiting and anti-Semitism seem to be increasing."[92] People, he concluded, should not "believe that more Jewish refugees are being admitted than can be absorbed by the country."[93]

In May 1938, when the immigration of Austrian scholars came to the agenda, the American Council of Learned Societies sensed only "a suspicion of anti-Semitism"[94] in the air. Yet by 1939 even the Emergency Committee in Aid of Displaced Foreign Scholars declared that there were no more chances to place Jewish refugees in the United States. The committee was shocked to receive David Cleghorn Thomson, general secretary of the British Society for the Protection of Science and Learning (formerly the AAC), who came from London to visit colleges in the Midwest and the West and to explore possible placements there for refugee academics from Europe. Leading Jewish members of the Executive Committee were troubled by the prospect of raising the level of existing anti-Semitism in the country. "Imagine a committee meeting in a city 29 percent Jewish, attended by Jewish leaders who have raised most of the $600,000 during the past five years for the academic placement of (mostly Jewish) exiles, but who in the face of a generally increasing anti-Semitism here are exceedingly sensitive about colleges and universities being asked . . . to accept any more Jewish emigres."[95] Alan Gregg noted, "it would be easy to exaggerate the dangers of the undercurrent of anti-Semitism now running in this country and its universities, but it would be hard to exaggerate the intensity of the anxiety of American Jews lest English efforts . . . expose . . . all Jews to the very resentments they are powerless to control."[96]

Jewish Notables from Hungary

However, the United States ultimately did support a large number of refugees, particularly those of use in war-related science, education, the film industry, and the economy. Among the many Jewish-Hungarians who found refuge were well-known scientists such as Theodore von Kármán, Cornelius Lanczos, Leo Szilard, and Edward Teller; mathematicians such as Paul Halmos, John Kemeny, George Pólya, Otto Szász, and Gábor Szegő; designers such as Marcel Breuer, George Kepes, Laszlo Moholy-Nagy, and Eva Zeisel; filmmakers such as Paul Fejos, Ernest Laszlo, Peter Lorre, George Pal, Joseph Pasternak, and S. Z. Sakall; musicians such as Paul Abraham, Gitta Alpar, Gabor Carelli, Antal Dorati, Otto Herz, Emmerich Kálmán, Alexander Laszlo, Jenő Léner, Alfred Sendrey, and Margit Varró; psychologists such as Franz Alexander, Robert Bak, Therese Benedek, Michael Erdélyi, George Gero, Sandor Lorand, Margaret Mahler, Sandor Rado, David Rapaport, René Árpád Spitz, and Thomas Szász; and photographers such as André Kertész and Martin Munkacsi.

Jews arriving from Hungary seemed to have been more Hungarian than Jewish, though further research is needed to find out more about the exact nature of their religious affiliation. Assimilation in Hungary certainly left a lasting imprint on their faith. Many of the U.S. citizens initiating or participating in the rescue missions were themselves Jewish and were driven by the special sensitivity of shared background and a more keenly felt danger.

Contrary to common belief, not all émigré Hungarians were Jewish in the period between 1919 and 1945. Though the overwhelming majority of exiles was Jewish, the country was also left by a relatively small group of gentile Hungarians, politically liberal, radical, or leftist, and some eventually just hoping for a more rewarding career. Some of these returned to Hungary at a later point.

Notes

1. See Tibor Frank, *Double Exile: Migrations of Jewish-Hungarian Professionals through Germany to the United States 1919–1945* (Oxford: Peter Lang, 2009).

2. Péter Hanák, "Magyarország társadalma a századforduló idején" [Society in Fin-de-Siècle Hungary], in Péter Hanák, ed., *Magyarország története 1890–1918* [A History of Hungary, 1890–1918], 2nd ed. (Budapest: Akadémiai Kiadó, 1983), 405, 414, 420; Iván T Berend, "A magyar társadalom a két világháború között" [Interwar Hungarian Society] in György Ránki, ed. *Magyarország története 1918–1919, 1919–1945* [A History of Hungary, 1918–1919, 1919–1945] (Budapest: Akadémiai Kiadó, 1976), 765, 767, 768.

3. Katalin N. Szegvári, *Numerus clausus rendelkezések az ellenforradalmi Magyarországon* [Numerus clausus provisions in counter-revolutionary Hungary] (Budapest: Akadémiai Kiadó, 1988), 52–53.

4. Endre Ady, "Korrobori," in *Ady Endre publicisztikai írásai* [The Journalism of Endre Ady] Vol. III (Budapest: Szépirodalmi Könyvkiadó, 1977), 520.

5. William O. McCagg, Jr. *A History of Habsburg Jews, 1670–1918* (Bloomington and Indianapolis: Indiana University Press, 1989). Cf. Elzbieta Ettinger, *Hannah Arendt/Martin Heidegger* (New Haven, Conn.: Yale UP, 1995), quoted by Alan Ryan, "Dangerous Liaison," *New York Review of Books*, January 11, 1996, 24.

6. Sander L Gilman, *Jewish Self-Hatred: Anti-Semitism and the Hidden Language of the Jews* (Baltimore/London: Johns Hopkins University Press, 1986), 22–67, 139–308; Viktor Karády, *Zsidóság Európában a modern korban* [Jewry in Modern Europe] (Budapest: Új Mandátum, 2000), 125–284; McCagg, *A History of Habsburg Jews, 1670–1918*, 47–158; Raphael Patai, *The Jews of Hungary: History, Culture, Psychology* (Detroit: Wayne State University Press, 1996), 230–441; Jacob Katz, *From Prejudice to Destruction: Anti-Semitism, 1700–1933* (Cambridge, Mass. / London, England: Harvard University Press, 1980), 203–9, 221–42.

7. McCagg, *A History of Habsburg Jews, 1670–1918*, 190.

8. Cf. Gyula Illyés, *Magyarok. Naplójegyzetek*, 3rd ed. (Budapest: Nyugat, [1938]), 2:239.

9. István Sőtér, *Eötvös József* [József Eötvös] 2nd rev. ed. (Budapest: Akadémiai Kiadó, 1967), 314.

10. István Deák, *Weimar Germany's Left-Wing Intellectuals: A Political History of the Weltbühne and Its Circle* (Berkeley / Los Angeles: University of California Press, 1968), 13.

11. Information from Budapest Opera conductor János Kerekes, August 1994. Cf. Antal Doráti, *Notes of Seven Decades* (London: Hodder and Stoughton, 1979), 90–125.

12. Cf. W. M. Johnston, *The Austrian Mind: An Intellectual and Social History, 1848–1938* (Berkeley: University of California Press, 1972); Allan Janik and Stephen Toulmin, *Wittgenstein's Vienna* (New York: Simon & Schuster, 1973); László Mátrai, *Alapját vesztett felépítmény* [Superstructure without Base] (Budapest: Magvető, 1976); Carl E.

Schorske, *Fin-de-Siècle Vienna: Politics and Culture* (New York: Knopf, 1980); Kristóf Nyíri, *A Monarchia szellemi életérő l: Filozófiatörténeti tanulmányok* [The Intellectual Life of the Monarchy: Studies in the History of Philosophy] (Budapest: Gondolat, 1980); J. C. Nyíri, *Am Rande Europas. Studien zur österreichisch-ungarischen Philosophiegeschichte* (Vienna: Böhlau, 1988), *Wien um 1900. Kunst und Kultur* (Vienna-Munich: Brandstätter, 1985); John Lukacs, *Budapest 1900. Historical Portrait of a City and Its Culture* (New York: Weidenfeld & Nicolson, 1988); Péter Hanák, *The Garden and the Workshop: Essays on the Cultural History of Vienna and Budapest* (Princeton: Princeton University Press, 1998).

13. Geoffrey Barraclough, ed., *The Times Atlas of World History,* rev. ed. (Maplewood, N.J.: Hammond, 1984), 265.

14. Linda K. Kerber, "Toward a History of Statelessness in America," *American Quarterly* 57(September 2005): 727–49.

15. Information obtained from Budapest Opera conductor János Kerekes, August 1994.

16. Éva Gábor, "Mannheim in Hungary and in Weimar Germany," *Newsletter of the International Society for the Sociology of Knowledge* 9 (August 1983): 7–14; Lee Congdon, "Karl Mannheim as Philosopher," *Journal of European Studies* 7 (March 1977): 1–18.

17. Michael Polanyi to G. Bredig, Berlin, June 23, 1923 (German), Michael Polanyi Papers, box 1, folder 20; Brian Longhurst, *Karl Mannheim and the Contemporary Sociology of Knowledge* (New York: St. Martin's Press, 1989), 5; Gabor Szegő, "Otto Szász," *Bulletin of the American Mathematical Society* 60 (May 1954): 261 .

18. Ephraim Katz, *The Film Encyclopedia,* 476–77, 665, 1181, 1187, 1194; 293–94, 741–42.

19. Mrs. Gábor Szegő to Mrs. Michael Polanyi, K[önigs]berg, May 15, 1929 (Hungarian), Michael Polanyi Papers.

20. Count Kuno Klebelsberg, "Szabad-e Dévénynél betörnöm új idő knek új dalaival?" [May I Break in at Dévény with the New Songs of New Times?] *Pesti Napló,* May 5, 1929.

21. Ibid.

22. Szent-Györgyi mistakenly remembers 1932 as the date of his return on which he accepted the chair of medical chemistry at the University of Szeged, Hungary. Cf. Albert Szent-Györgyi, "Prefatory Chapter—Lost in the Twentieth Century," *Annual Review of Biochemistry* 32 (1963): 8.

23. Béla Bartók discussed this plan with the conductor, who wanted membership in the upper house of the Hungarian Parliament, an effort that Bartók discouraged. Cf. Béla Bartók to Fritz Reiner, Budapest, October 29, 1928, published by János Demény, ed., *Bartók Béla levelei* [Letters of Béla Bartók] (Budapest: Művelt Nép Könyvkiadó, 1951), 109; K[ároly] K[ristóf], "Reiner Frigyes," in *Magyar Zsidó Lexikon* (Budapest: Magyar Zsidó Lexikon, 1929), 788.

24. Personal memories of Mrs. Éva Kerekes, August 1994.

25. The author's interview with conductor-composer János Kerekes, 1988.

26. John von Neumann to W. Blaschke, Princeton, January 28, 1935 (German), John von Neumann Papers, 1933–37, box 4, Library of Congress, Washington, D.C.

Cf. Johann von Neumann, *Mathematische Grundlagen der Quantenmechanik* (Berlin: Julius Springer, 1932).

27. Stefan L. Wolff, "Das ungarische Phänomen—ein Fallbeispiel zur Emigrationsforschung," *Deutsches Museum Wissenschaftliches Jahrbuch 1991* (Munich: Deutsches Museum, 1992), 228–45.

28. Eugene Rabinowitch, "James Franck 1882–1964, Leo Szilard 1898–1964," *Bulletin of the Atomic Scientists* 20 (October 1964): 16–20 [quoted material on 20]; Eugene P Wigner, "Leo Szilard 1898–1964," *Biographical Memoirs of the National Academy of Sciences* 40 (1969): 337–47 [quoted material on 337].

29. Leo Szilard, "Petition to the Budapest Police, December 11, 1919," Leo Szilard Papers, box 1, folder 11; Palló, "Lanouette," 164–65.

30. His hotels included the Imperial Hotel in London, the International House and King's Crown Hotel in New York City (opposite Columbia University), the Quadrangle Club in Chicago, and the Webster Hotel and Dupont Plaza in Washington, D.C.; even the small cottage in which the Szilards lived during the last few months of his life in early 1964 in La Jolla, California, was connected to a motel; see Lanouette, *Genius*, 136, 149, 163, 173, 230–31, 274–75, 321, 329, 383, 398, 430–32, 466–67.

31. Wolff, "Das ungarische Phänomen," 236; Lanouette, *Genius*, 110, 115.

32. Freud, Sigm[und]. "Über die Berechtigung, von der Neurasthenie einen bestimmten Symptomencomplex als 'Angstneurose' abzutrennen." *Neurologisches Centralblatt*, vol. 14, part 2 (Leipzig: Verlag von Veit & Comp., 1895), 50–66; reprinted in Sigmund Freud, *Gesammelte Werke*, 6th ed., vol. 1 (Frankfurt am Main: S. Fischer Verlag, 1991), 315–42; translated by James Strachey in *The Standard Edition of the Complete Psychological Works of Sigmund Freud*, vol. 3 (London: Hogarth Press, 1999), 90–115; on the translation of "Angst," see 116–17.

33. Joachim Radkau, *Das Zeitalter der Nervosität: Deutschland zwischen Bismarck und Hitler* (Munich: Propyläen Taschenbuch, Econ Ullstein List, 2000), 201, 534, 598, where Radkau rightly quotes Budapest hypnotist Ferenc Völgyesi's book, *Botschaft an die nervöse Welt! Nervosität, Hypnose, Selbstbeherrschung* (Zürich: Orell-Füssli, 1936); translated by Barnard Balogh as *A Message to the Neurotic World* (London: Hutchinson, 1935), as a contribution to his own thesis on Nervosität. The international popularity of Völgyesi's book (it was published in at least four languages) demonstrated the timeliness and importance of this problem. Völgyesi was one of the most popular psychiatrists in Budapest for forty years; he had altogether around forty thousand private patients; Mrs. Ferenc Völgyesi (who served as his assistant), personal communication, February 3, 1992.

34. Franz Alexander (1891–1964), Michael Bálint (1896–1970), Sándor Ferenczi (1873–1933), Imre Hermann (1889–1984), Hans Selye (1907–1982), and Leopold Szondi (1893–1986) were among the most widely known Hungarians in the history of twentieth-century psychology; see Lívia Nemes and Gábor Berényi, eds., *Die Budapester Schule der Psychoanalyse* (Budapest: Akadémiai Kiadó, 1999).

35. Radkau, *Zeitalter*, 357–62; Lanouette, *Genius*, 466. Jonas Salk recalled after Szilard's death: "There was something driving Leo;" ibid., 476.

36. Norman Bentwich, *The Rescue and Achievement of Refugee Scholars: The Story of Displaced Scholars and Scientists 1933–1952* (The Hague: Martinus Nijhoff, 1953), 11; Fermi, *Illustrious Immigrants,* 63–64; Edward Shils, "Leo Szilard: A Memoir," *Encounter* 23 (December 1964): 38–39; Weiner, "New Site," 211; Stefan Wolff, "Frederick Lindemanns Rolle bei der Emigration der aus Deutschland vertriebenen Physiker," in Anthony Grenville, ed., *German-Speaking Exiles in Great Britain: The Yearbook of the Research Centre for German and Austrian Exile Studies,* vol. 2 (Amsterdam and Atlanta: Rodopi, 2000), 28.

37. Szilard (Brussels) to Friedrich A. Paneth, May 14, 1933; Nachlass F. A. Paneth, Archiv zur Geschichte der Max-Planck-Gesellschaft, Berlin-Dahlem, Jewish Refugees Committee, 1933, III. Abt. Rep. 45.

38. Szilard (London) to Max Delbrück, May 7, 1933, Leo Szilard Papers, box 7, folder 9.

39. Jacques Errera (Bruxelles) to Szilard, June 5, 1933 (French), Leo Szilard Papers, box 7, folder 2; Szilard (Brussels) to unknown, May 14, 1933, ibid., box 12, folder 21; [Leo Szilard], "Report," May 23, 1933, ibid., box 4, folder 30.

40. Szilard (London) to Delbrück, May 7, 1933, Leo Szilard Papers, box 7, folder 9; Szilard (Strand Palace Hotel, London) to Friedrich A. Paneth, November 26, 1934, and Szilard (Brussels) to Friedrich A. Paneth, May 14, 1933 (handwritten notes), Nachlass F. A. Paneth, Jewish Refugees Committee, 1933, III. Abt. Rep. 45; Szilard (London) to Wigner, August 17, 1933, Michael Polanyi Papers, box 2, folder 12.

41. I. Zinn, secretary of the Jewish Refugee Committee, to F. A. Paneth, June 7, 1933, Nachlass F. A. Paneth, Jewish Refugees Committee, 1933, III. Abt. Rep. 45; R[alph] E. Oesper, "Fritz A. Paneth (1887–)," *Journal of Chemical Education* 16 (July 1939): 301; J. Mattauch, "Friedrich A. Paneth," *Verbandsausgabe der Physikalischen Verhandlungen* 8, Lieferung (1958): 165–69.

42. Szilard (London) to Maxwell Garnett, May 9, 1934, Leo Szilard Papers, box 8, folder 23; Julian Huxley (London) to Szilard, May 3, 1934, ibid., box 9, folder 12.

43. Karl Polanyi (London) to Michael Polanyi, October 31, 1934 (in Hungarian), Michael Polanyi Papers, box 17, folder 5; [Lawrence] Bragg (Manchester) to Michael Polanyi, July 10, 1933, ibid., box 2, folder 12.

44. Paul György, Biographies, Paul György Papers, American Philosophical Society Library, Philadelphia, Penn.; Fritz Zilliken, "Paul György 7.4.1893–1.3.1976," *MPI Berichte und Mitteilungen, Sonderheft* (1977), 15–17; Paul György Papers, Archiv zur Geschichte der Max-Planck-Gesellschaft, Berlin-Dahlem, IX. Abt. Rep. 1. György received an honorary doctorate from the Ruprecht-Karl-University of Heidelberg in 1960 and the U.S. National Medal of Science from President Gerald R. Ford in 1976.

45. Patterns of networking were occasionally different in Britain, where intellectual organizations occasionally welcomed distinguished Hungarian newcomers such as Karl Mannheim and Michael Polanyi, who joined, for example, the progressive circle of "The Moot" between 1937 and 1946. Cp. Éva Gábor, "Michael Polanyi in The Moot," *Polanyiana,* 2, nos. 1–2 (1992): 120–27. See also Lee Congdon's excellent recent book on Hungarian exiles in Britain, *Seeing Red: Hungarian Intellectuals in Exile and the Challenge of Communism* (DeKalb: Northern Illinois University Press, 2001).

46. Dr. Josef Szűcs to Theodore von Kármán, and enclosure, Vienna, June 29, 1938, Theodore von Kármán Papers, file 29.20.

47. Miklós Hoff to Theodore von Kármán, Budapest, September 19, 1938, and Palo Alto, Calif., April 20, 1940, Theodore von Kármán Papers, file 13.20.

48. Wilhelm Szilasi to Theodore von Kármán, Lisbon, May 20, 1941, Theodore von Kármán Papers, file 29.20.

49. Gábor Szegő to Theodore von Kármán, Stanford, July 24, 1940, Theodore von Kármán Papers, file 23.35.

50. Ibid.

51. Ibid.

52. G[abor] Szegő to George Pólya, Stanford, June 11, 1940; President Henry M. Wriston to Georg Polya [sic], Brown University, Providence R.I., July 31, 1940; George Polya Papers, S.C. 337, 86–36, Department of Special Collections and University Archives, Stanford University Libraries, Stanford, *The Life of Mathematician George Pólya, 1887–1985*, Department of Special Collections and University Archives, Cecil H. Green Library, Stanford University Libraries, December 13, 1987–June 1988 (exhibit guide).

53. Gyula Holló to John von Neumann, n.d. [1939?], John von Neumann Papers, box 6.

54. *Magyar Életrajzi Lexikon*, vol. 3 (Budapest: Akadémiai Kiadó, 1981), 311.

55. Dr. C. W. Mayo to Emil Lengyel, May 19, 1941, Emil Lengyel Collection, Bakhmeteff Archives, Butler Library, Columbia University Library, New York, N.Y.

56. Theodore von Kármán to Lajos Bencze, February 19, 1940, Theodore von Kármán Papers, file 2.24.

57. On Michael Polanyi and the Galileo Circle, see John M. Cash, *Guide to the Papers of Michael Polanyi* (N.p.: Joseph Regenstein Library, University of Chicago, 1977), 8; Michael Polanyi Papers, box 46, folder 5; on other, allegedly pro-Soviet involvement, see Malcolm D. Rivkin, "Teachers Protest Bar of Anti-Commie Prof," *Harvard Crimson*, November 14, 1952; Toni Stolper, "Letter to *The New York Times*," *New York Times*, May 10, 1952; William Taussig Scott, and Martin X. Moleski, S.J., *Michael Polanyi: Scientist and Philosopher* (Oxford: Oxford University Press, 2005), 222–23.

58. Emil Lengyel to Ingrid Warburg, New York, October 25, 1940; Sandor Rado to Bettina Warburg, October 28, 1940; Bettina Warburg to Ingrid Warburg, October 28, 1940; Sandor Rado to Ingrid Warburg, November 11, 1940; Rustem Vambery to Lotta Loeb, February 22, 1941; International Rescue Committee, box 6, Archives of the Hoover Institution on War, Revolution and Peace, Stanford, Calif.

59. Emil Lengyel to Ingrid Warburg, New York, October 25, 1940; International Rescue Committee, box 6, Archives of the Hoover Institution.

60. Sandor Rado, Affidavit, November 18, 1940; Ingrid Warburg to George Warren, January 28, 1941; International Rescue Committee, box 6, Archives of the Hoover Institution.

61. Rustem Vambery, "Biographical Sketch of Dr. Hugo Ignotus," New York, January 28, 1941, International Rescue Committee, box 6, Archives of the Hoover Institution.

62. Ingrid Warburg to George Warren, January 28, 1941; Lotta Loeb to Thomas Mann, November 13, 1940, International Rescue Committee, box 6, Archives of the Hoover Institution.

63. Oscar Jaszi to Felix Frankfurter, August 21, 1942, Felix Frankfurter to Oscar Jaszi, New Milford, Conn., August 27, 1942; Oscar Jaszi Papers, Rare Book and Manuscript Library, Butler Library, Columbia University Library, New York, N.Y.

64. Excerpts from letter of Janet Siebold, August 21, 1944, International Rescue Committee, box 6, Archives of the Hoover Institution.

65. Ibid.

66. Sheba Strupsky to Jewish Labor Committee, September 15, 1943; Eva Lewinski (IRRC) to Jewish Labor Committee, January 10, 1946; IRRC Case Department—Hugo Ignotus Correspondence, 1947–1949; International Rescue Committee, box 6, Archives of the Hoover Institution.

67. Excerpts from Letter of Janet Siebold, August 21, 1944, International Rescue Committee, box 6, Archives of the Hoover Institution; cf. *Magyar Irodalmi Lexikon*, vol. 1 (Budapest: Akadémiai Kiadó, 1963), 491.

68. Minutes of a January 8, 1945, meeting at ACCR, International Rescue Committee, box 6, Archives of the Hoover Institution.

69. Charles Sternberg (IRRC) to Samuel Estrin (Jewish Labor Committee), January 31, 1949, International Rescue Committee, box 6, Archives of the Hoover Institution.

70. Oszkár Gellért, *Kortársaim* (My Contemporaries; Budapest: Művelt Nép, 1954), 179–80.

71. Agatha Fassett, *Béla Bartók: The American Years* (New York: Dover, 1970).

72. Béla Bartók to Harold Spivacke, Budapest, November 9, 1939, Coolidge Collection / Béla Bartók, Library of Congress, Music Division, Washington, D.C.

73. Nicholas Murray Butler to Béla Bartók, April 1, 1940; Frank D. Fackenthal—Béla Bartók Correspondence, November 1940, Rare Book and Manuscript Library, Butler Library, Columbia University Library, New York, N.Y.

74. Columbia University to Béla Bartók, February 3, 1941; Béla Bartók to Douglas Moore, April 18, 1941, and January 21, 1942; Rare Book and Manuscript Library, Butler Library, Columbia University Library, New York, N.Y.

75. Béla Bartók to Theodore von Kármán, June 27, 1942, Theodore von Kármán Papers, file 2.5.

76. For a complex analysis of U.S. refugee policy between 1933 and 1945, see Richard Breitman and Alan M. Kraut, *American Refugee Policy and European Jewry, 1933–1945* (Bloomington and Indianapolis: Indiana University Press, 1987). On anti-Semitism in the United States before and during World War II, see David S. Wyman, *Paper Walls: America and the Refugee Crisis 1938–1941* (1968; repr., New York: Pantheon Books, 1985), as well as David S. Wyman, *The Abandonment of the Jews: America and the Holocaust 1941–1945* (New York: Pantheon Books, 1984).

77. Cecilia Razovsky, "The United States and the German Refugees," NBC radio broadcast, New York, July 23, 1934, Columbia University, Rare Book and Manuscript Library, Herbert H. Lehman Suite and Papers, James G. McDonald Papers, National Coordinating Committee, Cecilia Razovsky file, D356 H21.

78. Walter M. Kotschnig to A. Wurfbain, March 5, 1935, Columbia University, Rare Book and Manuscript Library, Herbert H. Lehman Suite and Papers, James G. McDonald Papers, Walter M. Kotschnig file, 1935–April 1936, D356 H20.

79. Louis Adamic, *America and the Refugee,* Public Affairs Pamphlets no. 29 (New York: Public Affairs Committee, 1939; rev. ed., 1940), 10.

80. Ibid., 11.

81. Ibid., 19.

82. "Thank You, Hitler," *New Republic,* November 10, 1937; Adamic, 15.

83. Report of the Institute for Propaganda Analysis, January 1, 1939, quoted by Adamic, 22.

84. Adamic, 23.

85. Henry S. Haskell, assistant to the director, Carnegie Endowment for International Peace to Susan Huntington Vernon, New York, March 13, 1939, Columbia University, Rare Book and Manuscript Library, Carnegie Endowment for International Peace, Aid to Refugees, box 271, folder 1, 94619.

86. The Alaska Colonization Society for Refugees, n.d. CEIP, Committee to Aid Czechoslovakia, box 288, folder 3, 102441.

87. Henry S. Haskell to Jan Mašek, New York, March 27, 1939, CEIP, Aid to Refugees, box 271, folder 1, 94625.

88. Phelan Beale to Nicholas Murray Butler, New York, November 29, 1938, CEIP, Committee to Aid Czechoslovakia, box 286, folder 4, 100930.89. Ibid.

90. C. Ledyard Blair to Nicholas Murray Butler, New York, November 23, 1938, CEIP, Committee to Aid Czechoslovakia, box 286, folder 4, 100931.

91. Delavan M. Baldwin to Nicholas Murray Butler, New York, December 21, 1938, CEIP, Committee to Aid Czechoslovakia, box 287, folder 1, 101194.

92. Adamic, 28–29, 30.

93. Ibid., p. 30.

94. Mortimer Graves to Dr. Stevens, May 27, 1938, Rockefeller Archive Center, Rockefeller Foundation Archives, RG 1.1, series 200, box 46, folder 529.

95. Alan Gregg to A. V. Hill, New York, April 13, 1939, Rockefeller Archive Center, Alfred E. Cohn Papers, RG 450 C661–U, box 4, folder 29.

96. Ibid.

Contributors

RICHARD BODEK earned his Ph.D. in 1990 at the University of Michigan with his dissertation, "We Are the Red Megaphone!" He is a professor of history at the College of Charleston, where he specializes in German cultural and intellectual history. His works include *Proletarian Performance in Weimar Berlin*. At present he is at work on a history of Berlin in 1932, tentatively titled *Berlin 1932: City on the Verge of a Nervous Breakdown* (1997).

GUDRUN BROKOPH-MAUCH is a professor of German at St. Lawrence University. She received her Ph.D. at the University of California, Davis. She is an internationally renowned scholar of Austrian literature and is the author of *Robert Musil, Essayismus und Ironie* and *Robert Musils "Nachlass zu Lebzeiten"* (1992).

YAEL EPSTEIN earned her M.A. in American studies in 2005 at Michigan State University with "European Jewish Refugee Chemists in the United States: Adjustment, Achievements and Jewish Identity." At present she resides In Israel.

SABINE FEISST is an associate professor of musicology at Arizona State University. She holds a Ph.D. in Musicology from the Free University of Berlin. Her research interests focus on the music of the twentieth and twenty-first centuries, including the music of Arnold Schoenberg, improvisation, experimental music, film music, and eco-criticism with respect to music. Her publications include the books *Der Begriff "Improvisation" in der neuen Musik* (1997; The Idea of Improvisation in New Music) and chapters in *Schoenberg and His World*.

TIBOR FRANK is professor of history and director of the School of English and American Studies at Eötvös Lorand University in Budapest (1994–2001, 2006–), where he is head of the Ph.D. program in American studies. He has been doing research on transatlantic relations, international migrations, imagology, and historiography. He was a Fulbright visiting professor at the University of California, Santa Barbara, at UCLA (1987–90), and the University of Nevada–Reno (1990–91) and a visiting professor as the Deak Chair of Columbia University (2001 and 2007). A recipient of the Humboldt Award, he spent the academic year 2003–4 in Berlin at the Max-Planck-Institut für Wissenschaftsgeschichte. He is a corresponding fellow of the Royal Historical Society (London, 2006–). His recent books include *From Habsburg Agent to Victorian Scholar* (2005) and *Double Exile: Migrations of Jewish-Hungarian Professionals through Germany to the United States 1919–1945* (2009).

DAVID KETTLER is research professor at Bard College (New York) and professor emeritus in political studies and cultural studies at Trent University, Ontario. His most recent co-authored book is *Karl Mannheim and the Legacy of Max Weber* (2008). In the past six years, he has published eleven articles and coedited four publications arising out of the "Contested Legacies" exile studies project, http://www.bard.edu/contestedlegacies.

SIMON LEWIS was born in England, went to school there and in South Africa, worked as a high school teacher for nine years in England and in Tanzania, earned a Ph.D. from the University of Florida in 1996, and has been teaching African and world literature at the College of Charleston ever since. He has published on a range of African writers, especially South Africans, is editor/publisher of the annual little literary magazine *Illuminations,* and has directed the Carolina Lowcountry and Atlantic World (CLAW) program at the College of Charleston since 2003.

COLIN LOADER received his Ph.D. from UCLA in European intellectual history. He began teaching at the University of Nevada–Las Vegas in 1986 and teaches courses in modern German history and modern European intellectual history. Although he has written on subjects such as Sherlock Holmes and German silent films, his primary research interests are in the history of German sociology between 1890 and 1933 and that discipline's relationship to others such as history, economics, and philosophy. Among the sociologists he has studied are Karl Mannheim, Max Weber, Alfred Weber, and Werner Sombart.

DAVID PICKUS earned his Ph.D. in German intellectual history from the University of Chicago in 1995. His publications include *Dying with an Enlightening Fall: Poland in the Eyes of German Intellectuals, 1764–1800* (2001). David is currently working on a study of the German American philosopher Walter Kaufmann.

JAMES SCHMIDT earned his Ph.D. in political science from the Massachusetts Institute of Technology, Cambridge. He is professor of history and political science at Boston University. He is the author of *Maurice Merleau-Ponty: Between Phenomenology and Structuralism* (1985) and the editor of *What Is Enlightenment? Eighteenth-Century Answers and Twentieth-Century Questions* (1996), and *Theodor Adorno* (2007), and coeditor, with Amelie Rorty, of the forthcoming *Critical Guide to Kant's Idea for a Universal History* (2009).

JEREMY TELMAN earned his doctorate in modern European intellectual history from Cornell University and his J.D. from the New York University School of Law. He is now an associate professor at the Valparaiso University School of Law, where he teaches contracts, business associations, and public international law. His recent scholarship, including two articles in the *Temple Law Review* and one in the *Maryland Law Review,* has focused on the intersection of international law and U.S. constitutional law.

DONALD WALLACE is assistant professor of history at the United States Naval Academy. He earned his Ph.D. in 2006 at the University of California, San Diego, with his thesis "Death of Civilization: Ethics and Politics in the Work of Hermann Broch, 1886–1951."

Index

acculturation, 103, 109, 110, 114, 121,
Adamic, Louis, 212–13
Adorno, Theodor, 1, 2–4, 7–10, 12, 14–15, 20–21, 30, 31, 40, 73, 107–10, 181, 183, 185
Ady, Endre, 198, 202
antifascism 191–92
anti-Semitism, 8–9, 29, 30–32, 35–37, 82, 102, 106, 128, 132–34, 192, 205, 211–14
Arendt, Hannah, 35, 36
assimilation, 30, 72, 106, 108, 191, 198–99, 214
atomic bomb, 127–28, 204

Bard College, 178, 188
Bartok, Bela, 104, 109, 113, 201, 208, 210–11
Beiser, Arthur, 134–35, 139
Benda, Julien, 158
Bergmann, Max, 129, 135, 140, 144–46
Berlin, 135, 136, 137, 142, 147, 156, 178, 189, 200, 201, 202, 203, 204, 205
Bikerman, Jacob J., 129, 131
Bildung, 59–69, 189–92
biochemistry, 133, 136–37, 140–41, 147, 148–49
Bloch, Konrad, 129, 131, 140–41, 147, 148, 150
Boston, 96, 104, 111, 132, 133
Bowman, Isaiah 132
Broch, Hermann, 71–86
Budapest, 191, 198–99, 200, 202–5, 208–10

Cage, John, 112
Carter, Jimmy, 134
Chargaff, Erwin, 129, 147–48, 150
Cassirer, Ernst, 1, 2
Christianity, 29, 32, 34, 75, 79, 170
City University of New York, 188
Civil Service Law (Germany), 127
Clarke, Hans, 140–41, 147
Columbia University, 1, 3–9, 11–13, 19, 20, 140–41, 146–47, 148, 211, 213
communism, 59, 75, 82, 86, 107, 180, 183

Danto, Arthur, 163
Das Lied der Bernadette (Werfel), 91
democracy, 10, 46, 60, 64, 65, 67, 71, 72, 73, 75–86
Dialectic of Enlightenment (Horkheimer and Adorno), 2, 3, 7, 9, 15, 30, 31, 32, 37
Diner, Dan, 31, 32, 37, 191
Displaced Persons Act (USA), 129
Dworkin, Ronald, 48

Eclipse of Reason (Horkheimer), 2–5, 9, 11–13, 15–17, 19–21
Eisler, Hanns, 108, 109
Einstein, Albert, 145, 204
Emergency Committee in Aid of Displaced Scholars, 137, 145, 149, 214
Emergency Rescue Committee, 143, 209–10
Emergency Society for German Scholars in Exile, 145
engaged music, 107, 110

228 Index

fascism, 8, 30, 32, 35, 36, 46, 62, 71, 72, 73, 75, 76, 78, 80–85, 107
Ferguson, Adam, 181–83, 185, 191
Fischer, Emil, 145, 147
Fischer, Hans, 140
Fledermaus, Die (Strauss), 94, 97, 98
Förster-Nietzsche, Elizabeth, 159, 173 n.11
Forty-Fourth Street Theater, 97
Franck, James, 129, 132–35, 141–42
Frankfurt School, ix, 2–28, 29–32, 35–36, 72–73, 178, 181, 183, 185, 186, 191
Freud, Sigmund, 31, 35, 36, 100, 205
Fromm, Erich, 5, 6
Fry, Varian 143

Garbo, Greta, 95
genocide, 83, 158
George, Stefan, x, 160–62, 163, 164, 166, 168, 169, 170–71
German (language), 179, 198–200
Germany, 2, 3, 12, 29, 32, 35–36, 40, 42, 59, 64–65, 76, 79, 82, 93, 97, 108, 127, 129, 130–32, 136, 139–40, 143, 145, 148–50, 156, 158, 160, 162–64, 169, 177, 183, 186, 189–90, 197–206, 211–13
Gesamtkunstwerk, 106
Great Depression, 61, 80, 82, 105, 113, 212

Habermas, Jürgen, 17, 47, 183, 185
Harvard University, 2, 42, 141, 146, 157
Hebrew (language), 148, 156, 199
Hegel, Georg, 15, 19, 88, 162
Heidegger, Martin, 28, 166–69, 189
Helen Goes to Troy (adaptation of Offenbach), 94, 98
Hertz, Gustav, 132
Hill, A[rchibald]. V., 143–44, 206
Hitler, Adolf, 3, 36, 71, 76, 79, 91, 107, 110, 127, 131, 151, 158, 181, 200, 202, 203, 204, 205, 209, 212

Hoffmann LaRoche, 139
Hofmannsthal, Hugo von, 95
Hollywood, 91, 92, 93, 104, 108, 110, 112
Horkheimer, Max, 1–20, 30, 31–35, 36, 73, 181–83, 185, 192
Hungary, 59, 183, 197–203, 205, 208–12, 214–15

Ignotus (Hugo Veigelsberg), 209–10
Institute for Social Research, 3–8, 11, 12, 13, 19, 20, 30, 182, 183, 184, 192
International Rescue Committee, 143

Jacobowsky and the Colonel (Werfel), 96
Jedermann (*Everyman*, Hofmansthal), 95
Jews, 30, 31, 36, 37, 149, 177, 179, 197, 198, 200, 207, 213, 214
"Jews and Europe, the," (Horkheimer), 31–33, 35–36
Joel, Karl, 163–66, 169
Johns Hopkins University, 132, 141
Judaism, 29, 36, 106, 108

Kaiser Wilhelm Institutes, 127, 131, 136, 137, 142, 145
Kant, Immanuel, 17, 29, 33, 34, 174
Karman, Theodore von, 202, 203, 208, 209, 214
Kaufmann, Walter, x, 156–76
Kelsen, Hans, 40–50
Kiebelsberg, Kuno, 202–3
Korngold, Erich, 97, 98, 109
Kristallnacht, 156
Kubin, Rosa, 129, 133

Ledebour, Graf, 93
legal positivism, 41, 43, 46
legal realism, 42, 43, 46, 48, 50
Leipzig, 178, 179, 191
Loewi, Otto, 129, 131, 146
Los Angeles, 4, 5, 7, 8, 102, 103, 209
Lowenthal, Leo, 1–10, 12–16, 19, 20, 29
Lukács, Georg, 59, 180, 183, 185

Mann, Thomas, 140, 164, 169, 210
Mannheim, Karl, 6, 59–70, 178, 180, 181, 182, 183–86, 188–92, 201
Marcuse, Herbert, 3, 4, 20, 86, 178, 181, 183, 185
Marx, Karl, 180, 181, 182
Marxism 33, 34, 37, 73, 88, 158
Mayo Clinic, 203, 209
Meja, Volker, 186, 188, 191
Merchant of Yonkers, The (Wilder), 94, 96
monopoly capitalism, 12, 15, 30
Merck (company), 136
Meyerhof, Otto, 129, 135, 137, 142–44, 146
Mount Sinai Hospital, 146, 148

Natural Law, 43, 44, 79
Nazi Party. *See* NSDAP
Nazism, 29, 32, 36, 110, 128, 130, 158, 159
Neuberg, Carl, 129, 135, 136–37, 146–47
Neumann, Franz, 3–8, 20, 32, 33, 34, 73, 178, 180–83, 185, 187, 189–90, 192
Neumann, John von, 202, 204, 208
New Opera Company, 97, 98
New School, 127, 145
New York City, 1–11, 21, 30, 59, 92–95, 98, 99, 104, 111, 132, 136, 140, 145, 146, 148, 188, 209, 210, 213,
Newlin, Dika, 103, 112
Nietzsche, Friedrich, x, 156–76, 182
Nilson, Einar, 93
Nobel Prize, 93, 127, 131, 132, 135, 137, 139, 140, 143, 146, 150, 151, 201, 206, 207, 210, 213
NSDAP, 29, 71, 203

Ohio State University, 178, 182, 184–85
O'Neill, Eugene, 95
Ode to Napoleon (Byron), 106, 107, 110
Oxford University, 131, 185, 206

Paris, 11, 142–43, 201
Paulsen, Johannes, 93
"Philosophische Fragmente" (Horkheimer and Adorno; original title for *Dialectic of Reason*), 8, 9, 30

Plato, 15, 19, 181
Polanyi, Michael, 202, 203, 207, 209
Polymer Research Institute, 134, 136, 147
polymer science, x, 134, 136, 146–47, 148–50
Polytechnic Institute of Brooklyn, 134, 136, 146, 147
Pollock, Friedrich, 2, 4, 7, 10, 20,
Popper, Karl, 86, 158, 180, 181
Posner, Richard, 41, 47, 48, 50

quota system (for immigration to the United States), 198, 201, 207–9, 212

Reinhardt, Max, 91, 92, 93, 94, 95, 96, 97, 98
Reinhardt Seminars, 93
Romanticism, 10, 163–64
Rosalinda (adaptation of Strauss's *Die Fledermaus*), 94, 97, 98
Rubin, Edith, 148
Rubinstein, Nina, 188–90
Rutgers University, 134

Said, Edward, 190
Salzburg Festivals, 91, 93
Schmitt, Carl, 41, 42, 62, 189
Schoenberg, Arnold, 102–15. See also *Survivor from Warsaw*
Schoenheimer, Rudolf 130, 141, 147
Schoeps, Hans-Joachim, 40
"second-wave" refugees, xi, 177–78
Self-help of Émigrés from Central Europe, 14
Shaw, Irwin, 94, 95
Simha, Robert, 130, 146–47
Sinzheimer, Hugo, 178, 187, 188, 189
Smith, Adam 191
Stalin, Joseph, 158, 181
Stalinism, 181, 192
stepmigration, 130–31, 197–221
Stern, Kurt G., 129, 146–47
Stern, Otto, 129, 135–36
Sternbach, Leo, 129, 139–40
Survivor from Warsaw, A (Schoenberg), 103, 104, 110

Szego, Gabor, 201, 202, 208, 214
Szilard, Leo, 203, 204–7, 214, 217 n.30

Theater in the Josefstadt, 93
Theater Guild, 96
Thimig, Helene, 91, 93, 95
Third Reich, 18, 32, 147
twelve-tone music, 107, 108

University of Chicago, 105, 132, 134, 141–42, 209

Valium, 139–40

Wagner, Richard, 161
Wallerstein, Leo, 140
Weber, Alfred, 60
Weber, Max, 59, 62, 64, 192
Weimar Republc, 3, 6, 63, 65, 79, 179, 184, 187, 188, 190, 191, 200, 203
Werfel, Franz, 91, 92, 96. See also *Das Lied der Bernadette; Jacobowsky and the Colonel*
Wolfe, Thomas, 95

Zeitschrift für Sozialforschung, 3, 9, 178
Zionism, 102, 106
Zuckmayer, Carl, 72, 98